Dissent on Development

Dissent on Development

Revised Edition

P. T. Bauer

Harvard University Press
Cambridge, Massachusetts
1976

HD
82
.B328
1976b

Contents

2. Dissent on Development

3. The Economics of Resentment: Colonialism and Underdevelopment

4. Marxism and the Underdeveloped Countries

5. Asian Vistas

6. A Critique of UNCTAD

7. Economics as a Form of Technical Assistance

8. The Study of Underdeveloped Economies

Acknowledgements

I discussed the topics examined in these essays with many colleagues and friends both in Britain and abroad. I have benefited greatly from their comments, criticisms and suggestions, on both specific subjects and wider issues. I hope they will accept such a general expression of thanks. Those who have helped me are too numerous for individual acknowledgement. Moreover, this benefit is among the perquisites of academic life, so that too many specific acknowledgements would be out of place.

I must, however, record my thanks to Professor B. S. Yamey and Mr John B. Wood, collaborators of many years' standing, with whom I have discussed many of the issues and ideas examined and developed in this book. Their many comments and criticisms have been most helpful.

Parts of these essays have appeared in various periodicals, and in one instance in the proceedings of a symposium. For permission to use this material I wish to thank the editors and publishers of the following periodicals: *Afrika Spektrum*; *Economica*; *The Journal of Contemporary History*; *The Manchester School of Economic and Social Studies*; *The Scottish Journal of Political Economy*; *The Spectator*; *Weltwirtschaftliches Archiv*. The original version of essay 4 appeared in a symposium entitled *Marxist Ideology in the Contemporary World*, edited by Dr Milorad M. Drachkovitch, published by Messrs Frederick Praeger. Part of essays 1 and 2 formed the substance of the Sir William Meyer Endowment Lectures at Madras University in 1970.

P. T. BAUER
January 1976

Introduction to the Revised Edition

This volume reproduces eight essays from my book *Dissent on Development: studies and debates in development economics* (1971).

The first part of that book examined some of the most widely canvassed and influential ideas of contemporary development economics in the light of the experience in many countries both in the recent and the more distant past. The second and third parts consisted of case studies and review articles. The essays reproduced here are the bulk of the first part of the book. They have been chosen on the basis of their interest to the student or to the general reader, and have not been revised in any way.

The re-issue of a book is always gratifying for an author, especially so when, as in this instance, one of its major thrusts is fundamental criticism of widely accepted ideas and methods of approach. The ideas examined in this volume include the notion (or hypothesis) of the vicious circle of poverty and stagnation in less developed countries; the allegation that the rich countries have caused the poverty of the less developed world; the assertions that any substantial progress of poor countries must result in balance-of-payments difficulties, that their terms of trade decline persistently, that economic development depends largely on monetary investment, and that central planning and foreign aid are indispensable for the development of poor countries.

Since the Second World War these ideas, many of which had their origin in academic writings, have dominated development literature and policy. They will be familiar to readers exposed to public discussion or to the literature on the position and prospects of less developed countries. In the 1960s, when most of these essays were written, the dominance of these ideas was manifest. They are still dominant, although they are occasionally expressed in a more sophisticated way than they were in the 1950s and 1960s.

In these essays I argue that the most prominent and influential of these ideas are demonstrably invalid. Their inadequacy is obvious on very little reflection. For instance, no elaborate reasoning is required to dispose of the hypothesis of the vicious circle of poverty (the notion that societies cannot escape from poverty without external help or prohibitive sacrifices), or the assertion that balance-of-payments difficulties are inevitable concomitants of economic development. Yet, as is clear from many extensive quotations reproduced in this book, these notions are both influential and very widely prevalent.

The exposure of the inadequacy of such ideas is not of itself very difficult, but the enquiry nevertheless seems worthwhile. The notions in the development literature examined in these essays are endowed with academic respectability which adds to their effectiveness; they are often presented in a variety of different ways which obscure their shortcomings; and they have often come to be protected by a façade of ostensibly technical analysis, which can impress, discourage or deter non-technical readers with no experience of less developed countries. While the presentation and the analysis are often more involved, the ideas are no more substantial now than fifteen or twenty years ago.

I stand by the argument of the essays reprinted here. But I realise that their presentation could be much improved. I think it appropriate to draw attention here to certain subjects which I would present in a different manner if I were writing these essays today.

The first of these subjects is the relation of population to development. It has come to be widely agreed in the academic, official and popular development literature that population growth and population pressure are major independent causes of the poverty of less developed countries, and population growth is therefore a misfortune; and that extensive birth control is indispensable for material progress. These ideas extend across the political spectrum. I discuss this set of ideas in essays 1, 2 and 5; and I argue that its principal components are inconclusive, misleading or even invalid. Unfortunately the discussion is scattered. For the convenience of the reader, the principal strands of the discussion are presented here in summary form.

Some of the simplest and least disputed facts about the less developed world must cast doubt on the idea that population pressure or population growth is a major independent cause of the poverty of the less developed world. For instance, most of Africa, Latin America and much of Asia are sparsely populated. Some of the poorest and most backward groups live in areas which are largely empty (even where the land is not particularly infertile) – for instance Papua, Borneo, Sumatra, Central Africa and much of Latin America. Indeed in many parts of the less developed world the population is too sparse for the construction of transport facilities. Conversely, some of the most advanced areas of the less developed world are very densely populated, for example Hong Kong, Singapore, parts of Malaysia and West Africa.

The relation between population density and living standards cannot be examined usefully without noting people's aptitudes and attitudes. This is obvious from the wide differences in economic performance between different ethnic and religious groups in the same country or region with the same physical resources – Chinese, Indians and Malays in Malaysia; Asians and Africans in East Africa; and Chinese, Lebanese and West Indians in the Caribbean. For example, the West Indies are supposed to be heavily over-populated and there is substantial emigration from there, while at the same time there are severe restrictions on the entry of Chinese and Lebanese. But the few Chinese or Lebanese who have been admitted, even without capital, have prospered, saved and built up substantial enterprises, often employing native-born West Indians.

In recent decades the population of the less developed world has increased greatly, appreciably faster than in most developed countries. This rapid growth of population in the less developed world, the much-canvassed and widely deplored population explosion, reflects a fall in mortality with a resulting longer expectation of life of both adults and children. But this is an improvement, not a catastrophe, because most people prefer to live longer and to see their children live longer. There is a great improvement in the standard of living of those who have survived. Most people who have children enjoy their generation and possession. All this is concealed in conventional income statistics, which do not take into account life expectation, health and the possession and generation of children as components of welfare. In recent decades life expectation has increased much more in the less developed countries than in the West. It is still higher in the latter than in the former, but the difference is much less than even a few decades ago. Thus life expectancy at birth in the less developed world increased from about 35–40 years in 1950 to about 52 years by the early 1970s, that is, by about 30–50 per cent; in the developed world the corresponding increase was from about 62–5 years to about 71 years, that is, an increase of about 9–14 per cent. This differential increase reduced the advantage of the developed world from about 70 per cent to about 35 per cent. Thus this gap, which is relatively free from conceptual ambiguities, has not widened but sharply narrowed in recent decades.

Reduction in population growth by itself is most unlikely to raise living standards appreciably. The prime determinants of the level of income and the rate of progress are not physical resources per head, but, as noted in these essays, personal, social and political factors.

Substantial economic improvement of entire societies has often been accompanied by a reduction in birth rates. Both the economic improvement and the decline in birth rates were the result largely of a change in outlook and motivation, especially increased interest in material living standards. Both developments should be seen appropriately as facets of change in the underlying determinants of economic performance. A reduction in the rate of increase of the population is most unlikely to be an independent cause of a simultaneous improvement in living standards. A decline in population growth represents a change in the rate of change of numbers. Unless it is a concomitant of other changes, this cannot by itself bring about significant improvement in the level of living standards over a few years – or even decades. In the conditions in many parts of the less developed world (though not everywhere) a reduction in the rate of population growth is unlikely to raise living standards appreciably in the foreseeable future. The conditions under which it could do so are noted in essay 5, section 11. As suggested there, changes in numbers, age composition and attitudes are closely interrelated. And, as also noted there, assessment of the result of these changes is affected by conventions about the interpretation and measurement of the national income and of living standards.

In short, the most widely encountered views on population and material progress ignore much empirical evidence, and treat the birth of children and longer life expectation as misfortunes. And by focussing on numbers and on physical resources, such views ignore the prime determinants of material progress.

In many parts of the book, especially in the context of central planning and foreign aid, I would now say much more about the process and effects of the politicisation of economic life in poor countries, a subject mentioned rather incidentally in these reprinted essays. The imposition of close and extensive state economic controls – irrespective of whether this has taken the form of state ownership – has resulted in pervasive social, political and economic consequences. In many poor countries the question who has the government has often become decisive for the economic position and prospects or even for the physical survival of millions of people. This situation provokes social and political tensions and reinforces the operation of centrifugal forces. It has inevitably much affected the direction of people's ambitions, energies and activities, and the deployment of their resources, which in turn must affect the economic progress of a society substantially or even decisively. These considerations are relevant to important issues of development policy, including central planning and its implementation, and on the scope and design of investment programmes and official controls.

Official foreign aid reinforces the widely prevalent tendency in less developed countries to politicise economic life. This repercussion of official aid is largely inevitable and is reinforced by the way it is administered, including the criteria of allocation. Examination of the effects of foreign aid in essay 2 would have benefited if I had covered the treatment of the social and political repercussions of aid in one or perhaps two sections, instead of the present, more scattered, exposition. This might have brought out more clearly that official aid is not a simple inflow of resources. Unlike manna from heaven, official aid does not descend indiscriminately on the population of the recipient country; it accrues to specific groups of people in positions of power and sets up repercussions often damaging to development, notably by contributing to the politicisation of economic life. The pertinence of these repercussions extends beyond the ex post assessment of the results of official aid. They are pertinent also to the framing of aid policy, to the arrangement of its methods of operation, including the criteria of its allocation. Failure to take account of the wider repercussions of aid must be detrimental to its effectiveness.

In the context of official aid I would now discuss at some length the anomaly or paradox of continued official aid to governments which maltreat by expropriation or other measures millions of economically highly productive, but politically ineffective, people, especially – but not only – ethnic minorities. Large-scale expropriation, expulsion and even massacre has been perpetrated, encouraged or tolerated by governments which receive official aid from the West. Ethnic minorities whose maltreatment is the order of the day over much of Africa and Asia have often been the main agents of economic progress in poor countries. These minorities have usually had incomes much above the average for the country. Their maltreatment has reduced both current and prospective incomes in these countries, and thereby widened income differences between them and the West, most obviously when they have been expelled or massacred. The receipt of official aid by governments pursuing such policies enables them to conceal from their own people, at any rate temporarily, some of the economic consequences of these policies, and for this reason (as well as for others) facilitates or even encourages their pursuit and continuation. This anomaly is touched on in the discussion of the widening gap in essay 1, section 11. But the anomaly has become even more glaring in recent years, and would deserve more extended discussion along the lines of my articles, 'Foreign Aid Forever?' in *Encounter*, March 1974 and 'Western Guilt and Third World Poverty' in *Commentary*, January 1976.

The issues noted in the foregoing three paragraphs are instances of the repercussions of changes in the familiar variables of economic theory on factors normally regarded as parameters, that is, taken as constant in the particular context. I note these limitations of the conventional treatment in essay 2, section 7 and at greater length in essay 7.

In essay 1, sections 8 and 17 and in essay 2, section 11, I consider possible reasons for the frequent elementary and basic transgressions in the literature of development economics. Examples will be found in the extended passages quoted from prominent authors in essays 1 to 5. Part of the introduction and part of another essay in the original version of this book, neither of which is reproduced in this volume, were also on this topic. I made it clear in the original version, and I hope it is also clear in this abridged edition, that reflections on the possible reasons for such lapses have no bearing on the substantive argument. I wrote about this matter because I thought that this would make the discussion more acceptable, since readers might not believe, even in the face of extensive quotations, that such misconstructions of fact and analysis are perpetrated by prominent scholars and – what is even more unexpected – that they should be widely accepted in serious academic and official publications and discussion. Such incredulity was precisely the response of some audiences whom I addressed on these topics. I also hoped that reflection on the reasons for these lapses might help to improve the level of discourse in this area. Moreover, a search for possible reasons why certain opinions flourish can inform us on various matters pertinent to development, such as the interaction of political and institutional forces with more narrowly economic factors, or the influence of ideas and of their purveyors on policy. Events since the publication of the original version of this book have supported the plausibility of some of these reflections – for instance, the continued official aid to governments pursuing the policies noted earlier in this introduction.

However, I now think that the treatment would be better without these reflections because they can so easily be misconstrued, in spite of explicit and repeated caveats. Perhaps more important, such reflections cannot be conclusive; they move necessarily on a plane different from the substantive argument; and they also break the flow of the discussion. In the present volume they occupy much less space than in the earlier version (both absolutely and relatively), and, as before, they are clearly marked off from the rest of the discussion. Even so, the exposition might be better if the sections noted at the beginning of the previous paragraph had been omitted.

Instead, I might have noted that the frequency and even ubiquity of elementary lapses in the development literature is perhaps best seen as an aspect of the confused state of contemporary economics, in the sense of a perplexing co-existence of substantial and at times rapid progress in some directions with stagnation or even retrogression in other parts of the subject. Examination of this curious situation is a major theme of an article by Professor A. A. Walters and myself, 'The State of Economics', in the *Journal of Law and Economics*, April 1975. For instance, in development economics instances of neglect of simple evidence and elementary lapses of analysis, often manifest concomitants of lack of reflectiveness, are so frequent and extensive that it is arguable that this branch of economics has retrogressed rather than progressed over the last thirty or forty years. Books by administrators, anthropologists, economists and economic historians published a few decades ago on conditions in less developed countries – as for instance books by Vera Anstey, Sir Keith Hancock and Allan McPhee – are often much more informative and exhibit greater power of explanation and prediction than most of the recent development literature. This situation reflects perhaps a characteristic of the contemporary intellectual climate, namely the presence of massive and rapid progress in some directions, coupled with frequent instances of the failure of highly trained people to understand elementary matters or ask simple questions pertinent to the issues they choose to discuss.

Because much economic discourse is so close to political debate and other practical issues, the subject is prone to mirror the contemporary intellectual and political climate. This may explain the frequent allegations in discussions on development and in the development literature, that income and wealth, especially the prosperity of relatively well-to-do persons, groups and societies, have been secured at the expense of those who are less well-off. If I were to write this book again I would examine this pernicious idea at greater length than I do in these essays. This notion has long been among the most disastrous of popular economic misconceptions. It has had devastating repercussions in the less developed world and has encouraged that maltreatment of economically productive but politically ineffective groups to which I have already referred. The same misconception has also often acted as a source of antagonism between countries at an international level.

No general theory of development is put forward in this book. Its absence does not in itself imply an unintellectual approach. It reflects recognition that economic development is a major aspect of the historical progress of entire societies, and is therefore not susceptible to general theory, in the sense in which phenomena studied by the natural and the social sciences are. Moreover, economic development depends largely on determinants which cannot readily be analysed with the tools of economic theory. The inability of economics systematically to analyse the major determinants of material progress does not mean that the subject cannot contribute materially both to analysis of phenomena and to assessment of policy in poor countries. As I hope will be clear from the essays in this volume, my scepticism about the possibility of a general theory of development (analogous to the theories of the natural and social sciences) does not mean that I believe that phenomena or sequences in economic development cannot be explained. As I argue repeatedly in this volume, patterns can often be discerned and probable results of different courses of action predicted, even when rigorous evaluation is not possible.

There is some overlap between certain essays in this volume, especially essays 3 and 4. Much of this was unavoidable because most of these essays represent critical discussion of major ideas of development literature, supplemented by criticisms of specific publications by prominent writers. The essays therefore discuss closely related and at times overlapping ideas. I have tried to minimise these instances of overlapping, but their complete removal would have destroyed the cohesion of particular essays.

Finally, I must also note certain matters of terminology. Many of the societies whose position is a principal theme of this volume have at various times been referred to as materially primitive, backward, poor, underdeveloped, developing and less developed. In recent years they have come to be termed collectively as the Third World, a particularly infelicitous expression, even apart from the inappropriateness of global aggregation implied by it. The term reflects a condescending attitude, not primarily because of the adjective 'third', but because we normally do not talk about the First or the Second World. It is only the rich variety of humanity which inhabits Asia, Africa and Latin America that is lumped together by this term, as if it were all much of a muchness. And the term also reflects a classification which confuses political and economic criteria. On the other hand references to developing countries represent an inappropriate euphemism; for instance they lead to such contradictions as references to the stagnation or retrogression of the developing world.

The expressions poor or technically backward seem the least inappropriate: they best describe the condition which serves as a basis of classification; they best convey the fact that the distinction implied in the terminology is simply a matter of degree; and they are neutral, in the sense that they do not suggest that the condition being described is abnormal, reprehensible and also, perhaps, readily rectifiable. The expression less developed countries, while perhaps not so appropriate as poor or technically backward, is much less misleading than underdeveloped, developing, or Third World used as an adjective. In the text of these essays I refer primarily to underdeveloped countries because this was the expression most widely used in the literature examined in this volume. But it must be understood that I use it as a synonym for poor or materially and technically backward. And, following the literature, I refer primarily to countries, though I now believe that societies would be the more appropriate term.

Much of the discussion in this field has been misdirected and distorted by the choice as the norm of a handful of highly industrialised societies, with the highest conventionally measured per capita incomes, thus designating the position of the great majority of mankind as abnormal. An extreme has been taken as the norm. In the same way, taking rich people as the norm, one can class the vast majority of the population of any country as impoverished. Once this practice has come to be adopted, the use of the term underdeveloped to describe the position of the great majority of mankind is only marginally less misleading than the use of other synonyms implying a deviation from the norm. It would be more appropriate to recognise that only a minority of the world's population has emerged from the surrounding sea of material backwardness; and that it is the position of this minority which requires explanation.

These problems of terminology and classification (as well as some other problems of presentation in development economics) reflect in part the play of political forces, and in part a quest for clear, unambiguous distinctions in contexts where this quest cannot be successful, because the distinctions are often arbitrary and shifting and at times based on political considerations or criteria. For instance the distinction between developed countries and less developed countries or between rich and poor people is not as clear or permanent as, say, the distinction between mammals and reptiles. The imprecision and arbitrariness of the distinctions and classifications are sometimes overlooked because of an unwarranted faith in the efficacy of quantification, whether genuine or spurious. It is widely believed in development economics (as in many other branches of social study), that quantification denotes exactness; that the quantifiable aspects of a situation are representative of its other characteristics; or that the quantifiable aspects are the most significant, or even the only significant aspects of economic phenomena. Quantification is mistaken for precision. and quantifiability for significance. These expectations and beliefs are unwarranted. Even when it is solidly based, quantification in no way ensures cogency of reasoning, nor is it normally sufficient for assessing a situation or as basis for policy. At best, quantification refers to certain aspects of a situation without examining its other aspects or its background. Yet these are normally pertinent both to worthwhile discussion of an issue and to the framing of effective policy.

I use interchangeably the terms material advance, material progress, and economic development. The former expressions are more appropriate than economic development, as they do not suggest that material progress depends on factors which economists are especially qualified or even uniquely qualified, to analyse or promote. Moreover, the reference to material advance and material progress may help to indicate that economic development is but one aspect of the total historical evolution of societies and one which, for many purposes of analysis and policy, is inseparable from other elements of social life. But having entered these caveats, I shall often refer to economic development, as it would be laboured or pedantic to try to ignore a term so widely used in this general context.

I refer repeatedly to certain categories of personal and group characteristics which I consider to be the main determinants of material progress, notably aptitudes, abilities, qualities, capacities and faculties;

attitudes, mores, values and motivations; and institutions and political arrangements. The terms used in the first of these categories embody a strong personal element and refer to traits which may be to a considerable extent hereditary; in the second group there is a larger cultural and social element; in the third category the cultural, social and political influences are predominant. (Most of these personal and cultural characteristics can be summed up in Alfred Marshall's phrase, the spirit of the people.) Within the categories I have used these terms interchangeably, according to what I felt to be the demands of the context. Of course the categories themselves are no more than a useful formula to express, in the context of the discussion, the relationship between the individual and society; the argument is nowhere affected either by acceptance or rejection of this broad classification, or by the choice of terms within these categories, or by opinions about the origins or persistence of the characteristics mentioned. These points of terminology should be borne in mind whenever these expressions occur, whether or not the qualifications are specifically mentioned in a particular context.

Throughout the book all references to these personal and group characteristics are in the context of material progress only. Many, perhaps most, of these characteristics do not confer either happiness or dignity or sensitivity or harmony on those who possess them. This is an obvious point, but one which is all too often overlooked; once it is perceived it explains why those who have achieved prosperity so often fail to find the happiness or even the contentment naively expected of material progress. This reservation, which is explicitly noted from time to time, should be remembered throughout the book.

Dissent on Development

1 The Vicious Circle of Poverty and the Widening Gap[1]

A. THE VICIOUS CIRCLE

The widely held notion that poor countries are caught in a vicious circle of poverty and stagnation, or, as the late Professor Nurkse put it, that a country is poor because it is poor, is not true; this essay explains why. The essay also challenges the popular idea that there is an ever-widening gap between per capita incomes in rich and poor countries and explains why this assertion is either untrue or meaningless.

The great upsurge of interest during the last twenty years in the economics of poor countries and in their development has not so far yielded many illuminating generalisations. The thesis usually known as the vicious circle of poverty claims to be a principal one. It is not quite so dominant now as it was a few years ago but it is still prominent in academic, official and popular literature. It also serves as the background or even as the basis for important policy proposals and measures, notably the suggestion that appreciable economic progress in poor countries requires drastic sacrifices at home, supplemented by large-scale aid from abroad.

1 *The Thesis Outlined*

The thesis states that it is poverty itself which sets up well-nigh insurmountable obstacles to its own conquest. The thesis is presented in several distinct and different formulations, which are not exclusive but cumulative. The most usual is that the low level of income makes saving impossible, thus preventing the capital accumulation necessary for an increase in income. Others include the suggestion that narrow markets in poor countries obstruct the emergence and extension of the specialisation necessary for higher incomes; that demand is too small to permit profitable and productive investment; that government revenues are insufficient for the establishment of effective public services; and that

---

[1] The original version of this essay was published as 'The Vicious Circle of Poverty: Reality or Myth?', in *Weltwirtschaftliches Archiv*, September 1965.

malnutrition and poor health keep productivity low, which prevents a rise in income. International private investment cannot, on this argument, alleviate the situation, since one aspect of the vicious circle is a lack of profitable opportunities for private investment.

I shall first quote at some length from influential sources to show the importance of the thesis in the literature, to illustrate the reasoning behind it and to forestall criticism that I am quoting out of context. A succinct formulation can be quoted from an early edition of Professor Samuelson's textbook:

They [the backward nations] cannot get their heads above water because their production is so low that they can spare nothing for capital formation by which their standard of living could be raised.[1]

The next example is from a study submitted to a United States Senate Committee by the Center for International Studies of the Massachusetts Institute of Technology, a well-known and influential organisation in this field:

. . . the general scarcity relative to population of nearly all resources creates a self-perpetuating vicious circle of poverty. Additional capital is necessary to increase output, but poverty itself makes it impossible to carry out the required saving and investment by a voluntary reduction in consumption.[2]

The emphasis on the impossibility of a voluntary reduction in consumption is notable. If it is the low level of incomes which prevents capital formation it is not clear how the exercise of compulsion would secure the required resources.

Yet another formulation, which has often been quoted, is by the late Professor Nurkse, whose book *Problems of Capital Formation in Underdeveloped Countries* is one of the best-known and most influential of the writings in this field. He writes under the heading 'The Vicious Circle of Poverty':

In discussions of the problem of economic development, a phrase that crops up frequently is 'the vicious circle of poverty' . . . .

A situation of this sort [of the vicious circle of poverty], relating to a country as a whole, can be summed up in the trite proposition: 'a country

[1] Paul A. Samuelson, *Economics: An Introductory Analysis* (2nd edn), New York, 1951, p. 49.
[2] *Study submitted by the Center for International Studies of the Massachusetts Institute of Technology to the State Committee investigating the operation of Foreign Aid*, Washington, 1957, p. 37.

is poor because it is poor'. Perhaps the most important circular relationships of this kind are those that afflict the accumulation of capital in economically backward countries. The supply of capital is governed by the ability and willingness to save; the demand for capital is governed by the incentives to invest. A circular relationship exists on both sides of the problem of capital formation in the poverty-ridden areas of the world.

On the supply side, there is the small capacity to save, resulting from the low level of real income. The low real income is a reflection of low productivity, which in its turn is due largely to the lack of capital. The lack of capital is a result of the small capacity to save, and so the circle is complete.

On the demand side, the inducement to invest may be low because of the small buying power of the people, which is due to their small real income, which again is due to low productivity. The low level of productivity, however, is a result of the small amount of capital used in production, which in its turn may be caused, or at least partly caused, by the small inducement to invest!

The low level of real income, reflecting low productivity, is a point that is common to both circles.[1]

Parts of this formulation are vague and indeed slipshod in their shift between what will, may, or is likely to occur. But the general conclusion is clear. Such quotations could easily be multiplied from the writings of such well-known authors as Professor Gunnar Myrdal, Dr H.W. Singer, and others.

This thesis can also be expressed in the form of a model, that is an analytical device setting out the crucial variables in the explanation of particular phenomena. The crucial variables and relationships in most growth models are these: the growth of income is a function of the rate of capital accumulation, that is of investment; investment depends on saving; and saving is a function of income. Hence the growth of income depends on the growth of capital and the growth of capital depends on the growth of income. The model behind the thesis of the vicious circle of poverty pivots on the notion that the low level of income itself prevents the capital formation required to raise income. It is designed to explain the continuation through time of a zero or negligible rate of economic growth.

2 The Thesis Invalid

The thesis is demonstrably invalid in that it is conclusively refuted by

[1] Ragnar Nurkse, *Problems of Capital Formation in Underdeveloped Countries*, Oxford, 1953, p. 4 *et seq.*

obvious empirical evidence. The model behind it is defective in that the variables specified or implied in it are either relatively unimportant as determinants of development, or they do not interact in the fashion implied. If the thesis were valid, for instance, innumerable individuals, groups and communities could not have risen from poverty to riches as they have done throughout the world, in both rich and poor countries. This in itself should be sufficient to disprove the thesis as a general proposition. But the thesis is also refuted by the very existence of developed countries, all of which started poor, with low incomes per head and low levels of accumulated capital, that is with the economic features which now define underdeveloped countries. Yet they have advanced, usually without appreciable outside capital and invariably without external grants, which would have been impossible according to the thesis of the vicious circle of poverty and stagnation. As the world is a closed system, the thesis is inconsistent with the phenomenon of development. The thesis of a general vicious circle of poverty thus conflicts with the most elementary empirical evidence.

3 *Empirical Evidence*

The thesis is also refuted by the rapid economic advance of many poor countries in recent decades, a phenomenon which is of obvious interest in this general context.

According to statistics of the Economic Commission for Latin America the gross national product in Latin American countries increased over the period 1935 through 1953 at an annual rate of 4·2 per cent, and output per head by 2 per cent.[1] Over the period 1945 through 1955 the rate of growth was even faster, as total output increased by about 4·9 per cent annually and output per head by 2·4 per cent, an appreciably higher rate than in the United States.[2]

Latin America is largely pervaded by the money economy, so that statistics of the gross national product are more meaningful than for most underdeveloped countries. The record of the substantial growth rates in the publications of the Economic Commission for Latin America is of special interest, because economists connected with that organisation have been prominent exponents of the thesis of the vicious circle of poverty.

[1] United Nations, Department of Economic and Social Affairs, *Analyses and Projections of Economic Development. I: An Introduction to the Technique of Programming*, New York, 1955, p. 10.

[2] United Nations, Department of Economic and Social Affairs, *Economic Survey of Latin America 1955*, New York, 1956, p. 3.

South-east Asia, particularly Malaya (broadly the present Malaysia), and West Africa are other underdeveloped regions which have achieved rapid and readily demonstrable progress since the latter part of the nineteenth century. However, there are no series of national income figures going back before the second world war in these areas and the present figures are unreliable. The national income per head in Malaya (gross domestic product per head per year) was about £100 in 1961,[1] the latest year for which official figures are available, and in Ghana about £75 in 1962, again the latest available figures. These are low figures by western standards, but they nevertheless represent substantial advances since the beginning of the century, when these countries were largely subsistence economies. The conventional statistics, moreover, much exaggerate income differences between the developed and under-developed countries. This is discussed at length later in this essay.

Apart from national income statistics there is much information about the rapid progress of these economies in recent years. The rubber industry of south-east Asia began only around 1900. In 1963 it produced about two million tons of rubber annually (in spite of the disorganisation in Indonesia, the country with the largest area under rubber), worth about £400 million. More than two-thirds of the output is from Asian-owned properties. In 1900 there were no exports of plantation rubber from Malaya; in 1963 they exceeded 800,000 tons. In 1900 total domestic exports from Malaya were worth about £8 million annually; in 1963 they were about £300 million.[2]

West Africa is another major region of the underdeveloped world where there has been large-scale material progress since the end of the nineteenth century. The progress of Gold Coast–Ghana[3] and Nigeria in particular has been rapid and is well documented; and in these areas, especially Gold Coast–Ghana, statistics are somewhat more reliable and meaningful than elsewhere in Africa. By the mid-1950s national income per head was about £70 to £75, approximately four times what it had been in 1890. The population also

---

[1] The statistics of national income per head in this paragraph are calculated from the figures of the gross domestic product presented in the United Nations' *Year Book of National Accounts Statistics 1963*, New York, 1964, pp. 85 and 107; and from the population figures in the United Nations' *Monthly Bulletin of Statistics*, vol. XVIII, New York, December 1964. More up-to-date figures are, of course, available since this essay was written, but they do not affect the argument.

[2] The external trade of Malaya and Singapore in 1963 is derived from data in the official *Monthly Statistical Bulletin of the States of Malaya*, Kuala Lumpur, October 1964, and from the Singapore *Monthly Digest of Statistics*, vol. III, October 1964.

[3] In this book we refer to this territory as Gold Coast, Ghana, or Gold Coast–Ghana, according to the period covered by the context.

approximately quadrupled between 1890 and 1960.[1] Material advance is reflected, too, in statistics of foreign trade, government revenues, literacy rates, school attendances, public health, infant mortality, and so on.

Statistics of foreign trade are of particular interest for West Africa because well over 99·5 per cent of the population is African: all agricultural exports (the bulk of exports) are produced by them and practically all imports are destined for their use. In 1890 there were no exports (or production) of Gold Coast cocoa; by the mid-1930s these were about 300,000 tons annually, and by the early 1960s they were over 400,000 tons, all from farms established, owned and operated by Africans; there are no foreign-owned cocoa farms. In 1890 combined imports and exports were less than £1 million annually; by the 1930s both imports and exports were in tens of millions; since the mid-1950s imports and exports have been about £100 million annually. Over this period there was a spectacular increase in imports of both consumer and capital goods. In 1890 there were no imports, or only negligible imports, of flour, sugar, cement, petroleum products, or iron and steel. In recent decades most of these have been on a massive scale. In the early 1890s there were about three thousand children at school; by the mid-1950s there were over half a million. In the 1890s there were neither railways nor roads, but only a few jungle paths, and transport of goods was entirely by human porterage or by canoe. By the 1930s there was a considerable railway mileage and a good road system; and journeys by road required fewer hours than they had required days in 1890.

Substantially the same applies to Nigeria between the end of the nineteenth century and 1960, when Nigeria became independent. Around 1900 exports and imports were each about £2 million annually; by the 1930s they were in tens of millions, and by the late 1950s they were about £150–200 million annually. Here again practically all exports are produced by Africans and practically all imports are destined for their use. In 1900 there were no exports (or production) of cocoa from Nigeria, and exports of oil palm products were one-tenth of their volume in the late 1950s. There was also a phenomenal increase in imports of mass consumer goods and capital goods over this period; in recent years there has also been a substantial increase in the local production of commodities previously imported.

[1] Details will be found in R.E. Szereszewski, *Structural Changes in the Economy of Ghana 1891–1911*, London, 1966; and in P. T. Bauer, *West African Trade*, Cambridge, 1954.

To take one more example. In the first half of the nineteenth century Hong Kong was an empty, barren rock. By the end of the century it was a substantial port and a minor entrepôt centre. It has now become a major manufacturing centre, exporting manufactures on a massive scale. Throughout the western world severe barriers have had to be erected to protect the domestic industries of the United States, Great Britain, Germany and France against imports from the unsubsidised competition of the industries of Hong Kong, an underdeveloped country, eight thousand or more miles away. This rapid progress has occurred in spite of the presence in Hong Kong of three features often said to reinforce the vicious circle of poverty, namely lack of natural resources, extremely severe population pressure, and a very restricted domestic market.

Statistical information of the kind presented in this section can be multiplied easily. But by itself it cannot convey the profound and pervasive changes which have taken place in many parts of the underdeveloped world in recent decades and which have changed the whole pattern of existence. In many areas this progress has meant the suppression of slavery and tribal warfare and the disappearance of famine and of the worst epidemic and endemic diseases. It has meant the development of communications, the replacement of local self-sufficiency by the possibilities of exchange, and the emergence and growth of cities. For instance, Malaya, which in the 1890s was a sparsely populated country of Malay hamlets and fishing villages, has been completely transformed by the rise of the rubber industry and has developed into a country with populous cities, thriving commerce and an excellent system of roads. In West Africa slave raiding and slavery were still widespread at the end of the nineteenth century; in 1900 the towns of northern Nigeria, which are now centres of the groundnut trade, were important slave markets.

The profound changes in the conditions of life which have occurred in many parts of the underdeveloped world over the last century also much affect the meaningfulness of discussions whether the differences in real income per head between rich and poor countries have widened or narrowed over this period. Indeed it is doubtful whether the concept of income conventionally measured is helpful in indicating or expressing such profound changes.

The level of income in underdeveloped countries is by definition low, but this is still compatible with advance, indeed even rapid advance, if that advance has begun only comparatively recently and has started from a very low level. This is the position in many underdeveloped countries. The thesis of the vicious circle of poverty postulates either that low average levels entail zero rates of change, which is readily refuted by observation, or alternatively that a low level is the same as a zero rate of change, which is a simple error in logic. This confusion between a level and a rate of change is neatly reflected in references to the vicious circle of poverty in *developing* countries.

4 *International Demonstration Effect*

In recent years one variant of the general thesis of the vicious circle of poverty has gained particular influence. This is the suggestion that the presence of the developed countries sets up a so-called demonstration effect, which is regarded as a further obstacle to capital formation and to economic development, in effect substituting another vicious circle of poverty and underdevelopment should the first vicious circle be broken through in some way or other. The suggestion was first advanced by Professor Nurkse, who argued that contact with advanced economies is damaging to underdeveloped countries because it raises the propensity to consume, thus discouraging saving and preventing investment. To quote:

Knowledge of or contact with new consumption patterns opens one's eyes to previously unrecognised possibilities. . . . In the poorer countries such goods are often imported goods, not produced at home; but that is not the only trouble. The basic trouble is that the presence or the mere knowledge of new goods and new methods of consumption tends to raise the general propensity to consume. . . . The vicious circle that keeps down the domestic supply of capital in low-income areas is bad enough by itself. My point is that it tends to be made even worse by the stresses that arise from relative as distinct from absolute poverty.[1]

The effects of contact with more advanced countries are, however, usually very different from those assumed in the international demonstration effect. International economic contacts almost invariably promote the development of less advanced communities by suggesting first of all that change is possible, and by undermining those attitudes and customs which most inhibit material advance. These contacts also promote new ideas, attitudes and modes of conduct, as well as new crops, wants and improved methods generally, besides encouraging production for sale. The provision of a market for export crops has often provided an outlet for surplus labour and unused land, a vent for surplus in

[1] Nurkse, *Problems of Capital Formation . . .*, pp. 61–2, 70.

Adam Smith's terminology, a sequence which has helped material progress in many underdeveloped countries.[1] Such sequences are commonplaces of economic history. They still operate, as is shown by the fact that at present throughout the underdeveloped world the more advanced sectors and areas are those in contact with the more developed countries.

The usual formulation of the international demonstration effect fails to note that new types of consumer goods can be bought only if incomes are first earned to purchase them. Indeed, until quite recently it was the absence of new wants, and the inelasticity of consumption and of standards of living, which were regarded as major obstacles to economic development, so that the role of new categories of consumer goods, often termed incentive or inducement goods, used to be emphasised as an instrument of economic progress. External contacts do indeed often suggest new wants, but at the same time they usually acquaint the population with new methods which make possible the satisfaction of these new wants. There would be no advantage in introducing new commodities to the population unless the population could pay for them.

These external contacts make possible the transformation of effort into desired commodities on more attractive terms. This development usually elicits a higher economic performance: more effort (at the expense of leisure), more productive saving and investment, especially direct investment in agriculture for production for the market. Specially important instances of such improved performance are direct investment in agricultural production for the market in addition to production for the family or instead of it. Moreover, by generating cash incomes these processes also promote investment in other parts of the economy; public investment made possible by increased revenues is only one obvious example.

The usual expositions of the international demonstration effect assume tacitly that the level of economic performance, notably the supply of effort to the exchange sector, is unaffected by the prospects of a higher and more varied level of consumption. At times these discussions seem to assume that the whole economy is already in the exchange sector, so that the question of advance from subsistence production to production for sale does not arise. Such assumptions are inadmissible

[1] The applicability of Adam Smith's concept of the vent for surplus to the expansion of export crops in underdeveloped countries is noted in H. Myint, ' The "Classical Theory" of International Trade and the Underdeveloped Countries', *Economic Journal*, June 1958.

in the conditions of underdeveloped countries. This is apart from the fact that these expositions also ignore the effects of external contacts in undermining traditional attitudes adverse to material progress, and in transmitting new ideas, crops and methods of production. Further, the exponents do not usually ask why the international demonstration effect should operate only on the consumption habits of the population and not on the production, saving and investment habits, or why an international demonstration effect should be singled out for comment when there are also differing levels and patterns of consumption locally which could set up such effects.

In the public sector of underdeveloped countries, however, an adverse demonstration effect does indeed often operate. Politicians and public servants in underdeveloped countries seem to be susceptible to it by adopting or seeking to adopt technical, educational and social standards which are inappropriate and wasteful. Governments and public servants in these countries are being pressed to rival the standards of developed countries. Readiness to yield to these pressures may be a condition of political survival; and in yielding to these pressures the politicians and the administrators do not spend their own resources. But such a situation is very different from the international demonstration effect envisaged by Professor Nurkse and by those who follow him.

A qualification to the general argument of this section which is more formal and apparent than it is substantial, may be noted. It is possible to devise models under which the international demonstration effect could operate in the way envisaged by Professor Nurkse and other exponents. It could so operate if economic performance were unaffected by expectations of a higher and more varied level of consumption; if people's ideas and attitudes and the methods and types of production were not affected by external contacts, but only their consumption patterns were so influenced; and if economic progress depended solely or very largely on the level of saving. While such a situation is conceivable, it is unrelated to the real world, as is clear from present and past experience of the transmission of economic progress. And even if such a situation did exist, it would simply reveal the preference of the population for current consumption over speculative and uncertain future benefits. The suggestion that external contacts (which, as we have noted, very greatly promote material progress) should be restricted to deny consumption opportunities to the population implies that consumer choice is largely irrelevant when development policies are being framed. This suggestion raises wide issues about the very meaning and purpose of economic development which cannot be pursued here though we shall note some of these issues in subsequent essays in this volume.

5 Some Objections Considered

I now turn to three points which may be of some interest in themselves and are also designed to forestall possible objections.

First, the foregoing discussion is not intended to suggest that there has been material progress *throughout* the underdeveloped world. There are substantial groups and large areas in the underdeveloped world which have progressed little in recent times. They include the aborigines in many parts of the world, the desert peoples of the Sahara and elsewhere, and the tribal populations of central and east Africa. And over large areas of south and east Asia (including large parts of rural India, Pakistan and China), progress has been comparatively slow, and much of it has been absorbed in the form of increased populations. These are areas largely of subsistence agriculture. There is nothing abnormal or unexpected even in extreme material poverty in such materially backward societies. But the reasons for this backwardness have nothing to do with a generally operative vicious circle of poverty. There is no general rule to ensure that all countries or regions should reach the same level of economic attainment or the same rate of progress at any given time or over any given period. Economic achievement and progress depend largely on human aptitudes and attitudes, on social and political instutions and arrangements which derive from these, on historical experience, and to a lesser extent on external contacts, market opportunities and on natural resources. And if these factors favourable to material progress are present, persons, groups and even societies will not stagnate, so that it is the absence of the favourable determinants, and not poverty, which is the causal factor in prolonged stagnation. The suggestion that it is poverty as such which acts as the principal obstacle to material progress has diverted attention from these underlying determinants of development.

Second, recognition of the material progress in so many parts of the underdeveloped world is not a plea for *laissez-faire* or for any other policy. The advance has often created formidable problems calling for government action. Progress has often been rapid and generally also uneven; it has affected certain areas and sectors earlier and more pervasively than others and its impact has been much greater on some activities, attitudes and institutions than on others. The differential incidence or impact of material advance in particular has often set up considerable strains. The resulting problems are often acute but they are totally different from those of stagnation. Problems of changes in land tenure arrangements and in property rights and inheritance; personal and social problems arising from the transformation of a subsistence economy into a money economy and from detribalisation; and congestion and delay in ports and on the railroads, are pressing issues in a number of underdeveloped countries. They would not arise in a stagnant economy caught in a vicious circle of poverty. Here again, insistence on the vicious circle of poverty has served to obscure these other problems and to divert attention and energy from attempts to deal with them.

The third point needs somewhat extended discussion. It is often said that the relatively advanced sectors in underdeveloped countries, particularly in Africa, are mere enclaves carved out of the local economies by the advanced countries, or outposts of the advanced economies which do not serve to improve the economic position or prospects of the local population.

It is not true that the local population does not participate in these relatively advanced sectors or does not derive material benefits from them. For instance, as already noted, all agricultural exports from West Africa and Uganda are produced entirely by the local populations on their own lands. Africans also have a large share in the transport, distribution and simple processing of these exports, as well as in the distribution of imports. In south-east Asia the bulk of the production of rubber is on Asian-owned properties. Even where enterprises in the advanced sectors are foreign, they normally still assist development by contributing to government revenues, by spreading skills, and by generally promoting the exchange economy.

These sectors are not, then, enclaves cut off from the rest of the economy, but the points where development makes its first impact. Economic advance always affects certain regions and activities first, from which it spreads outwards. The time required depends, among other factors, on the faculties of the population, on customs and attitudes, on institutional factors, and on physical communications.

The suggestion that the relatively advanced sectors of underdeveloped economies are enclaves which do not benefit the local population derives superficial but insubstantial plausibility from certain features of the economic and social landscape in the underdeveloped world which are especially pronounced in Africa.

All sub-Saharan Africa (outside South Africa) is poor; the incomes earned by Africans throughout Africa are low; apart from European-owned mines, estates and trading companies, small-scale agriculture is the main economic activity; in the advanced sectors, foreign personnel, enterprise and capital are prominent; and foreigners working in these sectors normally earn high incomes compared with the local population. The high incomes of expatriates reflect, of course, their command over skills and capital which could earn relatively high incomes in their own countries. But as is clear, both from general reasoning and from ample specific evidence, none of these features of the economies of underdeveloped countries warrants the suggestion that the material progress in the relatively advanced sectors in the economy has not benefited the living standards or the rates of material progress of the local populations.

6 Aspects and Implications of Change

The cultivation of cash crops by the local population both for export and for sale locally has been a major instrument of material advance in many parts of the underdeveloped world, notably in West Africa, south-east Asia, and parts of East Africa. The major products include cocoa, groundnuts, oil palm products and kola nuts in West Africa, and rubber in south-east Asia. And in East Africa there has occurred rapid, large-scale expantion in the production of coffee and cotton by the local population. The rapid and massive expansion of these products has a number of interesting implications.[1]

First, the cultivation of these products was promoted by contacts established by the west with these areas. The activities of foreign merchants and an inflow of human and financial resources from abroad played a crucial role. But large sections of the local population responded readily to the opportunities presented. The phenomenal expansion of production of these crops from a zero or negligible amount to leading staples of world commerce within a few decades effectively disposes of the suggestion that Africans and Asians do not respond to economic incentives. It also suggests that they can produce competitively for world markets, though the external marketing may be carried out by expatriates.

[1] Some of the factors behind the expansion of the production of cash crops in under-developed countries are examined in H. Myint, *The Economics of the Developing Countries*, London, 1964, and in 'The "Classical Theory" of International Trade and the Underdeveloped Countries'.

Second, the establishment of agricultural properties by Asians and Africans represents massive direct investment in agriculture. This type of capital formation is both quantitatively and qualitatively significant in many poor countries. It is important quantitatively because of the comparative importance of agriculture and its ancillary activities in these economies; and it is qualitatively important because it is generally necessary for the transition from subsistence production to production for wider exchange. This form of investment is important in many poor countries but is often ignored in estimates of capital formation. It is also yet another refutation of the argument that poverty precludes economic advance.

Third, the successful establishment and expansion of these crops shows that rapid and comparatively smooth progress is possible in poor countries. The comparative smoothness of this advance by way of the production of cash crops is not surprising since it involves less of a break with traditional pursuits and ways of living than do large-scale manufacturing or mining. From time immemorial the local population has engaged in various forms of subsistence production; the difficulties of adjustment involved in progress from subsistence production to production for wider exchange and sale are not exacerbated by violent changes in the pattern of life or by the additional need rapidly to acquire knowledge of unfamiliar techniques. The comparative smoothness of the advance is also demonstrated by the establishment of the kola nut industry, now a large-scale activity in western Nigeria, which passed unnoticed in official statistics until years after it had become quantitatively important (though it was reflected in railway returns, amongst other pieces of evidence). Similarly, in Sumatra and Borneo the rapid expansion of the acreage under smallholders' rubber also passed unnoticed for many years in the 1920s and 1930s.

Fourth, the substantial direct investment in agricultural properties producing cash crops also refutes the notion that individual Africans and Asians are invariably unenterprising. But the form of their enterprises, notably the establishment and production of cash crops, or transport and trading activity, differs substantially from that found in more advanced economies.

Fifth, the development of some of these cash crops conclusively refutes the suggestion that individual Africans and Asians cannot or do not take a long-term view, an opinion well known by anthropologists to be erroneous. Many of these crops, especially rubber, cocoa, kola nuts and coffee, are the products of trees or bushes which mature only four to six years after planting. Thus anyone planting these crops looks forward for a long period.

7 Impact of Change

The standard current ideology or orthodoxy about underdeveloped countries, of which the thesis of the vicious circle is an integral and indeed principal part, refers to the underdeveloped world almost wholly in terms of stagnation, starvation and retrogression. However, there also exists a substantial and authoritative body of writings, chiefly by anthropologists, historians, administrators and even a few economists, which is preoccupied with the rapid changes in these countries since the end of the nineteenth century, and the problems caused by them. This literature emphasises the difficulties of adapting institutions and attitudes to fast-changing conditions; the transition from communal to individual tenure of land; the results of detribalisation and disintegration of communal life and values; and the difficulties of rapid urbanisation. Here are a few examples.

In 1926, well before African development became a major international issue, Dr A. McPhee published a book with the revealing title *The Economic Revolution in British West Africa*. The following passages epitomise his conclusions:

In fact, the process since the 'nineties of the last century has been the superimposition of the twentieth century after Christ on the twentieth century before Christ, and a large part of the problem of native policy is concerned with the clash of such widely different cultures and with the protection of the natives during the difficulties of transition . . . . The transition has been from the growth of subsistence crops and the collection of sylvan produce to the cultivation of exchange crops, with the necessary implication of a transition from a 'Natural' economy to a 'Monetary' economy, and the innumerable important reactions from the latter phase.[1]

Much the same conclusions were reached by Sir Keith Hancock, judicious and critical historian of African development. This is what he says:

In some periods of European history – in our own day, for example, or in the day of the first steam engines and power mills – the European world has seemed to be transformed; Europe nevertheless has remained

[1] A. McPhee, *The Economic Revolution in British West Africa*, London, 1926, p. 8.

the same world, spinning very much faster. But in Africa change means more than acceleration. Europe's commerce and its money-measurements really have brought the African into a new world. . . . He retains something of his old social and religious and mental life and habit – these things are very slow in dying – but they are distinct from his new economic life and habit.[1]

Nor is this literature confined to Africa. The problems and strains of rapid advance are a major theme of J.S.Furnivall's *Colonial Policy and Practice*, which deals extensively with experience of Burma:

The dissolution of the political structure is only the first stage in social dissolution, and it is completed by the second, or economic stage, breaking up the village into individuals. In this process two factors are operative: economic forces are released; and the checks controlling their action are relaxed. . . . In such circumstances there remains no embodiment of social will or representative of public welfare to control the economic forces which the impact of the west releases.[2]

These writers were not simple sentimentalists deploring the passing of the good old days; they recognised the very rapid changes taking place and noted the problems which were thus created.

8 *Appeal of the Vicious Circle*

Our discussion of the thesis of the vicious circle of poverty has progressed from a description of the thesis, to examination and refutation based on empirical evidence and analytical reasoning; in technical language the discussion has been positive. I would now like to turn to more speculative issues and consider how a notion so crude as that of the vicious circle of poverty and stagnation should have come to be widely accepted. The explanation seems to lie in its congruity with certain intellectual fashions and methods of approach, and also in its effectiveness in forwarding certain political aims, especially the promotion of intergovernmental foreign aid and of the establishment in underdeveloped countries of economies closely controlled by the state.

The thesis has been a major factor in building up a picture of the underdeveloped world as a substantially homogeneous and stagnant mass, sharply distinct from the developed world. However, the under-

[1] W.K.Hancock, *Survey of British Commonwealth Affairs*, vol. II: *Problems of Economic Policy 1918–1939*, part 2, London, 1942, p. 283.
[2] J.S.Furnivall, *Colonial Policy and Practice, A Comparative Study of Burma and Netherlands India*, Cambridge, 1948, pp. 297 and 298.

developed world is a vast aggregate of different peoples, societies and countries with widely different faculties, attitudes, modes and conditions of living, as well as widely different densities of population, levels of income and rates of growth of population and income. It includes areas in which progress has been relatively slow, such as parts of Central America, Africa, India and Pakistan; and countries which have advanced very rapidly, such as Colombia, Venezuela, Malaya and Hong Kong; very densely populated regions such as Java and much of India and Pakistan; and the sparsely populated areas of Sumatra, Borneo, and most of Africa and Latin America. It includes traditional and highly stratified societies such as those of India and Pakistan and the Moslem middle east, and the much more fluid societies of south-east Asia and Latin America. It includes the semi-deserts of the middle east and the tropical jungles of Africa, Asia and Latin America; the thriving modern cities of south-east Asia, the tribal communities of Africa, and the millions of aborigines in Asia, Africa and Latin America.[1]

Many participants in discussions on economic development find it uncongenial to recognise this diversity, to note that the situation is complex, and that certain lines of distinction, especially that between developed and underdeveloped countries, are arbitrary and indeed impermanent. These participants have a predilection for the clear distinctions and high degree of simplification which rightly characterise the methods of natural sciences and which are at times also useful in certain branches of social study. Even severe abstraction is a valuable or even indispensable scientific device when it isolates principal variables or aspects of the phenomena or processes under review. However, in the economics of poor countries this procedure has often obscured rather than clarified major issues.

In economic discussion on underdeveloped countries, the predilection for sharp distinctions and for a high degree of abstraction has been further encouraged by the practice of negative definition, of treating the underdeveloped world as a residual, that is as the whole world outside North America, western Europe, Australasia and Japan. Special care and discrimination need to be exercised in discussions of residual

[1] Of course diversity in itself does not preclude the establishment of valid generalisations; indeed the recognition of uniformities underlying surface diversities is a principal task of scientific activity. Underdeveloped economies do indeed exhibit certain common features which justify limited generalisations for certain purposes, such as the comparative importance of subsistence production, or wide inter- and intra-seasonal price fluctuations in local markets, or a large proportion of children in the population. However, for many other purposes, including discussions on the background of policy and the framing of policy, it is essential to remember their deep-seated heterogeneity.

concepts and categories derived from negative definition, especially in view of the political potentialities often set up by arbitrary and shifting classification.[1] But the practice of negative definition itself has an appeal, since it conduces to a neglect of close examination of situations. It also makes more plausible the view of the underdeveloped world as a uniform and stagnant mass, which in turn promotes the acceptance of the vicious circle.

The intellectual attraction of the vicious circle is reinforced by certain political attractions; and the two sets of influences mutually reinforce each other. Insistence on the vicious circle of poverty and on the stagnation of the underdeveloped world has promoted the flow of foreign aid, which is a major object of policy for many people, both for its own sake as a supposed instrument for promoting the development of poor countries, and also as an instrument for the extension of progressive taxation from the national to the international level. The suggestion noted on page 32, that the operation of the vicious circle of poverty prevents a voluntary reduction in consumption and thus supposedly justifies compulsion, is a specific instance of the political basis of the thesis of the vicious circle.

Conscious or subconscious political motivations may also have played a part in the emergence and acceptance of the idea of the adverse international demonstration effect (a subspecies of the vicious circle of poverty). The notion is paradoxical that contacts which widen the consumption and production opportunities of people should damage their material position and prospects. It is a notion which conflicts with simple observation and elementary economic analysis. On the other hand, suggestions of western and especially American responsibility for the poverty of underdeveloped countries often serve to promote or reinforce feelings of guilt in the west, which in turn serves to further various political objectives, especially the flow of foreign aid.

Again, the notion that the advanced sectors in underdeveloped economies are foreign enclaves has proved acceptable because it appears to rescue the untenable thesis of the vicious circle of poverty and also because it vaguely confirms the unfounded but politically effective idea of external responsibility for the poverty of the underdeveloped world.

[1] A penetrating discussion of some of the motives and implications of negative definition will be found in Kenneth Minogue, *The Liberal Mind*, London, 1963, chapter 4. We shall note in several places in this volume, including the second part of this essay and essays 3 and 9, the significance, potentialities and dangers of classification, and of distinctions which are apparently clear but are in fact arbitrary.

It seems especially paradoxical that the notion of the vicious circle should have been championed most widely and uncritically in countries with a Protestant culture, that is a culture which values self-achievement and is generally opposed to charity in the form of giving something for nothing. On the other hand, the Protestant culture seems more vulnerable to feelings of guilt, and this as we have seen has played its part in the arguments in favour of foreign aid.

Finally, the notion of the vicious circle is attractive and useful to those numerically small but effective groups and persons, whose influence we noted in the introduction, who are opposed to major institutions of western society and who envisage the underdeveloped countries as instruments in the promotion of their beliefs and policies. The usefulness of the underdeveloped countries for these purposes depends largely on their assumed homogeneity and on the assumed uniformity of their interests in opposition to the west. Their usefulness would be greatly reduced, and might disappear altogether, if the wide differences in conditions, conduct, mores and abilities, and the bitter conflicts within the underdeveloped world, were recognised or admitted.[1] Hence the suggestion of the basic uniformity of the underdeveloped world. It is a suggestion which is so widely at variance with the truth that it could not possibly have gained any credence if it were not for a widespread predisposition among both the promoters of this suggestion and the population at large to believe that the people of the world outside the highly industrialised nations are all much of a muchness.

B. A WIDENING GAP?

9 The Vicious Circle and the Widening Gap

The thesis of the vicious circle of poverty suggests a clear distinction between developed (rich) and underdeveloped (poor) countries based

---

[1] The discussion in Britain over the enforced exodus of Asians from East and Central Africa in 1968–9 is an instance of the approach noted in the text. The discussion focused almost entirely on the failure of the British government to admit the people expelled from these areas and not on the action of the African governments in expelling these highly productive people. Examination of the action of the African governments and of the results of this action would expose the conflicts within the underdeveloped world and thus diminish the effectiveness of the suggestion that they are a homogeneous group with interests opposed to the west and for whose poverty the west is responsible.

on wide differences in per capita incomes between these two clearly distinct groups. Moreover, it follows from the thesis that these differences in per capita incomes between the two groups must increase, because while the developed countries progress the underdeveloped countries stagnate or even retrogress. Hence the suggestion of an ever-increasing international inequality of incomes, colloquially referred to as the ever-widening gap.

Examination of the wide and widening gap, that is of the extent of international differences in incomes, and of the changes in these differences, requires discussion of certain fundamental yet often ignored issues of concept, interpretation, measurement and comparison of incomes and of changes in incomes. Discussion of the concept of the widening gap is meaningless without reference to this range of issues; hence the extensive discussion of subsequent sections of this essay.

To begin with a point of terminology which is of some significance. Comparisons of incomes or wealth ought appropriately to be discussed in terms of differences rather than inequalities. The former term is neutral, while the latter (certainly in nontechnical discussion) implies an abnormal or reprehensible situation (an impression reinforced by the similarity between the words inequality and inequity), an implication often coupled with the suggestion that the situation is readily rectifiable. And the term difference does not prejudge either the origin of these differences or the possibilities or merits of their attempted removal. Moreover, the term inequality is often misleading, for instance in that equality of incomes by one criterion implies inequality by other criteria. Thus, equality in piece rates or hourly earnings implies differences in annual incomes. Again, in any comparison of average incomes between populations of different age compositions, equality of average incomes in the same age group very generally implies differences between average incomes of the populations as a whole.

It is also more appropriate to speak of a structure of incomes rather than the distribution of income. To the nontechnical reader, to whom so much of the development literature is addressed, the latter expression suggests apportionment of a pre-existing income instead of a range of incomes earned by factors of production for their participation in economic activity.

References to a wide or widening gap in incomes between developed and underdeveloped countries are advanced mostly in the context of proposals for policy, especially the advocacy of foreign aid. However, mere mention of the widening gap cannot serve as basis for rational policy without examination of the actual situation, and especially the conduct of the governments and populations of the underdeveloped countries. This consideration is fundamental to assessment of policy proposals. But for convenience of exposition we shall consider first certain issues of concept and measurement necessary for worthwhile discussion of the gap, and postpone until subsequent sections the necessary examination of the conduct of the recipient governments.

10 Ambiguities in the Concept of the Gap

The notion of the gap in per capita incomes between rich and poor countries and the suggestion of its increase encounter certain basic problems of concept which often go unrecognised.

A clear distinction needs to be drawn between differences in the absolute magnitude of per capita (that is average) incomes in developed and underdeveloped countries and in the ratios between these per capita incomes which denote the proportionate or relative differences. This distinction is obviously important because the two types of difference invariably change at different rates and often in opposite directions.

A simple numerical example will illustrate this obvious but widely overlooked point. Assume two groups of people whose average incomes are 100 and 50 units in the first period and 1,000 and 900 units in the second period. The absolute gap in incomes has doubled, but the relative difference has contracted by four-fifths.

Although the term gap suggests differences in absolute magnitudes, in most contexts it is relative or proportionate differences which are usually regarded as interesting or relevant.

In Britain in 1970 a difference between annual incomes of say £10,000 and £8,000 is regarded as less significant than that between £1,000 and £500, though the absolute gap (the difference in absolute magnitudes) between the former is four times that of the gap between the latter.

Further, when incomes increase at a uniform rate over time, the gap between the absolute level of average income between, say, the top 10 per cent of income earners and the bottom 10 per cent will increase, even though both groups are better off. Thus the absolute difference between the per capita incomes of the highest and the lowest decile of the population in Britain today is almost certainly larger than it was two hundred years ago because of the rise in the absolute levels in income, but the proportionate or relative difference has almost certainly narrowed with the improvement of the position of unskilled labour. The main influences which promote long-term increases in world incomes (especially the spread of skills and the accumulation of capital) normally widen absolute differences in per capita incomes between randomly chosen groups but simultaneously tend to reduce the relative differences between certain major groups by reducing the relative scarcity of the resources of the more prosperous categories compared with those of the poorer categories.

The allegations of the ever-widening gap do not usually specify whether they refer to changes in absolute differences in per capita incomes or to changes in relative differences. Nor is it possible to examine either the significance or the validity of these allegations, since they are rarely, if ever, supported by statistical evidence, least of all by statistics about the movement in the ratio of per capita incomes between rich and poor countries.

11 *Distinction between Developed and Underdeveloped Countries*

The notion of the gap implies a distinct and substantial discontinuity in per capita incomes of developed and underdeveloped countries. In fact, there is no such appreciable gap. There is continuous graduation in per capita incomes between different countries. There is no significant difference between the per capita income of the poorest developed country and the richest underdeveloped country – certainly any such difference would be a fraction of the errors and biases of these figures as they are given. And because the line of distinction is arbitrary, and countries are not homogeneous entities, there are groups and regions in many poor countries with higher per capita incomes than the per capita incomes of many countries classed as developed or rich, and *a fortiori* than per capita incomes of many groups and regions within developed countries.

The absence of a wide gap between per capita incomes in the poorest developed country and the richest underdeveloped country and the arbitrariness of the line of division between the two categories affects crucially this area of discourse. The gap in per capita incomes (both absolute and relative differences) of the two global categories, the developed world and the underdeveloped world, depends on where the line is placed. And in the absence of a clear discontinuity between the per capita incomes in the poorest developed countries and the richest underdeveloped countries any line of division on the basis of per capita incomes is arbitrary. Yet the extent of the difference in incomes (the gap) between the two categories depends on where it is placed.

The placing of the line of division depends quite often on accident, or on personal preference, but primarily on political pressures. For instance, in current discussion the underdeveloped world is largely equated with countries whose populations are mainly of non-European origin, a grouping which reflects the operation of political pressures. Again, communist countries are not usually included in the underdeveloped world, though on the basis of per capita incomes or living standards several of them could appropriately be classified as underdeveloped. Their omission again illustrates the play of political forces.

The arbitrary nature of the current distinction between developed and underdeveloped countries on the basis of per capita incomes is compounded by the fact that per capita income is in itself a seriously inadequate index of development. This inadequacy is at times recognised. For instance, some of the oil states of the middle east, habitually and appropriately classified as underdeveloped, have per capita incomes which are among the highest in the world. In many, perhaps most contexts, it is permissible to use interchangeably the terms developed and rich on the one hand, and underdeveloped and poor on the other. But this practice, as the above example shows, is inappropriate in discussions on an allegedly wide and widening gap in incomes.

The distinction between developed and underdeveloped countries on the basis of per capita incomes is not only arbitrary but is also shifting. Quite obviously all developed countries began as underdeveloped. And some countries, such as Japan and Italy, which until recently were classified as underdeveloped, are no longer so regarded. These changes in categories through time preclude any simple assessment of the long-term changes of difference in average incomes between developed and underdeveloped countries.

As a corollary of this situation, a widening difference in per capita incomes between two groups can always be established spuriously by changing the composition of the groups. Thus any worthwhile discussion of differences in average incomes and of changes in these differences depends crucially on the composition of the two categories.

The suggestion of a wide and widening gap between the developed and the underdeveloped world implies not only a clear distinction between the two categories but also substantial homogeneity within them. It implies that the underdeveloped countries are a substantially uniform mass. Such world-wide aggregation and averaging is meaningless. The aggregates are extremely heterogeneous, arbitrary and shifting categories whose composition is unstable and which are comprised of component elements which are themselves heterogeneous collectivities. One aspect of this diversity is the presence of wide differences in rates of material progress within both aggregates. As a result of these differences in rates of material progress, differences in average incomes (both absolute and relative) often move differently between significant groups within the two categories.

I have already noted some United Nations statistics according to which per capita output in Latin America as a whole grew faster between 1945 and 1955 than in the United States of America, so that over this period the relative difference in per capita incomes between these collectivities narrowed.[1] Such statistics could readily be multiplied from the publications of the international agencies. Other familiar examples of recent rapid material progress and substantial rise in per capita income in poor countries outside Latin America include Japan, South Korea, Taiwan, Hong Kong, Thailand, the Ivory Coast, Kenya, the oil states of the middle east and Israel. Indeed in recent years per capita incomes over large parts of the underdeveloped world have increased faster than in many developed countries, including the United Kingdom and the United States of America.

Four countries, India, Indonesia, Pakistan and Brazil, account for about three-fifths of the population of the underdeveloped world outside China; India alone, with a population of 550 million, accounts for well over one-third. Thus a slow rate of economic progress in these countries can mask the rapid progress of a score or more of other countries when their performance is aggregated. And since about 1960 the material progress of India, Indonesia and Brazil has been relatively sluggish. Once again the divergent experience of underdeveloped countries is obscured by world-wide aggregation.[2]

The choice of the period under review is also fundamental to discussions of a trend in the differences in incomes because the rate of change of incomes varies through time. Thus the period over which the gap is supposed to widen needs to be specified. The relevance of this simple conclusion is also clear from the changes in the relative economic position of different countries and populations in the course of history, changes which include economic decline, both absolute decline and

---

[1] These particular United Nations statistics refer to output, not to income per head, but the difference is immaterial in this context. Indeed, because of favourable changes in the terms of trade of the major Latin American countries over this period it is probable that the growth in per capita output understates the improvement in the position of Latin America compared to that of the United States between 1945 and 1955.

[2] I am indebted to Dr F. A. Mehta for this particular example.

decline relative to other countries. These phenomena, often noted by historians, are inconsistent with the supposedly ever-widening gap between rich and poor as a general trend. The allegacions of a supposedly ever-widening gap between rich and poor countries do not usually mention either the period envisaged or the phenomenon of economic decline.

The argument of this section is not affected by the wide margins of error in international comparisons of national income, notably the general undervaluation of national income in underdeveloped countries, which is noted subsequently in this essay. And much additional evidence could be produced to show that the ratio of per capita incomes between every rich and every poor country has certainly not widened in recent decades. But the foregoing should suffice to show that the allegation of an ever-widening difference in incomes between the developed and the underdeveloped world is at best unsubstantiated; as it is usually presented it is meaningless, and in so far as it can be evaluated it is largely untrue.

If it is felt useful to divide the world into two categories on the basis of differences in stages of development (an exercise of debatable usefulness), then differences in demographic patterns, notably in birth rates, which reflect differences in attitudes and institutions and which are often correlated with ethnic differences, would seem to provide a basis which would be potentially more illuminating than the present basis of conventionally measured per capita incomes. For instance, as part of this suggested basis, a distinction between societies in which fertility rates are close to the fecundity rate and those in which fertility rates are significantly below the fecundity rate, might prove useful; it has a certain amount of precision, it is more stable in time, and it could give a measure of insight into the underlying determinants of material progress.

12 *Problems of International Income Comparisons*

Estimates of differences in per capita incomes and living standards in rich and poor countries (that is the magnitudes between which the gap is supposed to be widened) are subject to very wide margins of error which are far larger than is usually recognised. On balance, however, the result is usually an underestimate of incomes in poor . countries and an overestimate in rich ones, thus exaggerating the difference in incomes and living standards between the two groups.

To begin with, even the population statistics of underdeveloped countries, which underlie calculations of per capita incomes and which are free from conceptual problems, are exceedingly unreliable. For instance, according to the official statistics the population of Nigeria in 1963 was 55·6 million. Professor Peter Kilby, a prominent scholar of Nigerian affairs, estimated it at 37·1 million. Again, the Second Indian Five-Year Plan estimated the population growth at about 1·25 per cent per annum over its duration; the figure was subsequently found to be over 2 per cent, thus exceeding the estimate by more than four-fifths.

Quantitatively even more important than the margins of error in statistics of population, are the huge margins of error and statistical bias in the estimates of the national income of poor countries and in the comparisons between the national incomes of rich and poor countries. There are many reasons for these errors and biases. This matter is so fundamental to this area of discussion and so little appreciated that it warrants extensive consideration.

One major reason for the underestimate of the national income of poor countries and the consequent exaggeration of the difference in incomes between rich and poor countries is the use of rates of exchange in comparing national incomes which greatly understate the domestic purchasing power of the currencies of underdeveloped countries relative to those of developed countries. Other reasons include the much greater quantitative importance of intra-family services and also of subsistence and near-subsistence output in poor compared to rich countries, categories which are either ignored or substantially under-valued in national income statistics.[1] Further, many goods and services conventionally included in national income are more nearly costs of production than income, for instance the journey to work, and these are relatively more important in rich than in poor countries.

These problems of international comparison have been known for some time.[2] But their most thorough and methodical examination has

---

[1] Subsistence production and intra-family services are not marketed, so that all prices placed on these must be largely arbitrary. There is an element of self-contradiction in pricing non-marketed output. The various methods adopted tend in practice to impart a strong downward bias to estimates of incomes and living standards in underdeveloped compared to developed countries.

[2] A pioneer work in this area is A. R. Prest and I. G. Stewart, *The National Income of Nigeria 1950–1951*, London, 1953; another important contribution is A. R. Prest, *Public Finance in Underdeveloped Countries* (Appendix I: The Valuation of Subsistence Output), London, 1962; other studies which note some of the conceptual and statistical problems of national income estimates of underdeveloped countries, and of international comparisons of income, include A. R. Prest, *The Investigation of National Income in British Tropical Dependencies*, London, 1957; Stephen Enke, *Economics for Development*, Englewood Cliffs, N. J., 1963; and also the important collection of essays by Professor S. Herbert Frankel, *The Economic Impact on Underdeveloped Societies*, Oxford, 1953.

come only comparatively recently from Professor Dan Usher, who has closely studied the extent of the major errors and biases and the reasons behind these. The following passages from Professor Usher's recent book, *The Price Mechanism and the Meaning of National Income Statistics*, epitomise his position.[1]

Our picture of economic life in poor countries is influenced significantly by statistics showing many countries to have incomes of as little as $50 per year and by estimates of the productivity of labour in agriculture of less than a tenth of the productivity of labour elsewhere in the economy. Using Thailand as an example, this book shows that statistics like these may contain errors of several hundreds per cent . . . the discrepancy is not due primarily to errors in data . . . the fault lies with the rules [of national income comparisons] themselves . . . [which] generate numbers that fail to carry the implications expected of them.

In Thailand I saw a people not prosperous by European standards but obviously enjoying a standard of living well above the bare requirements of subsistence. Many village communities seemed to have attained a standard of material comfort at least as high as that of slum dwellers in England or America. But at my desk I computed statistics of real national income showing people of underdeveloped countries including Thailand to be desperately if not impossibly poor. The contrast between what I saw and what I measured was so great that I came to believe that there must be some large and fundamental bias in the way income statistics are compiled. . . . Something is very wrong with these statistics. For instance, if the figure of $40 for Ethiopia means what it appears to mean, namely that Ethiopians are consuming per year an amount of goods and services no larger than could be bought in the United States for $40, then most Ethiopians are so poor that they could not possibly survive, let alone increase their numbers. . . . National income statistics are the principal medium through which we see the process of economic growth. We characterise countries as developed or underdeveloped according to their national incomes. Income statistics are also components of measures of the productivity of industries and of the equality of the income distribution. The main point of this book, brought out both by the theory and by the numbers, is that the picture conveyed by national income statistics is often distorted, not because the statistics themselves are inaccurate, nor because they fail to reflect accepted canons of statistical method, but because we attribute to income statistics a social meaning that they do not necessarily possess. Higher income is supposed to mean better off; higher productivity is supposed to mean contributing more to the economic welfare of the community. The theoretical part of the book

[1] Oxford, 1968, introduction and summary.

shows how this association can fail. The empirical part of the book shows that there can be a very great discrepancy between conventional statistics and revised statistics designed to reflect more closely the appropriate social facts.

The statistics of incomes examined by Professor Usher refer to per capita figures, as for instance the figure of $40 for Ethiopia, that is they refer to averages. Accordingly, a large proportion of the population would have significantly lower incomes, a consideration which reinforces Professor Usher's case about the utterly meaningless nature of these compilations. Professor Usher's reference to the contrast between what he saw and what he measured provides specific and remarkable confirmation of the importance of direct observation in this area and of the misleading nature of the results which emerge when direct observation is neglected.

Professor Usher writes elsewhere:

For example, the conventional comparison shows that the per capita national income of the United Kingdom is about fourteen times that of Thailand. Recomputations made by the author to allow for various biases in the comparison suggest that the effective ratio of living standards is about three to one. Even if the recomputed ratio is doubled, the change in order of magnitude is large enough to affect our way of thinking about the underdeveloped countries.[1]

Biases and errors of orders of magnitude must strike at the root of international statistics as indices of productivity or of economic development or of comparative living standards. These limitations and errors of comparison are distinct from the inevitable inaccuracies of national income computations in poor countries where even such comparatively straightforward information as population statistics is incomplete.

In the light of the evidence assembled and analysed by Professor Usher, it seems doubtful whether international comparison of national incomes retains any meaning at all, except when restricted to groups of countries which already have roughly the same standard of living.[2]

[1] 'The Transport Bias in National Income Comparisons', *Economica*, May 1963, p. 140.

[2] Professor Usher's arguments and the supporting evidence behind them not only expose the invalidity of international comparisons of per capita incomes between widely different societies, they also put into perspective such notions as the widely publicised suggestion by Professors Max F. Millikan and Walt W. Rostow (in *A Proposal*, New York, 1957) that if per capita incomes in an underdeveloped country rise by between 1 and 2 per cent annually for five years, that country can be assumed to be on the point of take-off (whatever that means) and thus qualify for as much foreign aid as it can absorb (in practice unlimited amounts). Thus changes of 1 per cent in per capita

It is necessary to insist on the presence of these huge margins of error and of bias in national income compilations of poor countries and in international comparisons. It is the conventionally measured per capita incomes which serve as usual or principal bases for classifying countries as developed or underdeveloped, rich or poor, and as a major criterion for the allocation of foreign aid.

International comparisons of per capita incomes, living standards and requirements are significantly affected further by differences in age composition. If per capita incomes of the same age group are equal between two populations, the average for the two populations as a whole will differ if the age composition is different. In underdeveloped countries the age composition usually differs significantly from that in developed countries because of the much higher proportion of children, who usually have appreciably lower incomes and requirements than have adults. Comparisons in per capita incomes unadjusted for differences in age structure confuse differences in levels of income with differences in age.[1]

This complication is again ignored in the standard international comparisons. The adjustment required to correct for differences in age composition are not marginal. The differences in age structure between poor and rich countries are substantial and so are the resulting understatements of per capita incomes in the latter, compared with computations on an age-standardised basis.

Comparisons of living standards, as distinct from per capita incomes,

[1] Quantification of the effects of age composition on differences in per capita incomes is difficult because of statistical and conceptual problems which include among others the interrelations of differences in age composition with differences in the length and effectiveness of education and in the period over which the returns from education are enjoyed.

Some of these difficulties are discussed by Professor Anne Krueger in an important article 'Factor Endowments and Per Capita Income Differences among Countries', *Economic Journal*, September 1968. Professor Krueger shows that in spite of a number of complications it can be established that differences in age composition explain an appreciable part of the differences in per capita incomes between the United States and some twenty underdeveloped countries examined in her article.

incomes are supposed to serve as bases for the most far-reaching policies when the statistics of those incomes are subject to errors of several hundreds per cent; and when these errors are compounded by the huge margins of error in estimates of population and population growth in underdeveloped countries. Quite apart from the other fundamental criticisms to which the suggestion of Professors Millikan and Rostow is subject, the notion that the increase in per capita national incomes in these countries can be assessed within 1 per cent reveals total unfamiliarity with their conditions.

Substantially the same criticism applies to major recommendations of the *Report of the Commission on International Development* (Pearson Report), New York, 1969, which also proposes to link foreign aid to specified rates of growth of the national income of the recipients.

are affected by differences in requirements, for instance in the (generally lower) requirements of food and clothing, and in the (generally higher) availability of leisure in underdeveloped countries. On the other hand, life expectation is generally higher in rich than in poor countries. Attempts to compare relative welfare conditions run into further, more deep-seated, problems. For instance, different economic processes have widely different effects in promoting or inhibiting people's capacities and opportunities for enjoying their incomes.

We may conclude this discussion of the problems of comparison of incomes by forestalling a possible reservation or objection. Most of these problems and limitations of international comparisons affect calculations and estimates of both the *levels* and the *changes* in incomes and living standards. It may be objected that if the errors and biases of comparison remain constant through time, their presence would not affect the suggestions of a widening gap in incomes. Such an objection would be invalid. First, the extent of the biases and errors could not remain constant because of changes in social and economic conditions, including the organisation and pattern of production and consumption within the huge aggregates under comparison. Obvious examples include changes in rates of population growth, and in the relative importance of subsistence production. Second, when errors and biases are so wide that they even affect the orders of magnitude, quantified discussion about international differences in incomes and about changes in these differences loses much of its interest and meaning. Third, if the gap is thought of in terms of absolute differences in incomes, its movement through time is affected by the presence of biases and errors, even if these remain constant as a proportion of estimated per capita incomes.

13 *Population Growth and the Widening Gap*

Estimates and comparisons of changes in per capita incomes and living standards are also complicated by certain fundamental problems of concept and measurement (besides those already discussed) arising from changes in rates of population growth in underdeveloped countries, and also from differences between rates of population growth in developed and in underdeveloped countries.

Over the last fifty to eighty years the population of most underdeveloped countries has increased greatly, mostly by a factor of between two and five. This increase has come about as a result of a fall in death rates, especially among children, which implies a longer life expectation. The position of those who have failed to die has certainly improved, as has the situation of those whose children continue to live, an improvement not reflected in conventional statistics compiled on a per capita basis. Indeed, as we shall shortly see, these statistics often register as a deterioration changes which are clearly an improvement. Thus the usual way of drawing conclusions from income per head obscures important conceptual problems in the definition and measurement of income in that the satisfactions derived from living longer and from having children are ignored.

Over considerable periods in recent times, notably since about 1930, rates of population growth in many underdeveloped countries have been higher than in most developed countries. A differential rate of increase in population in rich and poor countries brings about a change in relative numbers, which directly affects the measurement of international differences in incomes and of changes in these differences. Both absolute and proportionate differences in per capita incomes[1] between rich and poor countries can widen even when per capita incomes in poor countries grow faster than in rich countries, if the rate of population increase is fastest in the poorest countries within the poor countries' group.

Again, if population increases faster in poor than in rich countries, per capita income may fall in the world as a whole even if it has increased in every single country rich or poor. Further, within any one country the per capita income can fall, even if the incomes of all individuals and groups have risen, if the relative numerical importance of the poorer groups increases. In the absence of changes in attitudes and in methods of production, per capita income also falls as a result of an increase in the proportion of children in a population, since the income of children is generally below the overall national average.

These considerations underline again the need for care when referring to underdeveloped *countries*. What matters is the position and prospects of people, not of the country: as we have just noted, the average income in the country can fall even if everybody is materially better off than before, and the converse result is also possible, though in practice rather improbable. These considerations derive from familiar statistical results of a change in the relative importance of the components of an aggregate.

Thus when birth rates and death rates change, special care needs to

[1] The technical reader will note that this conclusion applies whether average is interpreted as arithmetic mean, median or mode.

be exercised in comparisons and interpretations of the movement through time of per capita incomes and of differences in incomes. An increase in the survival rate of the poorest groups usually promotes both a fall in per capita incomes and an increase in absolute and relative differences in incomes between rich and poor. Conversely, an increase in mortality among the relatively poor, or enforced reduction in their birth rates through government fiat would raise average incomes and reduce income differences. Yet the latter types of change could hardly be interpreted as an improvement in the conditions of the relatively poor.

The improved health, longer life expectation and the increase in the rate of population growth in underdeveloped countries have come about largely as a result of contacts established by the west. There are thus many more people alive in poor countries than there would have been in the absence of these contacts. It is only in this sense that the widely publicised notion is true that the west has caused the poverty of the underdeveloped world: it has enabled many relatively poor people to live longer.

The fall in death rates in many underdeveloped countries has come about largely through the suppression or reduction of famine, disease, infant mortality, slave raiding and tribal warfare. Some of these changes in turn reflect far-reaching changes in the conditions of existence which have occurred in many parts of the underdeveloped world in recent decades. Conventional statistics of national income accounting cannot adequately reflect such far-reaching and pervasive changes.[1] This limitation is quite apart from the conceptual and statistical problems, only some of which have been noted in this essay, which arise when the concept, derived largely from the study of societies pervaded by a money economy, is applied to societies in which subsistence production and intra-family transactions are important; or when it is applied to comparisons between such economies and largely monetised or industrialised economies, or is used as an index of change in such economies.

[1] A bias which often overstates the material progress of underdeveloped countries needs to be briefly noted. Economic progress in poor countries is usually accompanied by a reduction in the importance of subsistence output, which is often undervalued in national incomes statistics. Accordingly, a relative growth in production for the market and a corresponding relative decline in subsistence production can overstate material progress. The bias is not significant over the periods considered in the text and does not invalidate its argument.

14 *Further Implications of Population Growth*

Preoccupation with conventionally measured per capita incomes has resulted in some curious and paradoxical notions which bear on the concept of economic progress, standards of living, and also on the widening gap.

Health and life expectation, perhaps the most important components of well-being outside the field of emotions, are not included in the conventional national income compilations. Indeed, better health and longer life expectation often reduce conventionally measured per capita incomes (compared to what they would have been otherwise), with the paradoxical and indeed perverse result that what is clearly an improvement in people's conditions is represented as a deterioration.

Longer life expectation of people and of their children implies a psychic benefit, an increase in well-being, in psychic income. The reality of this benefit is obvious on reflection; and it is clear also from the readiness of people to pay for doctors' services to postpone their own death and that of their children.[1] The improvement in life expectation in underdeveloped countries (although still below that of developed countries), and the consequential survival of large numbers of people, ought to be taken into account in measuring and assessing both the trend in per capita incomes and the trend of differences in per capita incomes between developed and underdeveloped countries.

In statistics of national income the birth of a calf represents an increase in living standards but the birth of a child represents a fall. Discussions on economic development now widely regard children as a curse rather than a blessing; and an increase of population is treated as if it were the unavoidable result of uncontrolled factors rather than of human decisions and actions. But large numbers of people like the act of producing children, and also the children themselves. The generation and possession of children also yield obvious psychic income which people enjoy and which in their opinion exceeds the cost reflected in the reduction of the per capita income of the family. Their satisfaction is not diminished if the possession of children reduces the numerical value of the nebulous concept of the per capita national income.

It is now often thought that the generation of children beyond a small number, or indeed even of a small number, is an anti-social act,

---

[1] It is perhaps not too fanciful to suggest another more mundane illustration of the reality of the benefit of longer life expectation. It implies the personal consumption of a greater volume of goods and services. In this context, as in many others, discussion is meaningless without consideration of the time dimension.

especially in underdeveloped countries. For instance, at the conference of the Indian Family Planning Movement held in Bombay in December 1969 it was proposed to adopt the slogan that to have more than two children is an injustice to the nation. This type of suggestion implies that if a family has children it throws a burden on the rest of the community. But this is not so. There is no burden on the rest of the community if the parents bear the costs of rearing and educating the children. If they do not bear these costs, then there is a burden until the children become self-supporting. But this burden is unaffected by the size of the total population. Moreover it would be present even if a family had only one child.

The birth of a child, then, will always reduce the per capita national income even if it remains an only child. Whether it will reduce the per capita national income over the life span of the person will depend on whether its personal contribution to the national income exceeds or falls short of the national average, which depends on various factors which do not include the number of children in the family.[1]

15 The National Income as Index of Welfare

The shortcomings in comparisons of income and changes in income between rich and poor countries also throw into relief the basic defects of national income as an index of welfare. National income statistics are valuable tools as accounting concepts, primarily as instruments for estimating the volumes of goods and services available for different purposes in a country over specified periods. Their value for this purpose is unrelated to international and intertemporal comparisons and, *a fortiori*, to questions of the measurement of welfare.[2]

To express in a single figure of income the diverse components of the economic conditions of one person is already a simplification. The element of simplification is much greater when the conditions of a large number of diverse persons and groups, who comprise the population of a country, are averaged out and expressed as a single figure of per capita income.[3] And this process of simplification is carried yet

[1] This last issue is examined further in essay 5, where it is also noted that the considerations listed here do not exhaust the arguments for birth control or against it.

[2] This argument is a major theme of a penetrating and unduly neglected paper by Professor S. Herbert Frankel, 'Concepts of Income and Welfare and the Intercomparability of National Income Aggregates', in *The Economic Impact on Underdeveloped Societies*.

[3] For instance, to note a familiar and characteristic point, in cold climates people need heated houses. The cost of installing, maintaining and operating the necessary

further when these averages are compared between communities which differ in age composition and in physical and social living conditions, and which enjoy widely different amounts of leisure, work at different intensities, and whose members undergo different periods of training (expenditure on which is included in the national income although much of it, perhaps most of it, would be more appropriately regarded as cost of production rather than as income).[1]

The inadequacy of simple statistics of per capita incomes as an index of economic development is at times implicitly recognised. An example which we have already mentioned is the habitual designation of the oil states as underdeveloped countries even though their per capita incomes are among the highest in the world. Yet the designation is appropriate. Even when the rulers use their oil revenues for the benefit of their people, they discover that society cannot be transformed within a few decades so as to emulate the material conditions and modes of living of western-type societies with similar per capita incomes but with different attitudes and with centuries of sustained development behind them.

References to differences in average incomes and of changes in these differences are meaningful only if the social and physical living conditions of the populations under discussion are broadly similar. And even if the statistics were much more reliable and meaningful than they are, and also referred to people living in broadly similar social and physical conditions, they still would not serve as indices of welfare, because welfare is a psychological state. The extensive but unwarranted use of per capita incomes for international comparisons of economic conditions and of welfare reflects the naïve contemporary belief that virtually all aspects of personal and social life can be meaningfully reduced to simple quantitative expressions intelligible to all.[2]

[1] It is perhaps necessary to emphasise that recognition of the shortcomings and limitations of the concept of the national income for purposes of comparison between widely different societies does not invalidate the usefulness of the concept for various other purposes, notably for the purpose of national accounting.

[2] The misleading nature of conventional national income statistics as indices of welfare has recently come to be increasingly recognised in some writings on material progress. For instance, Dr E.J.Mishan has noted at some length certain major nonquantifiable aspects of the costs of economic growth in his book *The Costs of Economic Growth,* London, 1967. And some very recent observations by Dr Staffan B.Linder are also pertinent. 'As is well known, statistical difficulties make it impossible to construct an index of the gross national product which faithfully records changes in our material

equipment is included in the national income, which is thereby inflated, compared with those of countries where this expenditure is unnecessary. Of course, different climates imply different needs, but it is not legitimate to assume that these needs balance each other out.

International comparisons both of levels of economic achievement and of rates of progress (as well as of development policies) are in practice also obfuscated by frequent and often unacknowledged shifts in the criteria adopted for measuring economic attainment and progress. The numerous different and varying criteria include total income, per capita income, living standards (with or without allowing for life expectation), magnitudes of investment, industrial production, foreign trade, public expenditure, and many other criteria. Such shifts in criteria compound the difficulties of comparison and assessment presented by problems of concept, measurement, interpretation and of time lags.

16 *Wider Considerations on the Gap*

A possible interpretation of the concept of the widening gap which might provide it with a measure of precision would be a widening of the relative differences in average incomes (whether mean, median or modal) between specified ethnic groups over a specified period (especially if the appropriate adjustments for differences in age composition could be made). Certain populations may exhibit greater readiness and ability than others either to promote or to take advantage of technical progress, because of differences in capacities, attitudes, institutions or official policies. And there are also significant differences in demographic patterns, especially in birth rates, between different populations. These various differences could in turn reflect geographic, climatic, historical, cultural or even biological factors. In these circumstances a widening of differences in incomes would be neither surprising nor abnormal. However, this interpretation of the widening gap, while removing some of its ambiguities, still leaves some major problems of comparison of incomes and living standards between widely different societies untouched, including that of the period over which these differences are supposed to widen. Nor would such a development imply a decline in the living standards or incomes of the poorer groups; it is quite consistent with substantial increases in the real incomes and living standards of these groups. Still less would it warrant the suggestion often implied in current discussions on international

well-being. . . . But once an index, with all its imperfections, has been constructed, it assumes an importance in its own right. In order to wage political campaigns . . . governments will take actions designed to push up the index figures rather than the well-being of the population.' (*The Harried Leisure Class,* New York, 1970, p. 139.)

differences in incomes that the higher incomes of the populations of rich countries have somehow been extracted from the peoples of the poor countries.

Even if the extent and direction of the gap in living standards between different populations were clearly defined over a specified period, and the basic conceptual problems recognised and surmounted (conditions which are most unlikely to be fulfilled), statistical information would still reveal nothing about the causes either of the extent or of the changes in international differences in incomes.

Moreover, the domestic policies of governments in poor countries appreciably affect international income differences, yet this is rarely mentioned in the context. Restrictions of the activities of ethnic minorities in underdeveloped countries, often followed by their expulsion, are an example. The treatment of the Chinese in Indonesia, Indians in Burma, Asians in East Africa, Greeks and Armenians in Egypt, and Europeans in many underdeveloped countries, has reduced per capita incomes in these areas where the incomes of these groups were above the national average. And official policies such as these, directed against the most productive groups, are widespread, indeed almost general, throughout the underdeveloped world.[1] These policies have not only reduced current per capita incomes, they have also retarded their prospective rate of growth because these groups were especially productive. Thus the official restrictions on the activities of these groups, often compounded by expropriation and expulsion, widen the extent of the difference in per capita incomes between rich and poor countries, both at any given time and through time.

17 *Conclusion*

The assertions about the ever-widening gap usually do not even indicate what the widening gap is (that is whether it refers to changes in differences in the levels of per capita incomes or to changes in the ratio of these incomes), between whom it exists, and over what period it is supposed to widen. Yet recognition of these basic matters is a minimal requirement for sensible discussion of this issue. Worthwhile examination would also require recognition of the basic problems of concept, measurement and interpretation of international comparisons of per

---

[1] The enforced exodus of Asians and Europeans from many African countries is familiar. The inexperienced and often untrained personnel sent out by the international agencies, western governments and foundations do not generally serve to replace these emigrants even in numbers, let alone in productivity.

capita incomes and living standards. And for most purposes the reasons behind differences in per capita incomes and living standards also need to be considered.

In the first part of this essay we followed description and analysis of the notion of the vicious circle with reflections on the reasons for its appeal. We shall repeat this procedure here and follow out positive reasoning (again in the technical sense of that term) with more speculative reflections on the origins and the reasons for acceptance of the widening gap.

In one important sense the gap does not even exist because, as we have seen, there is continuous gradation in the international range of per capita incomes; there is no clear break.

As usually advanced, the ever-widening gap is merely a catch-phrase, in much the same way as is the thesis of the vicious circle of poverty, the precursor of the ever-widening gap. Like the vicious circle of poverty, the widening gap is in fact one of those expressions which appear to be descriptive (positive) statements but are actually prescriptive (normative) utterances. It appears to describe situations, but is actually designed to urge courses of action, especially the granting of foreign aid. Principally for two reasons, the allegation of an ever-widening gap is even more effective in the promotion of these purposes than is the thesis of the vicious circle of poverty. First, its defects and limitations are not so immediately obvious and cannot therefore be exposed so briefly and conclusively. Second, it adds a dimension of fear to existing feelings of guilt in the west. By introducing a trend factor into the discussion it promotes a sense of urgency, and an attendant feeling of the increasingly precarious situation of the west, in the face of undefined but mounting dangers, as the gap widens.

2 Dissent on Development[1]

The two parts of this essay examine two major policy axioms of the contemporary literature on economic development; these are that comprehensive planning and foreign aid are indispensable for the economic advance of poor countries.

Comprehensive planning means in this context state control of economic activity outside small-scale agriculture; and foreign aid means government to government grants and subsidised loans in cash or kind.

The case for comprehensive planning and foreign aid is usually taken for granted. At times it is supported by specific arguments, the more important of which are examined in the appendix to this essay (pp. 136–46).

Planning, central planning, comprehensive planning, and comprehensive central planning are generally used interchangeably in contemporary discussion. I shall follow this practice, though I think that attempted comprehensive central planning would convey best the policy under consideration.

A. COMPREHENSIVE CENTRAL PLANNING

1 *Axiomatic Case for Planning*

The thesis that comprehensive central planning is imperative can be illustrated with passages from two writers. I shall quote first from Professor Gunnar Myrdal who is perhaps the most influential, articulate and explicit exponent of the axiomatic necessity of this policy. He writes:

It is now commonly agreed that an underdeveloped country should have ... an overall integrated national plan.... All underdeveloped countries are now, under the encouraging and congratulating applause of the advanced countries, attempting to furnish themselves with such a plan....

---

[1] The original version of this essay, now rewritten and greatly expanded, first appeared in the *Scottish Journal of Political Economy*, February 1969. The article was in turn a revised version of a talk given at Glasgow University in May 1968.

... the national government is expected to assume by means of the plan ... responsibility for the direction of the entire economic development of the country.

The emergence of this common urge to economic development as a major *political* issue in all underdeveloped countries and the definition of development as *a rise in the levels of living of the common people,* the uncontested understanding that economic development is *a task for the governments* and that the governments have to prepare and enforce *a general economic plan,* containing a system of intentionally applied controls and impulses to get development started and to keep it going, is an entirely new thing in history. . . .

What we witness is how this much more than half of mankind living in poverty and distress is not only accepting for itself the pursuance on a grand scale of a policy line which we are accustomed to call 'socialistic', but that positive and urgent advice to do so is given to them by all scholars and statesmen in the advanced countries. . . .

Central economic planning is always a difficult thing and, when it has been tried, it has not been too much of a success in the advanced countries. Now, what amounts to a sort of superplanning *has* to be staged by underdeveloped countries with weak political and administrative apparatuses and a largely illiterate and apathetic citizenry.

There are all [kinds of] reasons [why we should] expect numerous mistakes and in many cases total failure. But *the alternative to making the heroic attempt is continued acquiescence in economic and cultural stagnation or regression which is politically impossible in the world of today*; and this is, of course, the explanation why grand scale national planning is at present the goal in underdeveloped countries all over the globe and why this policy line is unanimously endorsed by governments and experts in the advanced countries.[1]

He writes elsewhere:

The special advisers to underdeveloped countries who have taken the time and trouble to acquaint themselves with the problem, no matter who they are ... all recommend central planning as the first condition of progress.[2]

Professor H. Kitamura of Tokyo University supplies a much more succinct formulation of the alleged axiomatic necessity of planning:

[1] *Development and Underdevelopment,* Cairo, 1956, pp. 63 and 65. The italics are in the original except in the penultimate paragraph where the italicisation of 'has' is mine. That paragraph is notable in its insistence that comprehensive central planning must be undertaken regardless of the wishes of the population, the capacities of the government, and apparently regardless also of the likely results of the policy.

[2] *An International Economy,* London, 1956, p. 201.

Only planned economic development can hope to achieve a rate of growth that is politically acceptable and capable of commanding popular enthusiasm and support.[1]

Professor Kitamura's opinion is ironical in the light of the phenomenal progress of Japan which was achieved without the policies he specifies as indispensable. Of course any rate of progress can be described as inadequate or unacceptable on some criterion or other, and this alleged insufficiency then advanced to criticise social arrangements or government policies.

These are not the views of academic advocates only. Comprehensive central planning is now the essence of economic policy in many parts of the underdeveloped world, notably in India. And because such a policy is now widely regarded as a condition of economic advance, governments pursuing or purporting to pursue it are treated preferentially in the allocation of foreign aid.

Like love, freedom, democracy, equality, stabilisation, and many other abstract concepts, planning can mean widely different phenomena. It can mean orderly preparation for the future conduct of persons, enterprises and governments. It can describe the coordination of the activities of different government departments to reduce competition among themselves for scarce resources. It can denote plans for phasing fiscal policies to offset fluctuations in private expenditure. In the contemporary development literature it means actual or attempted extensive state control of most economic activity outside small-scale agriculture, especially of the composition of economic activity in the exchange sector.[2]

I shall again quote Professor Myrdal:

The plan must determine this overall amount of investment and must, in addition, determine the proportions of the capital which should be allocated in different directions: to increase the overall facilities in transport and power production; to construct new plants and acquire the machinery for heavy industries and for light industries of various types; to raise the productivity level in agriculture by long-term investments in irrigation schemes and short-term investments in tools, machinery and fertilisers; to improve the levels of health, education and training of the working people, and so on. To be practical and effective, the plan must be worked

---

[1] H. Kitamura, 'Foreign Trade Problems in Planned Economic Development', in Kenneth Berrill (ed.), *Economic Development With Special Reference to East Asia*, London, 1964, p. 202.

[2] A recent important reinterpretation of the concept is noted in section 2 of this essay.

out not only as a general frame, but must have this frame filled and concretised by careful segmental planning.[1]

Professor Myrdal says repeatedly that experts are unanimous in endorsing these policies. This is not true. There are many economists, some in prominent positions, who do not think that central planning promotes economic progress, let alone that it is necessary for it. On Professor Myrdal's definition, however, they cannot be experts, whatever their technical qualifications, academic positions or fields of study.

Although advocates of comprehensive planning take the case for it as granted, there is not even a *prima facie* case for its necessity. It played no part in the development of any one of the now highly developed countries. The Soviet Union is no exception to this statement: general living standards, the usual yardstick of development, are vastly lower there than in the advanced countries of the west. Nor did comprehensive planning play any part in the substantial progress of the many underdeveloped countries and areas which have advanced rapidly since the end of the nineteenth century.

It is not surprising that comprehensive planning was not found necessary either in the earlier history of the developed countries or for the recent progress of many underdeveloped countries. Comprehensive planning does not augment resources. It only concentrates power. And by concentrating power such a policy augments and creates power because in a decentralised system of decision-making there do not normally exist such positions of power as are created by comprehensive planning.[2]

Centralisation and thereby creation of power is, then, a necessary result of comprehensive planning.[3] Yet it is rarely discussed by its advocates. For instance, though this outcome is clear in the passages quoted above from Professor Myrdal, it is not noted explicitly. On the other hand, advocates of planning state or clearly imply that it somehow enlarges the volume of productive resources, without explaining how or why.

---

[1] *Development and Underdevelopment*, pp. 63–4.

[2] Power here means the capacity to restrict the choice open to other men. There are large corporations and rich men in a market system. But their resources do not confer power on them in this material sense, at any rate to nothing like the extent to which comprehensive planning confers it on politicians and civil servants.

[3] It follows from this that comprehensive planning necessarily affects the parameters of the conventional economic variables. This result in turn implies that the familiar assumption of other things being equal is inadmissible. Some implications of this outcome are noted later in this essay.

The state cannot create new additional productive resources. The politicians and civil servants who direct its policy dispose only of resources diverted from the rest of the economy. It is certainly not clear why overriding the decisions of private persons should increase the flow of income, since the resources used by the planners must have been diverted from other productive public or private uses.

It is even less obvious why the flow of goods and services which are desired by consumers and which makes up the standard of living should be increased by such a policy. A rise in general living standards is almost always instanced as the ostensible aim of comprehensive planning. For example, this is what Professor Myrdal writes in some of the passages I have already quoted. But he does not say how his policy of controls would bring this about; and indeed later in the same lecture he writes that comprehensive planning implies utmost austerity without resolving the contradiction.[1]

Professor Myrdal and other exponents of the axiomatic case for comprehensive planning do not refer to empirical evidence in their advocacy of planning. Indeed, once a case is treated as axiomatic empirical evidence becomes irrelevant. Whatever the actual course of events, it can always be adduced in support of a policy which is axiomatically deemed desirable: progress as evidence of its success and lack of progress as evidence of the need for its reinforcement.

2 *Some Points of Clarification*

Before examining the likely effects of comprehensive planning on material progress I would like to digress on two points: a recent reinterpretation of the concept of planning; and some implications of the references to human faculties and attitudes in this book.

A reinterpretation of the concept of planning has recently made its appearance in the literature. The central argument of Professor Myrdal's *Asian Drama* is an example. He envisages planning as wholesale transformation of people's attitudes, values and institutions, by compulsion

---

[1] 'There is no other road to economic development than a forceful rise on the part of the national income which is withheld from consumption and devoted to investments, and this implies a policy of the utmost austerity. . . . The frugality, which must be applied to the level of living of the masses of the people for the simple reason that they are the many. . .', *Development and Underdevelopment*, p. 64.

As discussed in subsequent sections of this essay, large-scale increase in investment expenditure through enforced increase in the savings ratio is neither a necessary nor a sufficient condition of economic development. Nor would increased investment necessarily imply utmost austerity though it often serves as a pretext for a scarcity of consumer goods.

if necessary. This reinterpretation of the concept envisages the policy not as state control of the economy but as attempted remoulding of man and society. If such a policy were pursued or pressed by coercion it would reduce the population to the status of malleable clay; such a population is more likely to become an inert mass rather than a vigorous society capable of material progress.[1]

Indeed, the widest moral and political issues are raised by the proposed attempts to coerce people to change or to attempt to change their beliefs, values, attitudes, mores, modes of living, social institutions and even their faculties. It is in fact improbable that indigenous governments, whose personnel are drawn from the local population and whose basic faculties and attitudes they usually share, would attempt such transformation as distinct from the introduction simply of close controls over economic life to promote the centralisation of power.[2]

In what follows I shall refer repeatedly to human aptitudes and attitudes. As noted in the introduction, these references are solely to those aptitudes and attitudes which influence economic performance. The attitudes and motivations which promote material success are not necessarily or even usually those which confer happiness, dignity, sensitivity, a capacity to love, a sense of harmony, or a reflective turn of mind. This important point is often overlooked.

A further point of clarification may be useful here. The references in this book to the significance of abilities, attitudes and institutions as determinants of material progress do not imply that official policy cannot promote material advance. To begin with, even when these determinants are not affected by official measures, the latter may nevertheless affect the deployment of the human, financial and physical resources of the society. Further, official policies can often appreciably react on the underlying determinants themselves.

3 *Determinants of Development*

An economy consists of people whose material needs it has to satisfy and whose performance largely determines the material achievement

[1] The establishment of compulsory labour services, or the imposition of poll taxes to force people to seek paid employment, raise issues somewhat analogous to those of the attempted transformation of human beings. However, the analogy is largely superficial, because the area, intensity and purpose of coercion in compulsory labour services have always been much more restricted than those envisaged by the proposals for attempts to transform people.

[2] This issue is examined at length in essay 5.

of the economy and its rate of advance. This is a platitude. But the implications and corollaries of the platitude are much neglected in discussions on economic development.

The prime corollary of this platitude is that economic achievement depends primarily on people's abilities and attitudes and also on their social and political institutions. Differences in these determinants or factors largely explain differences in levels of economic achievement and rates of material progress. It is, of course, true that these determinants not only interact among themselves but are also influenced by material progress, once it is under way, because those attitudes and institutions which blocked it in the past tend to be further weakened. This further influence does not, however, affect the significance of the determinants themselves.

Natural resources and external contacts and market opportunities also play a part in material advance. However, with the possible exception of climate and its effect on performance, which I shall consider shortly (climate is a significant natural resource though rarely classed as such), natural resources have been of only secondary importance, both in the development of the now advanced countries and in the development of many underdeveloped countries since the end of the nineteenth century.[1] And the exploitation both of natural resources and of external opportunities must depend on the required human capacities.

Capital resources, which are often thought to be crucial, are usually less important. Moreover their supply and productivity depend on personal faculties, motivations and social and political arrangements. These resources are thus primarily an effect, a result, a dependent variable in the process of economic development rather than a cause or an independent variable. When the basic determinants are favourable material progress will in the course of time occur unless forcibly repressed, notably by external action. Conversely, when they are absent even ample natural resources and ample capital (in these conditions the latter would represent a legacy of the past or externally supplied funds) will not secure development. The presence of the favourable determinants serves both to generate investible funds and to bring about their productive use, a sequence which provides superficial plausibility to the emphasis of the allegedly decisive role of the volume of investible

---

[1] Geographical configuration and accessibility of different areas are sometimes instanced as determinants of economic performance analogous to climate. This is true to some extent. However, as will be readily noted on some reflection, accessibility, unlike climate, is much influenced by human activity, so much so that it can be said to depend on human endeavour.

resources as a determinant of material progress.[1] But even if the supply of investible funds were a key independent variable in the development process, which it is not, this would be irrelevant to the case for comprehensive planning both because saving and investment can be increased without it, and because much of comprehensive planning is unrelated to increasing saving and investment. These issues are discussed in the appendix to this essay.

In intellectual, artistic, political and athletic activity achievement clearly depends on personal qualities and motivations. This connection is always taken for granted. Further, differences in achievement are obvious not only between persons but between groups, including ethnic groups. While in activities outside economic life the presence of such differences is recognised and accepted almost as a matter of course, the reality of differences in economic faculties and performances is often either ignored or denied, or regarded as abnormal and reprehensible. This differential approach is reflected in the habitual and revealing references to *differences* in the context of intellectual and artistic achievement and to *inequalities* in the context of economic performance and material rewards: difference is a neutral expression, while inequality suggests an abnormal and reprehensible situation.[2]

There seem to be several reasons why people recognise this relationship in other activities but not in economic life. The most important reason is perhaps that disregard of differences in economic aptitudes and attitudes spuriously justifies far-reaching proposals for compulsory standardisation of material conditions. Such proposals gain in plausibility if differences in economic achievement are treated as a result either of environment or of chance, since they then appear to be practicable, just and also neutral in their effects on material progress.[3] The refusal or reluctance to recognise the connection between economic faculties

[1] This conclusion is an instance of a general rule. If (a) and (b) together produce (c), and (a) without (b) also produces (c), but (b) without (a) does not, we are entitled to regard (a) as the cause of (c).

[2] A subsidiary reason why economic differences are termed inequalities may be that the results of economic performance can be more easily quantified than achievement in some of these other fields. But this is not the main reason for the difference in terminology. There are all sorts of other quantifiable differences between people which are not usually termed inequalities.

[3] Professor Myrdal has explicitly noted certain practical attractions of the disregard of differences in human aptitudes: 'On the whole, however, the social sciences and, in particular, economic theory stuck stubbornly to the naturalistic equality postulate that as a general rule men are equally endowed by nature; they could thereby also uphold the environmental approach.' *Economic Theory and Underdeveloped Regions*, London, 1957, p. 113.

and motivations and between economic performance thus partly reflects the influence of environmental determinism.

The appeal of environmental determinism in the social sciences, including development economics, derives primarily from the political attraction just noted. The significance of this attraction is further suggested by the neglect by social scientists of the effects of climate on economic performance and material progress, an influence which cannot reasonably be doubted. It is certainly far more obvious than most other environmental influences often cited. Yet this highly significant factor is habitually neglected by economists, including exponents of environmental determinism. This neglect in turn presumably reflects several factors: for instance, climate cannot readily be manipulated by policy;[1] it is not susceptible to formal analysis; and its effects on economic performance cannot easily be quantified.

Two further reasons may be noted for the greater acceptance of environmental determinism in economics than in many other disciplines. Preoccupation with material success has become especially pronounced in public discussion in the twentieth century, a period in which environment has come to be increasingly emphasised as a determinant of achievement compared to personal faculties and motivations. Also in public discussion attention has come to be increasingly focused on quantifiable phenomena, and the fruits of economic activity are on the whole readily quantified, certainly more so than those of artistic or scientific activity.

Whatever its appeal, the limitations of environmental determinism are quite as pronounced when applied to economic activity as to other spheres of endeavour. Its influence in economics is, however, most tenacious, partly because its limitations are less immediately obvious or demonstrable in economic activity than elsewhere; and also because much of its appeal is of political and emotional rather than intellectual origin. And the acceptance of environmental determinism in turn reinforces other possible reasons for not recognising the connection between economic faculties and economic performance.

Similarly the role of chance is probably not significantly more

---

[1] Forestry policy is a partial exception; and water control schemes in appropriate conditions affect some results of the climate itself, for instance irrigation schemes in arid climates.

Mr Nirad C. Chaudhuri, a writer whose grasp of the fundamentals of Indian life is exceptional, has emphasised at length in his books the effects of the Indian climate on economic performance; he discusses this influence especially in *The Continent of Circe*, London, 1965.

important in economic life than in other activities.[1] But its role in specific instances can be picked out more plausibly in economic activity.[2] Curiously, the most articulate critics of western-type economic activity, and of successful participants in it, never doubt the connection between capacity and achievement in their own fields.

What factors underlie the determinants of development or account for ethnic or geographical differences in their operation are matters about which little is known and which are much disputed. It is also conjectural how they have emerged or how far they are likely to persist. What is not in doubt is the presence in many underdeveloped countries of long-standing and interrelated attitudes, beliefs and cultural traditions uncongenial to material advance, and often also a comparative weakness of personal capacities which favour it. The more authoritarian tradition of most of Africa and Asia compared to western Europe has probably contributed to the persistence of attitudes and mores damaging to material advance. It is also highly probable that because these factors uncongenial to material advance are of long standing, they will not be eliminated or even substantially reduced (taking the community as a whole) over the comparatively short period of a few years or decades without large-scale immigration or emigration.

Examples of significant attitudes, beliefs and modes of conduct unfavourable to material progress include lack of interest in material advance, combined with resignation in the face of poverty; lack of initiative, self-reliance and of a sense of personal responsibility for the economic fortune of oneself and one's family; high leisure preference, together with a lassitude often found in tropical climates; relatively high prestige of passive or contemplative life compared to active life; the prestige of mysticism and of renunciation of the world compared to acquisition and achievement; acceptance of the idea of a preordained, unchanging and unchangeable universe; emphasis on performance of duties and acceptance of obligations, rather than on achievement of results, or assertion or even a recognition of personal rights; lack of sustained curiosity, experimentation and interest in change; belief in the efficacy of supernatural and occult forces and of their influence over one's destiny; insistence on the unity of the organic universe, and on the

[1] Pasteur's familiar remark that chance visits a prepared mind applies in economic life much as it does elsewhere.

[2] The advantages accruing to persons who have inherited wealth is sometimes noted as an influence analogous to the operation of environmental determinism. The significance of inherited wealth is often much exaggerated; it is of little practical significance in the context of economic development. Some observations on this point will be found in essay 5, section 3.

need to live with nature rather than conquer it or harness it to man's needs, an attitude of which reluctance to take animal life is a corollary; belief in perpetual reincarnation, which reduces the significance of effort in the course of the present life; recognised status of beggary, together with a lack of stigma in the acceptance of charity; opposition to women's work outside the household.

This list could of course be extended greatly. Moreover, the attitudes and aptitudes discussed here are not surface phenomena. Over large areas, with huge populations, especially in south Asia, some of the prevailing attitudes and beliefs most uncongenial to material advance are so deeply felt and strongly held that they have become an integral part of the spiritual and emotional life of many millions of people, probably hundreds of millions. Enforced removal of these attitudes or beliefs, or even energetic attempts in this direction, would probably result in large-scale spiritual and emotional collapse.[1] The effects of these attitudes on material progress are often compounded by the results of having lived for centuries or millennia in a debilitating climate. In Africa the attitudes uncongenial to material progress may be less deep-seated than in south Asia. But in Africa also there are many strongly held attitudes and beliefs which are inimical to material advance.

Personal aptitudes and attitudes, cultural conditions, and social and political institutions differ widely between societies both within the developed and the underdeveloped world and between them. As we have already mentioned, the underdeveloped world is not a substantially homogeneous and stagnant collectivity of uniform societies and human beings, basically similar themselves and different from those of developed countries only in being poorer. There are pronounced differences in the determinants of material progress between persons, groups and societies throughout the world. If the only relevant difference between

[1] Lord Clark has noted that the challenge of the Reformation to the position of certain values, beliefs and practices, such as the cult of the Virgin Mary and the Saints, was experienced by the peasants of southern Europe as a threat to their emotional lives: 'He must have felt something deeper than shock and indignation: he must have felt that some part of his whole emotional life was threatened. And he would have been right.' (Kenneth Clark, *Civilization*, London, 1970, p. 177.) In south Asia many of the attitudes and beliefs discussed in the text are certainly of greater antiquity, and probably of greater strength, than those discussed by Lord Clark in relation to southern Europe. Another distinguished art historian, Professor Gombrich, has insisted that certain attitudes and beliefs, particularly the sanctity of the cow, are deeply interwoven into the very fabric of the lives of the Hindu peasant (E. H. Gombrich, *The Tradition of General Knowledge*, London, 1962, p. 7).

The antiquity and strength of these attitudes and beliefs need special emphasis because they are apt to be so underrated, or even denied, both by western observers and by many westernised Asian intellectuals.

people and between societies were that in income it would probably never have emerged, and if it had would not have persisted for long.[1]

The practice of negative definition,[2] that is the lumping together as underdeveloped countries the whole world except for a few countries with relatively high conventionally measured incomes, has been at least partly responsible for the neglect of international differences in the presence and strength of the determinants of development. Various political motives, notably the wish to reduce international differences in conventionally measured incomes and to some extent standardise material conditions internationally through progressive taxation on the international level and possibly through the imposition of supernational economic controls, have also encouraged disregard of differences between groups other than those in conventionally measured incomes; and these motives themselves have helped to promote the practice of negative definition in this area.

The significance of the determinants of material progress has been underrated, or even ignored, in most of the development literature of the last two decades. These influences have either been ignored altogether or have been treated parametrically at best. Various reasons may account for this comparative neglect. These determinants are not among the familiar variables of economic analysis; they are not readily quantifiable; and they cannot easily be manipulated by official policy. But while these considerations may account for the relative neglect of these determinants of development, they do not affect their significance.[3]

---

[1] It is sometimes urged that differences in the presence of these determinants account for international differences in *levels* of economic development but not for differences in *rates* of development over a specified period. This objection is generally superficial. First, levels of economic attainment reflect past rates of change. Second, differences in the determinants of development affect people's ability to take advantage of changing conditions and thus affect rates of economic progress over specified periods.

[2] We have already noted the practice of negative definition and some of its implications in the introduction and essay 1.

[3] Professor Kaldor wrote in a paper presented to the 1962 Vienna Conference on Economic Development of the International Economic Association: '. . . it is limitation of resources, and not inadequate incentives, which limits the pace of economic development'. 'The Role of Taxation in Economic Development', in E.A.G.Robinson (ed.), *Problems in Economic Development*, London, 1965, p. 170.

'Resources' here seems to refer to money, and 'incentives' to attitudes and motivations. Such a cavalier treatment of mores and institutions may perhaps have been excusable in the heady early postwar years, when it was widely believed that capital imports were practically all that was required for the material progress of the underdeveloped world. But by 1962, after the failures of massive investment programmes in many underdeveloped countries, such an attitude was inexcusable. And it is a particularly surprising opinion from an economist who visited India at some length in the 1950s, when the statutory ban on the slaughter of cattle was being enacted in one Indian state after another.

Neglect of the basic determinants of material progress, together with certain related shortcomings of method (such as the intrusion of unacknowledged political objectives into the discussion, or the neglect of direct observation or of primary sources), have brought about an emphasis in the current development literature on topics which are of very limited substantive importance to the development prospects of poor countries. Examples include often lengthy discussions on how to improve the material prospects of underdeveloped countries by internalising external economies (that is, centralising production decisions to take into account all spillover effects of a decision) or on the construction of elaborate programming models for optimising public investment decisions.[1] Such subjects, though they may be useful in certain contexts, are almost wholly irrelevant as components of state activity designed to promote the material progress of societies attached to attitudes largely inconsistent with appreciable material progress, or which are still largely in the grip of magic, or which may not even have reached the level of a tribal culture. Preoccupation with such matters diverts attention from the major determinants of development and of the possibility of influencing these favourably, besides often issuing in policy proposals which in fact affect them adversely.

A further reason for the neglect of the crucial determinants of material progress in these discussions is that the discussions themselves are much influenced by modern macroeconomic models which address themselves to problems quite different from those of long-term economic development. The irrelevance of these models to an analysis or explanation of material progress is quite clear from the assumptions of Keynes' *General Theory*, the work from which most of these models derive.

Keynes wrote there:

We take as given the existing skill and quantity of available labour, the existing quality and quantity of available equipment, the existing technique, the degree of competition, the tastes and habits of the consumer, the disutility of different intensities of labour and of the activities of supervision and organisation, as well as the social structure. This does not mean that we assume these factors to be constant; but merely that,

---

[1] The presence of unacknowledged political objectives behind apparently irrelevant and jejune discussions is suggested by the conclusions which issue frcm these, which are almost always for more state control or operation of major economic activities. Thus the nebulous and (in the context) irrelevant notion of the internalisation of external economies leads to the proposal for state operation of the activities yielding these alleged economies.

in this place and context, we are not considering or taking into account the effects and consequences of changes in them.[1]

Thus the prime determinants of material progress are deliberately taken as given. Such models are appropriate, or at any rate may be appropriate, to a study of short-period fluctuations in aggregate output in technically advanced societies. But they are useless for an examination of the long-term determinants of economic progress and for the framing of policies for its promotion. A manual for driving a motor car or operating an engine will tell us nothing about the process of the machine's evolution nor about the principles lying behind its construction.

4 Effects of Climate

Material backwardness is heavily concentrated in extreme climates, and especially in the tropics. This would suggest, *prima facie*, that prolonged residence there, especially when it involves domicile over centuries or millennia, affect adversely the determinants of material progress.[2] There is as yet no conclusive evidence for assuming that extreme climate conduces to material backwardness, but it does seem that there is a causal relationship. Yet development economists have come largely to ignore this possibility.

That extreme climate has an enervating effect has certainly been remarked on in the past and indeed regarded as evident. Nor have expressions of this opinion been confined to casual observers, or applied only to visitors from temperate climates. Any possible adverse influences would not, of course, affect all groups equally. Nor would they preclude the emergence of first-class specialists in diverse fields. But it would seem that extreme climate affects adversely the energy and stamina of the population at large and conduces to comparative poverty. Moreover, those groups most interested in economic improvement, and capable of it, are those most likely to leave a poor society, in search of better opportunities. Climatic conditions are relatively long-lasting, and thus any possible adverse effects of climate on the material progress

---

[1] *General Theory*, p. 245.

[2] In the past very high civilisations emerged in tropical and subtropical areas and these produced outstanding monuments. But these civilisations did not produce widespread material achievement; nor were their leaders concerned with its promotion. The achievements of contemporary civilisations and those of the high civilisations of the past rest on very different aptitudes and attitudes.

of societies may over a long period have an effect which is not only important but also cumulative.

Geographical inaccessibility has in the past had adverse effects on the material progress of certain societies analogous to those of climate in that it too is difficult for a society to overcome. However, as a result of improvements in communications which have originated in the west, this is now a much less important factor than it was in the past.

A point may be noted here which bears on the possibly lasting effects of factors unfavourable to material progress. If attitudes, mores and institutions uncongenial to material progress have prevailed for long historical periods, with corresponding effects on material advance, it may be difficult or even impossible to reverse their effects except after long periods. Even if the attitudes and institutions are modified, the mental and physical capacities and the attitudes of appreciable sectors of the population may have been affected so greatly that their economic performance will compare unfavourably with those of other groups for a long time. Such a result is especially likely if these groups have lived for long in an unfavourable climate and if they remain in the same climate even after their attitudes and institutions have changed.[1]

In practice, of course, the various determinants of development, probably including climate, operate simultaneously, which makes it difficult or even impossible to disentangle their relative importance. An example is provided by the operation of the factors behind the differences in the economic fortunes of East and West Pakistan and of the refugees from these two areas now domiciled in India. These differences both in income and in rates of progress have become a major political issue in Pakistan. The pattern is confirmed by the experience of the refugee communities in India. The refugees from West Pakistan have on the whole adapted themselves much more successfully than those from East Pakistan. The climate of the north-western regions of the Indian subcontinent is widely regarded as much less debilitating than that of East Bengal; over the centuries there has been more intermarriage with ethnic groups from outside the subcontinent; and that region

---

[1] These considerations may explain the difference in economic performance between Chinese and Indian migrants in south-east Asia, which is specially clear in Malaysia. Both groups entered that country as extremely poor immigrants, very largely as unskilled labourers. In both groups the more enterprising categories of the countries of origin were presumably strongly represented. Within a few decades the Chinese far outdistanced the Indians.

The same difference is reflected on what may be termed the microeconomic level. Malaysian rubber estates frequently employ both Chinese and Indian rubber tappers who use identical equipment. The output of the Chinese usually exceeds that of the Indians by between one-quarter and three-quarters.

experienced a much greater variety and volume of external contacts than has East Bengal. The relative importance of these different and interacting influences, and possibly of other influences as well, is probably impossible to assess. The differential prosperity of the two regions, and also of the refugees from West and East Pakistan to some extent accords with what would have been expected from past experience. The Punjabis have for centuries been more successful as agriculturalists and craftsmen than the Bengalis. However, assessment of the reasons behind group differences in economic performance must rest on large elements of intuitive judgment.

5 *Planning and Progress*

As we have shown, the notion that comprehensive planning is indispensable for material progress is plainly unfounded. This still leaves open the question whether it is more likely to promote or to retard it. It can be shown that it is much more likely to obstruct economic progress than to advance it. This is particularly true when material progress is interpreted as an improvement in general living standards.

Economic development requires modernisation of the mind. It requires revision of the attitudes, modes of conduct and institutions adverse to material progress. The attitudes, mores and institutions of large parts of the underdeveloped world differ radically from those which have promoted the material progress in the west of the last millennium, especially those which have prevailed in recent centuries. The mores and institutions of underdeveloped societies are often closer to those of much earlier stages of development in the west.

Comprehensive planning does not promote favourable changes in these attitudes and mores. It reinforces the authoritarian tradition of many underdeveloped societies, which inhibits the development of faculties and motivations congenial to material advance. By continuing and extending state control over the lines of the population central planning reinforces the subjection of the individual to authority. Such a development discourages self-reliance, personal provision for the future, sustained curiosity and an experimental turn of mind.

Comprehensive planning means close economic controls. Such controls restrict the movement of resources to directions where they would be most productive. They inhibit the establishment of new enterprises and the expansion of efficient producers. This is a familiar result of such measures. Certain other results and implications of such controls are probably more important in the context of economic development. Restrictions on occupational and geographical mobility inhibit the establishment of new contacts, the spirit of experimentation and the opportunities to set up new enterprises. Mobility and experimentation promote material advance in familiar ways, including the erosion of attitudes and customs adverse to material progress.

These controls necessarily extend to external economic relations. Indeed the control of foreign trade is usually a pivot of comprehensive planning. External economic relations, that is migration, trade and capital movements, serve not only as channels and vehicles of the movement of human resources, including skills, physical commodities and financial transactions, but also of new ideas and attitudes, crops, methods of production, and wants. Throughout economic history and throughout the present underdeveloped world these contacts have often served to promote economic change and indeed to engender a new outlook towards material progress. Quite often these contacts have first suggested to the population the idea and possibility of a change in the existing scheme of things, including the idea of economic improvement. External economic contacts make possible such changes by voluntary adjustment to new opportunities, that is without the hardships and costs of compulsion. Thus in poor countries enforced restriction of external contacts is often extremely damaging to material progress.

The exercise of compulsion for the promotion of material progress is indeed often self-defeating. Even if it were effective, the right to exercise compulsion for the alleged material benefit of those over whom it is exercised is at best very doubtful.

6 Some Components of Planning and their Implications

The grounds for suggesting that close economic controls obstruct material progress is reinforced by the character and method of operation of the major types of control under comprehensive planning. The principal controls include the confining of major branches of industry and trade to state monopolies; extensive licensing of commercial and industrial activity, including imports, exports and foreign exchange; the establishment of many state owned and operated enterprises, including state supported and operated so-called cooperatives. Some of these measures, especially the ubiquitous state export monopolies of agricultural products and extensive commercial and industrial licensing, give governments close and direct control over the livelihood of people.

They greatly restrict people's range of choice, including their ability to choose between employers, and also their opportunities to set up new enterprises. They promote economies in which the opportunities of people as producers, consumers, workers and traders depend largely on the government. These policies also serve as a powerful source of finance and patronage for the rulers.

Moreover, decisions under central planning, including the imposition of controls, have largely to be standardised on a national or regional basis, and cannot therefore be adjusted to local, let alone to personal differences in conditions of supply, including access to complementary resources, and in consumer requirements. Failure to take account of these differences, which are often wide, diminishes the effectiveness of the deployment of resources.

Comprehensive planning implies further that much of output is unrelated to consumer demand and therefore to living standards. Thus even if the policy were to increase total output compared to what it would have been otherwise, which is improbable, this increase would be unrelated to living standards, the improvement of which is the ostensible objective of the policy. This divorce of output from living standards is in itself likely to retard a rise both in output and in living standards. This is because the prospect of a higher and more varied level of consumption is usually an important incentive to higher economic performance by way of additional effort, saving and enterprise. This is notably so in poor countries.

The controls imposed under comprehensive planning generally have nothing to do with raising popular living standards. Indeed, they usually depress them. Lip service is paid to the improvement of living standards. But this objective is rarely used as test of official policies. The usual tests are the volume of expansion of particular sectors and activities, or of investment expenditure or state spending. The extensive controls and the heavy taxation imposed under comprehensive planning are not only unrelated to the raising of general living standards but generally contrary to this ostensible aim of the policy. In fact the situation is created where it is the people who are serving the economy rather than the economy serving the people.

7 *Some Political Results*

Comprehensive planning is apt to provoke and exacerbate political tension at least until all political opposition is suppressed. When state control over social and economic life is extensive and close the achievement and the exercise of political power become all-important. Such a situation creates widespread anxiety and concern with the processes and results of political life, especially among the active elements of the population. The stakes in the fight for political power increase and the struggle for it intensifies. Such a development enhances political tension, especially in societies which comprise distinct ethnic, religious or linguistic groups. Moreover, when state control over economic life is extensive the population is certain to be especially prone to blame the government for all economic grievances, whether genuine or spurious, including adverse effects of economic change; and practically all change affects adversely some groups. This allocation of responsibility and of blame may or may not be justified in specific instances. But superficial plausibility is lent to it, both by extensive state control over economic life and by the claims advanced for state action by its advocates. Such a situation clearly exacerbates political tension. Finally, when political action is all-important, the energies and resources of able and ambitious men are diverted from economic activity to political life. And the direction in which the activities of able, energetic and ambitious people are employed is clearly a major influence on the level and progress of economic attainment of a society. These important corollaries of comprehensive central planning and their implications for material progress are widely ignored in discussions on this subject.[1]

Extensive economic controls also reinforce certain other familiar modes of conduct in underdeveloped countries which obstruct material progress, notably the preferential treatment of relatives in the allocation of licences and of responsible posts in the public service. Politicisation of economic life also increases the range of activities over which allocation of posts and of licences is determined by the need to balance or to satisfy the claims of different groups and communities. In practice this leads to formal or informal quota systems on a communal basis, superimposed on the quotas implicit in the specific licensing of imports, foreign exchange and of other controlled commodities and services.

---

[1] The relationship between economic controls, political activity and political tension noted in the text is an instance of the interaction of the variables of economic theory or of the policies designed to influence these with factors usually treated parametrically.

A parameter is an element in the situation which is treated as constant or given for the purposes of the particular analysis or discussion. When manipulation of the variables affects the parameters it is no longer appropriate to treat the latter as constants. We shall repeatedly note in this volume such instances of interaction between parameters and variables.

The various results and implications of central planning noted in sections 5 to 7 are some of the incidental but significant aspects of the wide discrepancy between theoretical formulation of a policy and its implementation in the real world. The implementation is subject to the political and administrative processes of the society and thus differs markedly from the simplified and idealised world of theoretical formulations and models sometimes invoked in support of central planning.[1] And as there is no likelihood that the real life situation will grow to resemble the textbook formulation of planning procedures, it would seem appropriate that in this instance textbook formulation should attempt to approximate to the real life situation.

8 *Two Objections Considered*

I may note two objections here which are sometimes raised against the general argument of the preceding sections.

The first objection is that state control of economic life in underdeveloped countries with ambitious development plans is in fact modest, as is shown by the relatively small size of the public sector when it is expressed as a proportion of national income. However, much of economic activity in these countries is traditionally small-scale agriculture. As a percentage of the exchange economy the public sector is much larger than is suggested by conventional statistics. And it is the size of the public sector relative to the exchange economy and not to the total national income which is relevant to the state control of the economy.

Moreover, the size of the public sector does not by itself indicate the extent of the state control of the economy. Government expenditure may be comparatively small, and yet government control over the economy close, if there are many state trading monopolies or if there is extensive licensing of economic activity. Conversely, even if government expenditure as a proportion of the national income is substantial, this need not imply close control over the economy, if the expenditure is on the performance of the familiar traditional functions of government. Thus in assessing the implications of state control of economic life, the character and the closeness of the control is of major relevance.

[1] The arguments in the last three sections of this essay refer to the effects of planning as a system of state control of economic life. We noted earlier in this essay (p. 74) a wider interpretation, namely the attempted remoulding of man and society. These arguments about the effects of planning apply with at least equal cogency to the results and implications of this wider interpretation.

Second, it is often objected that many of the widely publicised development plans of underdeveloped countries are in fact either fictitious or ineffective, or do not go beyond forward budgeting of fiscal policy. This may often be true. But the prevalent view that comprehensive central planning is necessary or indispensable serves as an ostensible justification for the imposition and maintenance of extensive and close economic controls. Such controls may be established piecemeal to achieve particular purposes, notably to placate particular interests, rather than as parts of a so-called comprehensive plan for development. Even fictitious plans are useful as spurious justification for the imposition of controls.

Thus these often heard objections are insubstantial. Moreover they do not affect the validity of the analysis of the implications of comprehensive planning. They only suggest that the scale of the policy may be modest or that it has not been put into effect.

9 *Planning and Living Standards*

Extension of state control over people's lives is the essence of comprehensive planning. Concentration of power and creation of positions of power are its necessary results. A prospective rise in incomes and living standards is highly improbable and based only on unsubstantiated assertion.

The adoption of comprehensive planning has nowhere benefited general living standards compared to different policies. It is in the Soviet type economies that comprehensive planning is the essence of economic policy. After decades of operation general living standards remain extremely low; they are almost certainly much lower than they would have been under different economic systems. The contrast in the development of living standards in East and West Germany makes this point even more tellingly because the populations of the two Germanys are ethnically identical. On the other hand, the nature and texture of communist societies reflect the pervasive character of sustained comprehensive planning. And it is these countries that have strict frontier controls to prevent people from leaving, which clearly suggests widespread dissatisfaction with the material and non-material conditions of these societies.

We have already quoted Professor Myrdal, one of the most ardent and influential advocates of the necessity of central planning, to the effect that such a policy implies the utmost austerity. And this suggestion has been amply borne out by the experience of the peoples of centrally planned societies. The policies of austerity in these countries have often been announced as a temporary necessity for future prosperity. Subsequent developments have contradicted these promises. Nor is this outcome surprising. Enforced current austerity does not in the least ensure future abundance and does not even generally promote it. Indeed, policies of current austerity tend to perpetuate it, in a number of different ways: by reducing the supply of incentive goods; by divorcing output from consumer demand; by politicising economic life; by provoking political tension; and in various other ways as well. *Souvent le provisoire dure longtemps.*

Any government which closely controls the economy can readily expand particular sectors and activities of the economy, by extracting resources from the population or transferring these from other sectors. Such governments can therefore develop or enlarge particular industries and sectors of the economy, and can erect impressive monuments or create substantial military machines. But such achievements have nothing to do with the advancement of general living standards.

Economic development is appropriately interpreted and normally understood as an increase in the total output of goods and services desired by the population, which implies a rise in general living standards, including life expectation. Its presence cannot be inferred from an increase in a particular sector to which resources have been diverted from the rest of the economy. Once this is understood the potentialities of state action in the promotion of development appear much more limited than is widely suggested in contemporary discussions, in which opinions about these potentialities are all too often supported either by unsubstantiated assertions or by reference to the growth of particular sectors of an economy, notably of certain types of capital goods, without reference to general living standards.

10 *Government and Material Progress*

This critical discussion of planning as allegedly indispensable for development again does not conceal a plea for *laissez-faire*. Preoccupation with central planning has, paradoxically, contributed to a serious neglect of essential governmental tasks in many underdeveloped countries. These tasks include the successful conduct of external affairs; the maintenance of law and order; the effective management of the monetary and fiscal system; the promotion of a suitable institutional framework for the activities of individuals; the provision of basic health and education services and of basic communications; and also agricultural extension work. These are important or even essential functions which must devolve on the government. This is so for two reasons. First, because part of the institutional structure within which the private sector functions does not emerge from the operation of market forces, and so must be established by law; second, because some of these activities yield services which, although there may be a demand for them, cannot be bought and sold in the market. The preservation and encouragement of external commercial contacts is of special importance in the conditions of underdeveloped countries. To be effective for material progress these contacts need to be widely dispersed among the inhabitants of the country.

It is by the discharge of these tasks that governments can best develop the framework within which people can improve their living standards, if that is what they want. Of course people can achieve this aim only if they are prepared to develop the required conduct and mores. It may well be that significant sectors of the population are not prepared to change their established ways. It is often difficult to predict how far people are ready in particular circumstances to modify attitudes and modes of conduct adverse to material progress. It is probable that in many underdeveloped countries significant numbers of people would respond to a widening of opportunities, especially to opportunities offered by a widening of markets and by the emergence of external contacts. Such changes might be cumulative. But for the purpose of our discussion it is not necessary to speculate on these possibilities. What is not in doubt is that comprehensive planning is not necessary for these changes and indeed that major elements of this policy obstruct them.[1]

This list of tasks largely exhausts the potentialities of state action in the promotion of general living standards. These tasks are extensive and complex. And their adequate performance would fully stretch the human, financial and administrative resources of all governments in poor countries. Yet governments frequently neglect even the most elementary of these functions while attempting close control of the

[1] We are concerned here with the likely effects of various policies in economic progress. For the purpose of this particular discussion we need not examine the wider and more fundamental issue of the right of some persons or groups to coerce others into changing their way of life on the ground, or ostensible ground, that such a change is required for the material progress of the society or its descendants. This issue is considered further in essay 5.

economies of their countries or even, occasionally, contemplating coercive transformation of societies. They seem anxious to plan and are unable to govern.

The performance of the essential governmental functions is onerous. Indeed, as I have just noted, even their adequate performance would stretch the resources of governments of poor countries. But these functions do not normally imply close control over people's lives and activities. This may be one reason why advocates of comprehensive planning are often so unperturbed when governments engaged in central planning neglect these elementary functions. The planners seem more interested in controlling people's lives than in liberating their minds or augmenting their resources.

11 *Appeal of Planning*

Comprehensive planning has thus not served to raise general living standards anywhere. There is no analytical reason or empirical evidence for expecting it to do so. And in fact both analytical reasoning and empirical evidence point to the opposite conclusion.

But the failure of comprehensive planning to raise general living standards has not affected its appeal for politicians, administrators and intellectuals, that is for actual or potential wielders of power. It is interesting to speculate on the reasons for this, some of which are more familiar than others. For instance, for intellectuals at least planning seems to imply conscious, rational and scientific control of economic life, in contrast to the supposedly irrational, blind and haphazard methods prevailing in its absence. Moreover, such a policy will lead to the creation of positions of power both for politicians and for intellectuals to which they could not aspire in a less centralised society. Another factor, somewhat less general but not unimportant, is that – at least in the initial stages of planning – major elements of the policy often benefit business enterprises by shielding them from competition or even by creating windfall profits; these business interests may also represent an active and influential element in the society.

There is another point to consider in this context. When a far-reaching policy such as comprehensive planning proves very costly over a long period its supporters find it difficult to question the basic principles for which the sacrifices have been exacted: indeed, the greater the cost and the heavier the sacrifices, the more absolute becomes the resistance to facing the need for radical re-examination of the principles. The most effective and articulate supporters of comprehensive planning, whose advocacy derives from political and emotional motives, will not confront its results with empirical evidence. They will insist on its beneficial results even in the face of the most obvious evidence to the contrary, an attitude which is indeed a corollary of the axiomatic assumption that the policy must be efficacious.

Comprehensive central planning is generally discussed as an instrument for development. It seems that some of its vocal and influential advocates have different objectives in mind. In particular they are more interested in the creation of highly centralised societies, which is the inescapable result of comprehensive planning, than they are in the raising of general living standards, the ostensible but unrealised aim of the policy. The advocacy and adoption of policies calculated to obstruct and not to raise the level of incomes and living standards often appears paradoxical. The paradox is resolved by recognising the precedence of ends which require policies unrelated to the ostensible aim of economic development, and which usually conflict with this aim. It would seem that many advocates of comprehensive planning regard the establishment of closely controlled societies rather than the raising of living standards as the objective of policy.

More unexpected and baffling than the appeal of central planning to intellectuals, politicians and administrators is the acceptance by large numbers of people in both developed and underdeveloped countries of policies designed to bring about extensive state control over social and economic life, to restrict the choices open to them as consumers, workers and traders, and more often than not to increase taxation and thus to reduce their disposable incomes, and even at times to impose extreme austerity. One reason that springs to mind is that people have no real choice in these matters, that they habitually accept, or that they have no alternative but to accept, the policies of the articulate and effective members of the society. Nevertheless it may still surprise that resistance to these policies is at times not stronger. One reason may lie in certain social and technical developments of recent decades, especially the exceedingly rapid rate of change, the growth of specialisation, and the huge increase in the number of messages and items of information reaching people, often about matters outside their immediate experience and direct concern. Many of these developments have led to sharp discontinuities in people's lives, to a contraction in the range and depth of people's shared experience, and to a decline in traditional beliefs and attitudes. These changes have eroded social cohesion and undermined people's feelings of community as well as of continuity. The consequent isolation of the individual, which has resulted from all these factors but especially from the erosion of social cohesion, has often produced a sense of impotence and hence of passive acceptance of the policies of the powerful and articulate groups in the country.

However, it would seem that, initially at least, acceptance of these policies is not merely passive, that this acceptance contains an element of welcome. We have just noted that the social and technical changes of the last decades have undermined the individual's feelings of continuity and community. Yet many people, perhaps most people, need this sense of continuity and community for a satisfactory and fulfilled life, and in its absence experience emptiness, isolation, bewilderment and loss of bearings. This element of welcome may be partly explained by the belief that these lost values may be recovered in the authoritarian structure of a centrally planned political system. That this belief is mistaken does not affect its appeal, an appeal which is particularly strong when the impact of change on a society has been sudden and violent, and when the resulting disintegration of traditional beliefs, attitudes and values has been rapid.

This last consideration also accounts at least partly for the special appeal of comprehensive planning to the intellectuals in underdeveloped countries. Apart from its attraction for reasons of political power and influence which we have already noted, intellectuals too feel this loss of continuity and community, perhaps even more sharply than the rest of their countrymen, though possibly subconsciously. They too may feel that comprehensive planning can act as a substitute for lost values.[1]

These suggested reasons for the appeal of central planning are neither conclusive nor exhaustive. But they may go some way to account for the attractions of a policy which has been a complete failure in terms of its ostensible objectives.

---

[1] This point is developed further in essay 4, in which among other matters the appeal of Marxism–Leninism is discussed.

B. FOREIGN AID[1]

The second major policy axiom of the current development literature is that foreign aid is indispensable for the development of poor countries. This belief supplies the main argument in the advocacy of foreign aid. Various other arguments are sometimes adduced: the most important of these are perhaps that foreign aid is a natural extension of progressive taxation; that it is an instrument for the relief of need; and that it is a discharge of the moral obligation to help the poor. I shall argue here that foreign aid is plainly not indispensable to economic progress, and is indeed likely to obstruct it, and that the other arguments are also defective.

Before turning to the substantive argument, however, I would like to note a significant anomaly in current discussions on foreign aid. In these discussions the burden of proof has come to be placed on the critics of aid instead of on its supporters. Yet it rests appropriately with those who advocate compulsory transfer of taxpayers' money to foreign governments rather than with the critics of such a policy. This judgment about the allocation of the burden of proof applies both to the overall case for aid and to the assessment of particular arguments. In most

[1] Foreign aid in this essay refers to intergovernmental grants and subsidised loans in cash or kind, which is what is meant by foreign aid in current discussions. It does not refer to external loans raised by governments abroad on commercial terms, nor to private foreign investment, nor to the activities of voluntary organisations. Private capital includes external loans raised abroad by governments on commercial terms. A few World Bank loans and investments have gone to private or to semi-public enterprises. But these transfers have had to be sanctioned by the governments of the recipient countries, so that this exception is not only quantitively negligible but also largely irrelevant.

Discussions on foreign aid to underdeveloped countries normally refer to economic aid and not to military aid; in fact, foreign aid appropriations of western donor countries now generally exclude military aid. The distinction is in any case often imprecise because most domestic resources in the recipient countries can be shifted between civilian and military uses. When military aid does in fact set resources free for civilian use, official statistics of foreign aid understate the amount of economic aid. The discussion of this essay is, however, unaffected by the validity or the significance of this distinction. The only point to which the distinction is superficially relevant is the experience of Taiwan noted in section 19 of this essay. But the argument there is not affected by the continuation of specific defence aid after the cessation of economic aid.

The discussion refers primarily to western aid to underdeveloped countries, though much of it applies also to aid from communist countries.

Some remarks on the composition and valuation of foreign aid may be appropriate here. Most of aggregate foreign aid consists of grants. According to the Pearson Report (p. 137), approximately two-thirds of all aid takes the form of grants and grant-like contributions. When aid takes the form of subsidised loans which are repaid (that is, if they are not defaulted on), the aid element is the difference between market terms and the subsidised terms. As interest and amortisation charges on these loans are generally extremely modest compared to market terms, most of the foreign aid loans are substantially akin to grants. When aid has to be spent in the donor countries its money value overstates its value in real terms; the difference represents subsidies to exporters in the donor countries. None of these considerations affects the argument of the text.

academic and popular discussion neither the general case for aid nor the specific arguments are set out in detail. The usual procedure is to take the case for aid for granted or to argue it in only the most general terms.

12 *Axiomatic Case for Aid*

A terse and convenient formulation of the axiomatic case for foreign aid is presented by a passage in a letter by Professor Wolfgang Friedmann of Columbia University in the *New York Times*:[1]

> It is the unanimous opinion of all foreign-aid experts that the total amount of development aid is grossly inadequate for even the minimum needs of the developing countries.

Thus, according to Professor Friedmann, those who dispute the necessity for aid cannot be experts. This statement is no more true than Professor Myrdal's allegations noted in Part A of this essay that all development experts insist on comprehensive planning. There are many economists, including some in prominent academic positions, who do not accept the prevailing ideology on foreign aid and who dispute that aid is an efficient, let alone an indispensable instrument for the advance of poor countries.

Foreign aid is a system of gifts. This fact is obscured but unaffected by calling the recipients partners in development. Indeed this last phrase patronises the recipients by suggesting that they do not understand simple realities or that they are minors whose illusions must be preserved and whose susceptibilities must be spared. The phrase also prejudges the effects of aid by implying that it necessarily promotes development.

As a system of gifts, foreign aid is more nearly akin to doles than to subsidies. A dole is generally plain charity; a subsidy is usually linked to measurable output or performance. Thus although the term foreign aid is now so widely used that it would be pedantic to eschew it, either gifts or doles would be much preferable on logical grounds as a description of these transfers because these words do not prejudge the effects of aid.

The argument that foreign aid is indispensable for the progress of the underdeveloped world means that without a system of doles, poor countries must stagnate. According to advocates of foreign aid, these doles are indispensable because the poverty of underdeveloped countries

[1] 30 July 1966.

prevents the capital formation required for higher incomes. This situation is supposed to be an instance of the operation of the alleged vicious circle of poverty. This advocacy is, however, no more than unsubstantiated assertion. Foreign aid is plainly neither a generally necessary nor a sufficient condition for emergence from poverty.[1]

As we have already seen in essay 1, foreign aid is clearly not necessary for economic development, as is obvious for instance from the very existence of developed countries. All of these began as underdeveloped and progressed without foreign aid. Moreover, many underdeveloped countries have advanced very rapidly over the last half century or so without foreign aid, a consideration particularly relevant in this context. There are many such countries in the far east, south-east Asia, East and West Africa and Latin America.

Nor is foreign aid a sufficient condition. It cannot, for instance, promote development if the population at large is not interested in material advance, nor if it is strongly attached to values and customs incompatible with material progress. An instructive example is provided by the results of large-scale American (domestic) aid to the Navajo Indian population, a large group with its own territory and government. The United States government has over decades spent huge sums of money in attempts to improve the material position of this group, with no perceptible results.

In fact, the advocates of aid as an allegedly indispensable instrument for development of poor countries are faced by an inescapable though largely unrecognised dilemma. If all conditions for development other than capital are present, capital will soon be generated locally, or will be available to the government or to private businesses on commercial terms from abroad, the capital to be serviced out of higher tax revenues or from the profits of enterprise.[2] If, however, the conditions for

---

[1] The term generally is introduced solely to allow for the extremely exceptional, perhaps freakish, instance where it may be necessary. Such an exceptional case where it may have been necessary is noted in section 19.

[2] It might be objected that the inflow of capital represented by aid would in itself promote the favourable determinants of development by transforming the society. Experience so far has pointed in the opposite direction. But if this were so, the government could achieve the same result by borrowing abroad commercially, without the internal and external complications resulting from aid.

For the sake of completeness we may note a qualification or proviso to the argument of the text which is, however, of little practical significance. There may be conditions in which expenditure financed from abroad increases the national income by more than the cost of the capital, but government revenues do not rise sufficiently to enable the government to service commercially borrowed capital. But if the benefit from the expenditure financed by external funds cannot be tapped by taxes or charges (whether because of the highly dispersed nature of the benefits or for other reasons) the amount of these benefits must be highly speculative. In practice it is also relevant that if a government is unable

development are not present, then aid – which in these circumstances will be the only source of external capital – will be necessarily unproductive and therefore ineffective. Thus, if the mainsprings of development are present, material progress will occur even without foreign aid. If they are absent, it will not occur even with aid. It is of course true that a country receiving aid benefits in the sense of obtaining cheap or free capital (though as we shall see its beneficial effects cannot be taken for granted), but this in no sense makes foreign aid indispensable for development.

There is only one possible but rather unlikely set of circumstances when foreign aid may be effective and also appear to be necessary: this is when the required conditions for development are present but for external political reasons neither the government nor private business can borrow from abroad, and when for these same reasons local enterprise and investment are inhibited. In these very exceptional circumstances, foreign aid from a politically powerful country may both supply necessary capital and restore confidence. But in these conditions aid will restore confidence only in so far as it is interpreted as guaranteeing political security; a military presence in the recipient country, supplied by the donor country, would restore confidence perhaps more effectively even without aid.

13 Foreign Aid and Material Progress

Foreign aid is thus indisputably not generally necessary or sufficient for advance from poverty. Whether it is likely to promote or to retard material progress cannot be conclusively shown. Time series can be presented of the flow of aid and of changes in certain other variables, such as the national income or income per head. But it cannot be ascertained confidently what would have happened without aid. This difficulty arises partly because of the familiar problem of discerning the causal, functional relationship between specified variables when a situation or process is affected simultaneously by numerous past and present influences operating with various time lags. And the difficulties are particularly acute when we examine the performance of a whole economy and try to relate it to the operations of a specific variable, in

to collect additional revenues out of an appreciably higher national income, either from taxes or from such charges as railway receipts or public utility charges, then it is unlikely that it will use aid productively.

This somewhat formal qualification applies also to parts of the argument of sections 16 and 18, where, however, we shall not repeat it.

this case the inflow of foreign aid. The economic performance and progress of entire societies are aspects of their general historical development which depends on literally countless past and present factors, many of which are outside the scope of economic analysis.

The difficulties are compounded further by major conceptual and practical problems in the interpretation and measurement of economic progress, notably the widely different and often shifting interpretations of economic advance frequent in discussions on development; and also by the enormous margins of error and bias in estimates and comparisons of income and living standards in underdeveloped countries. These are among the reasons why it is difficult conclusively to establish the effects of aid on development.

When we wish to ascertain what were the effects of aid on the performance of certain economies in the past, or what they are likely to be on their subsequent performance, it becomes, therefore, necessary to proceed by reference to certain general considerations supplemented by specific instances of empirical evidence. But it needs to be repeated that the difficulties of establishing conclusively the effects of aid on the rate of progress of the recipients apply only to the problem of ascertaining whether aid has advanced or retarded it. They do not affect the criticism of the idea that it is indispensable for material progress.

Foreign aid increases the resources of the recipient governments and countries, that is, it makes possible additional consumption and investment. But it does not follow that aid increases the rate of development. The result depends on the expenditure of the funds and also on the repercussions of the flow of aid on the basic determinants of material progress, notably attitudes, policies and institutions. Some of these effects and repercussions are adverse and can easily outweigh any favourable result of the inflow of resources.

To begin with a consideration which is within the purview of standard economic discussion. The positive economic productivity of a piece of expenditure cannot be taken for granted. This point is particularly relevant when the funds are spent by persons who neither bear the cost nor enjoy the economic return. In these conditions negative productivity is distinctly possible, especially when the funds are external gifts.

It is by no means unusual for projects to absorb domestic inputs of greater value than the net output, especially when the cost of administering the projects and the explicit or implicit obligation to maintain and replace the fixed assets originally donated is also considered. Large losses in activities and projects financed by aid have been reported in many poor countries. In fact they have been a recurrent theme of official reports in India and Ceylon. Though it is difficult to assess in each instance exactly what costs have been taken into consideration in these documents, the losses have often been so huge that it is safe to assume that the country would have been better off without the project.[1]

In assessing the effects of aid on material progress there are, however, repercussions to consider which extend beyond the direct productivity of the expenditure and which are generally more important. As we have argued in Part A of this essay, the prime determinants of material progress are people's economic aptitudes, their social institutions and political arrangements, and to a much lesser extent natural resources and external market opportunities. Foreign aid cannot affect these underlying determinants of development favourably to any considerable extent. If a country, or rather a people, cannot readily develop without external gifts, it is unlikely to develop with them. A low level of material achievement is a symptom, an effect of the absence or the weakness of the forces behind material progress; foreign aid focuses on symptoms and effects and diverts attention from the determinants of development. Thus even when aid improves current economic conditions in the recipient countries it need not promote their long-term development.

The advocacy and flow of aid tend in themselves to set up repercussions adverse to material progress. Indeed as aid has operated since the second world war these have probably outweighed the favourable effects. We shall now consider some of these adverse effects, which are frequent and perhaps general concomitants of aid. In subsequent sections we shall consider other more specific repercussions brought about by the criteria of allocation of aid since the second world war. The distinction between these categories is to some extent arbitrary; however, this does not affect the substantive argument but bears only on the order of exposition.

First, advocates of aid encourage the unfounded belief that the prime prerequisites of development can be had for nothing, and ignore or obscure the fact that the populations of developed countries themselves have had to develop the faculties, attitudes and institutions favourable

---

[1] The inability of a number of aid recipients to service soft loans also suggests the low or even negative productivity of aid, though it must be recognised that there may be other reasons for an inability or unwillingness to service soft loans. It must also be recognised on the other hand that the ability to service them does not necessarily provide an adequate test of the productivity of aid.

to material progress. This aspect of aid is related to one of the many paradoxes in this realm of discourse: the simultaneous insistence of the supporters of aid that the peoples of the underdeveloped world are the equals of those of the developed world, or even their moral superiors, and also that without large-scale aid they cannot work out their own salvation.

Second, the suggestion that foreign aid is indispensable for the development of the recipients implies that the progress of persons and groups depends on external forces. This suggestion reinforces the attitude widely prevalent in the underdeveloped world, notably so in south Asia, that the opportunities and the resources for the economic advance of oneself or one's family have to be provided by someone else – by the state, by one's superiors, by richer people, or from abroad. This attitude is in turn one aspect of the belief of the efficacy of external forces over one's destiny. In parts of the underdeveloped world this attitude goes back for millennia and, especially in south Asia, has been reinforced by the authoritarian tradition of the society. It is an attitude plainly unfavourable to material progress.

People react to poverty and material backwardness in different ways. Some may not even notice it. Such a response may be part of a wider attitude of unquestioning acceptance of the nature of things, a reaction which is especially likely if comparisons with other people are not readily available. Some may accept poverty consciously, either in the form of resignation or by unwillingness to change modes of conduct. Some may attempt to improve their position through beggary or blackmail. Finally, some may attempt to improve their economic performance. Only the last of these responses can lead to sustained material progress. And it is the one least likely to be encouraged by an insistence on foreign aid as allegedly necessary for material advance. Altogether pre-occupation with aid diverts attention from the basic causes of poverty and the possibilities of acting on them.

Third, the advocates of aid do not usually refer either to the relevant policies of the recipient governments or to the conduct of the population. Many recipient governments pursue courses of action which patently reduce the level of income or retard its increase. For instance, they expel the most productive groups of the population from their countries, or restrict the inflow and the deployment of private capital or the expansion of certain types of enterprise, both domestic and foreign. These policies, are not questioned by the advocates of aid. The flow of unconditional aid supports, underwrites and encourages such policies. And it is certainly not calculated to promote revision of popular mores and modes of conduct adverse to development. In these conditions foreign aid is at best irrelevant to economic advance. But it is more likely to set up responses adverse to it, especially by encouraging the governments to pursue policies or persist in policies which obstruct economic advance.

Fourth, the advocacy of aid often includes suggestions that the higher incomes of actual or prospective donors have been secured at the expense of poor countries rather than generated by themselves. Such suggestions obscure the nature of economic transactions and processes. They often spill over into the domestic discussions of poor countries, where they lead to the suggestion that the prosperity of better-off persons and groups has been secured at the expense of the rest of the population. They also lend plausibility to the imposition of damaging restrictions on external contacts. These notions thus promote policies harmful to material progress.

The repercussions of the flow of aid on motivations and institutions, and on government policy in the recipient countries (that is on major determinants of development) are habitually ignored in current discussions on foreign aid, which focus almost entirely on its effects on the volume of investible resources. This practice is an example of a wider issue, noted repeatedly in this book, namely the disregard of the interaction of the familiar variables of conventional economic theory with the prime determinants of development. These determinants are treated parametrically or ignored altogether, even when the policy designed to operate on the conventional variables substantially affects the major determinants of development.

Fifth, foreign aid has probably affected adversely the market opportunities, and therefore the material position and development prospects, of many aid recipients. The major donor countries erect substantial barriers against the exports of the same underdeveloped countries to whom they are giving aid. These trade barriers reflect the operation of sectional interests in the donor countries. Foreign aid diminishes the political resistance in the recipient countries to the erection of these barriers, both within the donor countries and by spokesmen of recipient countries.

The ideas that external financial support is a necessary and perhaps even a sufficient condition for the material progress of poor countries, and that its effects will always be favourable, are unfounded. They derive again from a view of the underdeveloped world – rejection of which is one of the major themes of this book – as a category which is substanially uniform and whose population differs from the people of the developed countries only in being poorer, that other differences between them are either negligible, or are irrelevant to economic advance.

14 *Domestic Growth and External Gifts*

There are certain substantial differences between resources developed locally and the receipt of resources gratis from abroad which bear on the effectiveness of aid as an instrument of material progress. When resources are received from abroad for nothing the valuable process of generating them is lost. When resources are both generated and used locally the personal qualities and attitudes, social institutions and economic opportunities required for their employment are encouraged to develop simultaneously. The interaction of these elements of social constituents and processes then serves as a basis for further material progress. There is plainly a great difference between the generation of resources and the acceptance of external gifts.

The interaction noted in the preceding paragraph also bears on the relationship between the accumulation of capital and its productive deployment. Capital is much more likely to be productive when deployed by those groups and persons who accumulated it, because accumulation and effective deployment require much the same abilities, motivations and institutions.

External doles also tend to bias the development process in directions based on external prototypes which are often inappropriate and therefore damaging. Such a sequence retards development rather than promotes it and provokes frustration and political tension. Adverse results are all the more likely when the expenditure within the country is undertaken by people who do not themselves bear the cost. Inappropriate external prototypes may come to be adopted in political life, the legal system, the organisation of the civil service, as well as many forms of industrial and commercial organisation.

An important instance of the adoption of inappropriate external models is that of the establishment and proliferation of universities based on western models when there are no employment opportunities for their graduates. This consideration applies especially to vocational training, the usefulness of which is closely related to the occupational pattern and salary structure of the society.

The unemployment of graduates is an important social and political phenomenon of the underdeveloped world. It is largely a result of this proliferation of western-type universities in inappropriate conditions. In many underdeveloped countries, especially in south Asia, the unemployment of graduates has induced governments to put pressure on people to retire relatively early. As a result, experienced and skilled civil servants, executives, technicians and university teachers have had to make way for less experienced and qualified graduates.[1]

The number and size of western-type universities in many underdeveloped countries is perhaps the most characteristic example of the adoption of unsuitable external models. Other familiar examples which may be less damaging include the proliferation of steel mills, advanced engineering works, or air lines, in countries with largely illiterate populations. Such activities require skills and experience which will have to be obtained from abroad for the foreseeable future.

These considerations apply also to the provision of technical assistance, which is a minor but not insignificant part of the total flow of aid. When the recipient government has to find the money for technical advice, it is much more likely to scrutinise the expenditure to adjust it to the requirements of the country than when technical assistance is provided gratis. In the half century between the Meiji restoration and the first world war the Japanese government drew readily on foreign technical instruction and advice. The expenditure was financed from their own funds and proved very productive.

The impact of foreign aid in biasing development policy in inappropriate directions is an instance of the wider issue of the difficulties presented by transferring institutions between widely different cultures and societies, especially between societies which although they are to be found in the world today are not really contemporary. They are not contemporary in the sense that the beliefs, motivations, institutions and occupational structure of some societies are often much closer to

---

[1] Some aspects of the unemployment of graduates are often baffling at first sight. For instance there is often substantial unemployment among graduates with skills which seem very scarce in the country. For example there is now (1970) heavy unemployment among engineering graduates in India when there are relatively few qualified engineers in that huge country. The training of these graduates is often poor but the reason for this substantial unemployment is more fundamental. Even very high skills are unmarketable if the ancillary services or consumer demand are insufficient. The volume of unemployment may be increased further by formal or informal minimum wage regulation, again based on inappropriate external models.

The Indian government has announced that it will give preference to unemployed engineering graduates in operating the petrol stations of Indian Oil, the public sector oil company. The government intends to use more than one graduate per station. Each of these graduates will have had five years of university education behind him. In most instances a reasonably competent owner or driver of a taxi without university education would almost certainly perform the operation better and more cheaply.

those of other societies in much earlier stages of the development of the latter. This consideration is obvious when extreme cases are observed such as, say, western societies and tribal groups which both are present in the world today but which are not contemporary in any real sense. But substantially similar considerations apply also to the comparative position of many societies, especially between societies in the developed and the underdeveloped world.

Economic development is a process which requires much more than the provision of money from abroad. And in this area, as in many other areas of life, experience, time and other qualifications and requirements of achievement cannot be bought. Social processes cannot generally be telescoped forcibly without affecting their nature as well as the outcome of the processes.

Recognition of the non-contemporary nature of societies bears on the operation of foreign aid. Certain perceptive remarks by Mr Guy Hunter of the London Institute of Race Relations set out some of the problems and difficulties of the transfer of institutions between societies. They show the results of setting up institutions for which there is no effective demand, in the sense of a gap which they could successfully fill.

... the moral and social conventions in a developing country may be wholly different from those upon which the institution was founded originally. Trade unions, as one example, depend upon a complex set of conventional codes between the union and the employer, developed over a long period of trial. It is easy to transfer the set of rules which finally emerge, but impossible to transfer the morality and experience which made the rules workable. Again, the university in its modern shape in developed countries corresponds to a certain employment (and salary) pattern in the surrounding society, to a certain state of technology, and to a certain proportion between primary, secondary and tertiary employment, the tertiary sector being enormously expanded. There is no need to point to the contrast with a society such as Uganda, or Burma or Malawi.

Again, aid represents the import of resources not generated within the receiving economy. This may mean that the skills which would have been generating these resources were never in fact called for or learned, and are not available to use the resources when it is provided. In a more complex case, the educational system of a country has to be paid for from its productive resources: as resources grow, skills are needed and education is expanded to provide them; thus the graduates are likely to find employment; but if education is rapidly expanded by the use of unearned aid resources (without corresponding growth in the economy) there may well not be employment for its graduates – and this in fact is happening in many countries.[1]

Observations along these lines are not confined to European observers. They are discussed repeatedly in the writings of Mr Nirad C. Chaudhuri, especially in *The Continent of Circe* and *The Autobiography of an Unknown Indian*. In an African context the problems have been clearly and succinctly noted by Miss Noni Jabavu:

I thought about these and many other aspects of the problem [of advancing the welfare of Africans in Uganda], feeling more convinced than ever that it is impossible to introduce to other people in other circumstances those things in life that one considers desirable; such other people do better to be left alone to find out for themselves what suits them. They then adapt what they know and want, to what they gradually discover by trial and error that they do want in their new setting. Little is achieved ... by those who 'have' being softhearted and solicitous towards those who seem to 'have not'. The best things in life are learnt the hard way. And need there be unanimity about what everyone means by 'best'?[2]

The arguments in support of aid rarely examine the presence, significance and implications of these differences between societies. In this general context a distinct ambivalence or even inconsistency, related to a paradox noted in section 14, is noticeable in much of the advocacy of aid, especially in the insistence on its alleged necessity. The advocates emphasise the duty of the west to provide aid. They often even seem to imply that the west should abase itself before underdeveloped countries for its alleged responsibility for their poverty. At the same time a distinct suggestion of western superiority underlies the suggestion that without aid the underdeveloped countries could not work out their salvation, that they must follow our ways and that they cannot progress without us. But it is generally neither easy nor appropriate to transfer attitudes and institutions from one culture to another. And this is especially so when the population of the latter has not shown readiness to accept them.

15 *Criteria for Allocation and Practical Implications of Aid*

Foreign aid augments the resources of recipient governments compared to those of the private sector, thereby promoting concentration of power

---

[1] Mr Guy Hunter, from an unpublished memorandum which he has kindly allowed me to consult and quote.

[2] Noni Jabavu, *Drawn in Colour* ,London, 1960, p. 116.

n the recipient countries. This effect is much reinforced by the preferential treatment in the allocation of aid of governments engaged in comprehensive planning, a criterion based, at any rate ostensibly, on the ground that such a policy is a condition of economic development.[1] However, as we have seen in Part A of this essay, such a policy is demonstrably not a condition of material progress and is much more likely to obstruct it. However, this preferential treatment of governments engaged in comprehensive planning is likely to continue. As we have also noted in Part A of this essay, failure of central planning to promote a rise in living standards does not diminish its appeal and indeed often reinforces the zeal of its advocates. At the same time the continued low living standards and the persistent economic difficulties of centrally planned economies in underdeveloped countries serve as justification for continued aid. These sequences promote extensive politicization of life which for reasons noted in Part A above is most damaging to material progress.

The flow of aid is also often linked to the balance of payments deficits of the recipient countries. This is particularly so when such deficits are regarded, as they often are, as inevitable concomitants of government efforts to speed up material progress by means of development plans. Balance of payments crises emerging in the course of development planning have proved especially effective bases of appeals for securing foreign aid. This particular usefulness of payments difficulties and crises encourages governments to make their development plans as ambitious as possible, to pursue inflationary monetary and fiscal policies, and to avoid the accumulation of foreign exchange reserves. Such policies may in any case accord with the inclination of governments because they lead to an expansion of the public sector and provide useful arguments for the imposition of both domestic and external controls.

The pursuit of inflationary policies, the recurrence of balance of payments crises, the imposition of higher taxation and of specific controls, notably exchange controls, all lead to a widespread feeling of insecurity and may engender a crisis atmosphere. Such developments obstruct domestic saving and investment and promote the export of capital.

Practically all recipients of foreign aid impose severe restrictions on the inflow and deployment of private capital. For example, in India this inflow is strictly controlled. Foreign capital is barred from a wide range

---

[1] The term ostensibly is introduced because some advocates of aid may wish to encourage such policies regardless of their effects on material progress.

of industrial and commercial activities. The expansion and even the current operation of foreign enterprises are often severely restricted. Many of these enterprises are not allowed to expand even if they are prepared to finance their expansion from their own resources and even when they are prepared to bring in foreign exchange for the purpose. Quite often both foreign and domestic enterprises are forced to work below capacity while the government receives foreign aid to expand its own enterprises in competition with them.

Analogous restrictions are enforced by many other aid recipients. The public in the donor countries is rarely informed about these measures. The operation of these policies, which are facilitated by foreign aid, shows again that the inflow of aid need not bring about an increase in net investment.

It is highly probable that without aid the governments of many underdeveloped countries would have borrowed more from abroad on commercial terms. This would have been more expensive than the grants or subsidised loans under foreign aid, but there can be no doubt that it would have been used more carefully and productively. Much of the aid received by underdeveloped countries, notably India, Indonesia and Ghana, has been in the form of heavily subsidised loans, but because the use of aid has not served materially to improve the income-earning capacity of these countries they are now saddled with large debts without a commensurate increase in the capacity to service them. The result must be either a drain on their resources or a default on their obligations. The reality of the default may be partly obscured by euphemisms such as rescheduling, rephasing, or harmonising of obligations. But a default, even if it is called rescheduling, must affect the future credit-worthiness of a country. Moreover, it also provokes or reinforces attitudes harmful to material progress, for example a readiness to default on contractual obligations.

The claim that it is necessary to finance certain projects or categories of expenditure through foreign aid implies that the return is expected to be less, often significantly less, than the market returns on private capital, as otherwise the project or expenditure could have been financed commercially, including by means of government loans raised on commercial terms. We have already noted the inability of some recipients to service even the soft loans under foreign aid; and that this suggests that the return secured by the investment of these funds was extremely low, perhaps even zero or negative.

It is also probable that in the absence of aid at least some governments of underdeveloped countries would have permitted or encouraged the inflow and deployment of private capital to a much greater extent. Private capital (including loans raised abroad commercially by the government) is likely to be more productive than foreign aid. This is because it is more closely geared to specific market conditions than is foreign aid, both in the narrower sense of the presence of skills, natural resources, and market demand for the product, and in the wider sense of the presence of the appropriate faculties, motivations and institutions. Moreover, private capital does not bring about the creation and concentration of power in the recipient countries in the way foreign aid does, for the reasons and with the results already indicated.[1] Without aid not only would private capital be given more scope, but it would presumably be treated more favourably and would be less subject to expropriation.[2]

Quite apart from the *de facto* or *de jure* erection of obstacles to the inflow and deployment of private capital in underdeveloped countries, the flow of aid is also likely to reduce the volume of private foreign investment simply by curtailing the supply of investible funds in donor countries.[3]

Thus certain repercussions of aid may reduce rather than increase net investment within the recipient countries. And the reduction of domestic saving and investment and the export of capital usually affects types of capital and capital formation which are likely to be more productive than the expenditure financed by foreign aid.

In many instances, of course, expenditures made possible or easier by foreign aid are quite unrelated to any type of capital formation. They may serve such diverse aims as the equipping of an expeditionary force to invade another country or expenditure on training so-called freedom fighters.

The flow of aid and the preferential treatment of governments engaged in comprehensive planning or experiencing balance of payments difficulties have reinforced the tendency of governments of underdeveloped countries to neglect agriculture. They assume that aid givers

---

[1] For obvious reasons this consideration applies less cogently to government borrowing on commercial terms than it does to the inflow of capital into the private sector.

[2] Partial compensation for expropriation is often financed by foreign aid, directly or at one remove, which poses interesting questions on the incidence of tied aid.

[3] Because capital supplied under foreign aid yields a much lower return than it would in the donor countries its flow reduces the potential combined income of donor and recipient countries. It is a corollary of this uneconomic use of capital that in principle a larger volume of goods and services could be given to the present recipients if the aid funds were invested in the donor countries and the return given away. This point is of considerable interest for an assessment of foreign aid as a policy but it is of little practical significance.

will come to their rescue in the event of a serious food shortage, and consequently feel freer to divert their resources to industrial and to prestige projects.

Another untoward result of the operation of aid has been a certain misdirection of emphasis and attention about the conditions and determinants of economic development. Preoccupation with aid, with planning and with investment expenditure has encouraged the facile belief that economic development is possible without cultural change. It has inhibited the exploration of ways to promote institutional change designed to promote development, especially change without coercion. In the sphere of institutional change recipients of foreign aid have so far largely confined their activities to the expropriation of unpopular classes in the name of land reform, social justice or the removal of alleged exploitation. Such measures retard material progress.

The arguments of the above three sections do not mean that there is no possibility of foreign aid assisting the material progress of the recipients. But they certainly point to the conclusion that it is unwarranted to assume that it necessarily does so. Whether it in fact does so or not depends on the specific circumstances of each case. And because the volume of investible resources is far less important as a prerequisite of material progress than are people's attitudes, motivations (including the direction of their activities), social institutions and political arrangements, and also less important than the efficient deployment of resources, all of which are likely to be affected adversely by the advocacy and the flow of aid, there can be no general presumption that in practice aid is more likely to promote development rather than retard it. And in fact these considerations suggest that as it has operated and is likely to operate, any general presumption would favour the opposite conclusion.

16 *Aid and Infrastructure*

A variant of the case for foreign aid as an instrument to promote investment links aid specifically to the financing of the infrastructure (sometimes termed social overhead capital) supposedly necessary for the development of poor countries.

In this context infrastructure refers to such installations as ports, railways and roads, which do not produce commodities directly but promote general economic activity. It is often said that without these installations economic advance is not possible. And it is argued further that the high cost puts them beyond the means of poor countries, especially because the economic return is either too long delayed or too indiscriminate for private financing. But these arguments are again invalid. First, governments of underdeveloped countries can borrow from abroad commercially and service the loans from tax revenues, which is indeed what has happened in many underdeveloped countries in the recent past. Further, much of the infrastructure in underdeveloped countries has been financed and operated privately until comparatively recently.

Nor is it true that a substantial infrastructure is a precondition of development. The infrastructures of highly developed economies represent substantial capital, which has absorbed much of total investment over decades or even centuries. The suggestion that a ready-made infrastructure is necessary for development ignores the fact that the infrastructure develops in the course of economic progress, not ahead of it. The suggestion is yet another example of an unhistorical and unrealistic attitude to the process of development. Much of the literature suggests that the world was somehow created in two parts; one part with a ready-made infrastructure of railways, roads, ports, pipe lines and public utilities, which has therefore been able to develop, and the other which the Creator unfortunately forgot to endow with social overhead capital. This is not the way things have happened.

Nowadays the problem of financing the infrastructure has been made more difficult by various factors. One such factor is the poor record of many underdeveloped countries in the treatment of foreign capital. Another familiar factor is the tendency to divert resources into subsidised manufactures, which reduces the funds available for the construction and maintenance of the social overhead capital. But these factors are rarely mentioned in the literature.[1]

17 *Further Repercussions and Implications of Aid*

The considerations reviewed in the foregoing sections of this essay make it clear that any favourable effects of the inflow of resources represented by foreign aid can be offset or even outweighed by significant unfavourable repercussions, and also by ineffective use of the resources themselves. It is indeed probable that the flow of aid since the

[1] A. J. Youngson, *Overhead Capital: A Study in Development Economics*, Edinburgh, 1967, examines perceptively the ambiguities and complexities in the concept of infrastructure or social overhead capital, especially in the context of economic development.

second world war has inhibited rather than advanced the material progress of many recipients.

There are many examples from the experience of the last two decades of the comparative ineffectiveness of foreign aid as an instrument for raising general living standards and promoting long-term economic development in poor countries. For instance, fifteen years after the inception of western aid and of the five-year plans, India experienced, in 1966–7, the most acute of its recurring food and foreign exchange crises. India has depended on foreign aid for so long that this dependence has come to be taken for granted. Indeed the economic history of that country since about the mid-1950s has been one of progression from poverty to pauperism. Yet it was an explicit objective of Indian planning to reduce or eliminate economic dependence.[1] There are many other aid recipients where general living standards have shown no significant rise and where the countries face persistent economic difficulties after many years of aid.

After over fifteen years of foreign aid its relative ineffectiveness to promote higher living standards in poor countries has perforce had to be recognised. At the same time the supporters of aid insist that the absence of appreciable improvement in the economic conditions of the recipients is an argument for extending foreign aid in amount and in time. Such demands are corollaries of considering its operation as axiomatically beneficial and the case for it as granted. Once it is so treated either progress or lack of progress can be invoked in support of its continuation or expansion: the former as evidence of its success, the latter as evidence of the need for more. As we have already noted in the discussion on central planning, empirical evidence and the analysis of evidence become irrelevant to the merits of an axiom.[2]

---

[1] The experience of India is instructive in this context. Until about 1956, when both comprehensive planning and substantial aid got under way, India generally had a surplus on its current external trade. During the Second Five-Year Plan (1956–61), large-scale deficits emerged and have continued ever since. Exports on private account continue to exceed imports on private account but there was a huge increase in imports on government account, which by the late 1960s accounted for over three-fifths of all imports. About one-half of total imports were by then financed from aid. It was large-scale foreign aid which substantially financed the trade deficit and made possible the maintenance of an overvalued rate of exchange, which discouraged exports and pulled in imports. Professor B.R. Shenoy has analysed these relationships in many publications, notably in *Indian Economic Policy*, Bombay, 1968.

[2] Supporters of aid often argue that its duration has been too short and its volume, at least on a per capita basis, too small for its effectiveness to emerge. This insistence on its inadequacies in time and amount is an instance of the axiomatic approach noted in the text. There can be no limit in time or volume for the assessment of the effects of aid if it is axiomatically assumed to be beneficial.

Nor is it clear what is meant by 'small' in this context. But even if aid figures are

The axiomatic assumption that foreign aid is beneficial, together with the diversity of its ostensible objectives (noted in section 18 of this essay), are responsible for another of its anomalies. In public discussions on aid, giving more has come to be equated with doing better, without reference to the circumstances in the recipient countries or to the results of aid. To assume that giving more is the same as doing better is to measure result by cost, or even to identify the two. This is tantamount to saying that the more a process costs the better it is. Such an approach does not promote effective use of scarce capital, least of all when it is expended in distant areas and unfamiliar conditions about which the public in the donor countries has little reliable information.

We have so far focused on certain anomalous repercussions of the advocacy and flow of aid. I would like now to note another significant anomaly which belongs to the field of social psychology. The emphasis on the poverty, that is the material backwardness, of the underdeveloped world, and on the alleged necessity for foreign aid to relieve it, which lies at the centre of the advocacy of aid, directs attention precisely to those elements of life and activity in underdeveloped countries in which their peoples compare least favourably with those of rich countries, and especially so on the conventional criteria adopted in these discussions. These discussions suggest that the only relevant differences between people are those in conventionally measured incomes; that apart from these differences humanity consists of homogeneous, undifferentiated stuff; and that these differences are somehow correlated with well-being, happiness, satisfaction, and indeed general excellence.

The emphasis on the indispensability of aid is especially likely to exacerbate any feelings of inferiority which some sections of the populations of underdeveloped countries may experience in their relations with the west, a feeling which is widely present though not always apparent and rarely acknowledged. It also enhances any sentiments of

expressed on a per capita basis, in the context of the effects of aid they are meaningful only if they are shown as a percentage of per capita incomes in the recipient country, and not in absolute terms or as a percentage of the per capita aid received by others. Moreover, even as a percentage per capita figure it would be more meaningful to relate it to the occupied population rather than to the total population. Alternatively, it could be related to the total flow of monetary saving in the recipient country. Those who complain about the allegedly small volume of aid do not usually undertake such calculations. However, on all worthwhile criteria it is plain that over the last ten years or more many aid recipients have enjoyed substantial amounts of aid: and yet further and indefinite continuation of aid is envisaged because of continued low living standards and payments difficulties.

superiority indulged in by certain sections of the population in rich countries, by encouraging a patronising attitude to the recipients.[1]

In poor countries the agreeable sensation of superiority conveyed by the giving of aid, and the impulse to counterbalance any feelings of inferiority brought on by the acceptance of aid, may together help to explain the anomalous phenomenon that some aid recipients themselves act as aid givers, albeit on a small scale. In fact it seems that aid has assumed the role of an international status symbol, to use an expression from current jargon; it is a term which aptly describes the trappings of a superiority which is hoped for or pretended rather than felt or achieved.

When it comes to the flow of aid from rich to poor countries, however, there are obvious emotional, political and financial attractions for the latter to consider themselves, and be considered by others, as victims of circumstances beyond their control, especially of external oppression and exploitation. Conversely, feelings of guilt which allegations of oppression and exploitation arouse in persons and groups so accused are often accompanied by an agreeable sense of superiority in the guilty self or community as these suggestions serve as indicators of past or present power. These various sentiments are manifest in discussions on the relationships between colonies and ex-colonies and metropolitan powers, and between rich and poor countries, and their presence and operation is apt to strain the relations between donors and recipients.[2]

18 *Specific and Subsidiary Arguments in Support of Aid*

The principal argument or axiom in the advocacy of foreign aid is the suggestion that it provides resources indispensable for the development of poor countries. But there are also a number of subsidiary arguments or assumptions which are often more prominent than the main argument itself, especially in nontechnical discussion. However, these too usually turn out to be mere assertions about the merits and likely effects

---

[1] As Dostoievsky put into the mouth of one of his characters: '. . . the enjoyment derived from charity is a haughty and immoral enjoyment. The rich man's enjoyment [lies in] his wealth, his power, and in the comparison of his importance with the poor. Charity corrupts giver and taker alike; and, what is more, [charity] does not attain its objects as it only increases poverty.' (*The Possessed.*)

A patronising attitude towards peoples of underdeveloped countries is manifest in literary and academic pursuits, a patronisation reflected in the attitude that one cannot and should not apply the same standards in judging their performance as one would to peoples of the west.

[2] Analogous results are often brought about by the manner in which the economic position and prospects of coloured immigrant populations are discussed in western countries.

of foreign aid, not arguments based on reason and supported by evidence.

Aid as redistributive taxation. These subsidiary arguments tend to overlap and to reinforce each other. For instance, it is often argued that the west has a moral duty to help poor countries and that aid should be offered to meet their needs, especially in view of the allegedly ever-widening gap between rich and poor countries. Both views lead to the conclusion that taxation must be raised in the west to finance foreign aid, which thus becomes an extension of progressive taxation into the international field. In the development literature aid is often instanced as an inevitable and desirable extension of the welfare state from the domestic sphere to the international plane by means of redistributive taxation.

However, foreign aid differs radically from domestic redistributive taxation, whatever the merits of the latter. Foreign aid is paid by governments to governments; it is not a redistribution of income between persons and families. It cannot be adjusted to the incomes and circumstances of payers and recipients. It is therefore inevitably partly regressive, because many taxpayers in donor countries are poorer than many people in recipient countries. This regressive aspect is increased in practice by the fact that foreign aid benefits better-off people within the recipient countries, notably members of the urban population and especially politicians, civil servants, academics and certain sections of the business community. Hence the gibe that foreign aid is a process by which poor people in rich countries help rich people in poor countries.[1] Further, it should be noted that the materially poorest groups in the underdeveloped world, the aborigines, the tribal populations and the desert peoples, are hardly touched by aid, if at all; and substantially the same applies to the poorest sections of the rural and urban proletariat, especially the former.

Moreover, the case for redistributive taxation rests on an assumed basic uniformity in the circumstances of the people among whom it is to be effected. In fact, however, social and physical living conditions, and therefore requirements, which are reasonably uniform within one country, differ enormously between many rich and many poor countries. It follows from this that if redistributive taxation is deemed desirable it

---

[1] The discussion in the text refers to the real value of aid reaching the recipient countries. If aid is tied, part of the nominal value is a subsidy from the taxpayers to the exporters within the donor countries.

is appropriate to conduct it primarily within countries rather than internationally. In fact, however, not only is there relatively little effective domestic redistributive taxation in many recipient countries, but (as we have already noted) foreign aid, advocated as an instrument of redistributive taxation, benefits the better-off in the recipient countries. Furthermore, the sharing of the cost of aid among donors and its distribution among recipient governments is not determined by the canons and criteria of redistributive taxation, but by political pressures, vagaries of public sentiment and sheer chance.

The analogy between foreign aid and redistributive taxation is also affected by the enormous margins of error to which the interpretation of comparisons of national incomes between rich and poor countries is subject. The biases and margins of error involved amount to several hundreds per cent of the conventional estimates.[1] Margins of error of such magnitude preclude the valid application of redistributive taxation between developed and underdeveloped countries. This is quite apart from the other more fundamental issues already noted, notably the fact that intergovernmental aid cannot serve as an instrument for redistribution between persons and families.

As a minor variant of the argument that foreign aid is a form of redistributive taxation it is sometimes urged that aid is analogous to a system of regional grants by central governments in advanced countries, such as the development area grants of the British government. This argument is invalid. Regional grants reflect the pursuit of a variety of domestic policies and the operation of political pressures. They are not redistributive taxation in the sense of redistribution between rich and poor any more than is assistance to particular industries.

We have already noted that the materially most backward groups are not reached by aid. As they are inarticulate and politically ineffective their presence affects neither the international flow of aid nor the domestic allocation of aid funds. Quite possibly because of their primitive conditions they could not benefit from aid except in forms carefully geared to their conditions. However, the problems raised by their position and the fact that they are substantially untouched by aid show that it differs fundamentally from redistributive taxation.

The prominence of aspects and developments of international trade in discussions on foreign aid also underlies the fundamental differences between redistributive taxation and foreign aid. For instance, changes in

[1] The reasons for these biases and errors have been examined in essay 1.

the terms of trade of underdeveloped countries often figure prominently in the advocacy of aid.[1] This again shows that the beneficiaries of aid are not the poorest groups; the poorest countries and communities in the underdeveloped world have no external trade or practically none; throughout the underdeveloped world the materially poorest countries and groups are those with fewest external contacts. External trade plays a significant role only in the lives and activities of the relatively better-off countries and societies.

The general case for redistributive taxation implies a basic uniformity in living conditions and requirements of income recipients. But physical and social conditions plainly differ widely between rich and poor countries. This is obvious for physical conditions; but there are also wide differences in expectations and requirements dictated by social conditions. The meaning and significance of income differences and of the concepts of riches and poverty depend greatly on the specific physical and social context, and thus comparisons in incomes between persons or groups in widely different societies are often meaningless. For instance, recipients of national assistance in Britain who are normally regarded as poor often have larger conventionally measured incomes than many landowners in India, or for that matter than many African chiefs, persons who would be regarded as men of substance in their community. The inappropriateness of the analogy between redistributive taxation and foreign aid reflects the dangers of aggregation even when applied to bilateral aid and applies even more when such global aggregates as the developed world and the underdeveloped world are under consideration.

Discussions about the extension of redistributive taxation to the international sphere often assume, explicitly or by clear implication, that international differences in per capita incomes are inequitable, whether genuine or merely apparent. Once again it is assumed that the peoples of underdeveloped countries are much like those of developed countries except for being poorer, and that they share the same living conditions. In short, the differences regarded as significant are those

[1] Measures to raise export prices of underdeveloped countries by commodity agreements, often advocated and introduced as a form of aid, clearly benefit the better-off countries and groups in the underdeveloped world. And the resulting higher prices of foodstuffs and raw materials are a regressive form of taxation in the importing countries. The operation of commodity agreements usually requires restriction or even total ban on the creation of new capacity in the producing countries, which bears harshly on people excluded from the production of these commodities who are almost always poorer than established producers. These various considerations show again how little foreign aid helps the poorer groups of the community.

which can be quantified plausibly: relevance and significance are equated with quantifiability, genuine or spurious.

Advocacy of international redistribution of income, then, ignores wide differences in modes of conduct, mores and institutions, as well as in living conditions and requirements. This advocacy often even implies that it is somehow reprehensible for certain societies and groups to have emerged from poverty, and also that these differences in material conditions can be removed relatively easily. However, international income differences reflect the operation of the underlying personal and social determinants of material achievement. Attempts to reduce or eliminate these differences therefore require close and intensive control over people's lives, that is the creation of great inequalities of power. The more diverse the conditions and the more deep-seated the causes of diversity, the more intensive is the compulsion required to standardise them. A substantial measure of international standardisation of material conditions requires not only world government but world government with totalitarian powers.

As yet the international redistribution brought about by foreign aid is small, largely because of the absence of world government. But if the powers of the international organisations and agencies were to grow, further steps towards international standardisation of material conditions could then confidently be expected. For both political and psychological reasons such a process is likely to be escalating and self-reinforcing: the greater are the resources of those committed to policies of standardisation, the further the process is likely to be carried; and once an appreciable measure of standardisation has been achieved, the residual differences will appear ever more irksome and less defensible.

The advocacy of aid as a form of redistributive taxation is often based on allegations of a wide and widening gap in incomes between developed and underdeveloped countries.[1] As was shown in essay I, this idea of a wide and widening gap is untrue in so far as it can be given any definable meaning. We have also shown that even if it were clearly defined, and a valid description of a situation, it still could not serve as worthwhile basis for policy without examination of official policies and popular attitudes and behaviour in the poorer societies. But even if the extent and movement of differences in incomes between groups of rich and

---

[1] This argument is supported by the insistence that the situation is morally and politically intolerable, and that it is becoming more intolerable as the gap widens. The question of the moral element in foreign aid, and its international political implications, are discussed later in this section.

poor countries were agreed to be excessive on some specified and agreed criterion, foreign aid would not necessarily be the appropriate policy for their reduction for the simple reason that it does not necessarily promote the development of poor countries. The suggestion that it does so prejudges the effects of its operation.

If the basis of the advocacy of aid is simply the need to reduce the allegedly wide and widening gap in incomes then such advocacy would not be affected even if it were recognised that aid need not promote the material progress of the recipients as long as it impoverished the donors. Indeed, the frequent assertion that to give more is to do better, without examination of the effects of aid on the material progress of the recipients, suggests that this is in fact the position of some advocates of aid. But not only does impoverishment of the donors not ensure the material advance of the recipients, it does not even ensure reduction of international differences in income: the net effects of aid in the recipient countries may be sufficiently adverse to retard their progress to an extent which would actually widen the gap. Such an outcome would, of course, again spuriously justify indefinite continuation and extension of aid.

Finally, the general case for redistributive taxation is not even self-evident on the national level, let alone on the international plane. Compulsory redistribution of income involves many unresolved problems. These include the difficulties of tracing through the incidence of a tax as distinct from its impact. More deep-seated and significant are problems of equity presented by differences in the volume and intensity of effort behind differences in income, and in the sacrifice of leisure and pleasure; indeed, the sacrifice of pleasure includes significantly not only immediate pleasures forgone but also the effect on a person's capacity and qualifications subsequently to enjoy the good things of life.[1] These differences in the cost of securing income are ignored in the advocacy and in the practice of redistributive taxation. Other major social, political and economic issues often ignored or understated in discussions on redistributive taxation range from relatively simple issues of incentive to much wider matters of social cohesion, political tension and, especially in the case of death duties, the continuity of the family. The unquestioning acceptance of the case for redistributive taxation is yet another instance of the belief that the only significant and

---

[1] This consideration explains why references to the poor rich man are so often apposite. The argument in the text does not, of course, apply to inherited wealth.

relevant aspects of a situation or phenomenon are those which can be easily quantified, at least with superficial plausibility.[1]

The basic assumption and overriding objective behind redistributive taxation, whether on an international or on the domestic plane, is that it improves the material position of the poor. But making the rich poor does not make the poor rich. In fact it often makes the poor poorer. For instance, the arguments used in the advocacy of international redistributive taxation, notably the suggestion that differences in wealth are reprehensible, helps to promote egalitarian domestic policies (at least ostensibly egalitarian policies) in the recipient countries which retard their material progress, including the material position and prospects of the poorest groups. Such policies often obstruct the growth of capital and enterprise and the acquisition and deployment of skills, and also divert human and financial resources from more productive employment into less productive directions, including tax avoidance and evasion.

The relief of need. Another argument for foreign aid is based on need. According to this argument it must be given simply because of the need of poor countries as shown and measured by their low incomes.

Before discussing the substantive issue of the merits of this argument, we should note that relief of need and promotion of development are completely different as bases and criteria for foreign aid. Donations to a beggar or an invalid are distributed on bases and criteria very different from loans to promising young people for their training or for the establishment of businesses. Expectations about the results and the duration of the two kinds of monetary transfers are also very different. This obvious consideration is ignored and even obscured in the terminology and activities of the aid organisations.[2]

Simple references to need provide neither an argument nor a criterion for aid. Indeed its adoption leads to absurdities. For instance, should aid be given or increased if incomes are reduced and their increase

---

[1] The quantification employed in progressive taxation is indeed often incomplete, arbitrary and crude. It is incomplete in that it does not take into account such quantifiable aspects of a situation as the age of the income recipient. A single man of twenty-one with an income of £3,000 is obviously much better off than is a single man of forty-five with an income of £3,500; yet the older man pays more tax. This neglect of differences in age in progressive taxation is relevant also to its international extension, because of the substantial differences in age composition of the populations of different countries. The crudeness and arbitrariness of its procedures is clear from its neglect of the considerations listed in the text.

[2] That promotion of development and relief of need are seen as different functions is reflected in the content of aid when it is supplied in kind.

inhibited by the expulsion of groups whose productivity is above the national average? The expulsion of the Asians from East Africa and the Indians from Burma reduced per capita incomes in these countries; on the basis of the argument from need aid should be given or increased in these circumstances, which might encourage further expulsions, this in turn reinforcing the case for aid, and so on *ad infinitum*.[1]

Expulsion or slaughter of productive minority groups are extreme cases. But practically throughout the underdeveloped world governments restrict the activities of various productive minority groups, which both reduces per capita incomes and retards their rates of growth.

Similar considerations apply when recipient governments spend heavily on armaments, or on political propaganda directed either against the donors of aid or against other recipients of aid. Countless other examples could be instanced of policies of recipients which impoverish their own countries or other aid recipients. Thus need plainly does not offer a worthwhile argument nor a sensible criterion for aid.

Some considerations already noted in the discussion on progressive taxation bear also on the argument from need. These include the significance of international differences in physical and social conditions and thus in requirements; the huge margins of error and the large biases in international income comparisons; and also the fact that the poorest communities of the underdeveloped world are generally not reached by aid. This last point is especially relevant because it shows that allocation of aid is unrelated to need.

The rapid growth of population in underdeveloped countries is often instanced as presenting a special need calling for foreign aid. Because this issue is so widely canvassed we shall deal with it separately in a later subsection, but we may note here that population growth by itself cannot support the argument from need since it reflects a fall in mortality and thus an improvement in the position of the people. This particular argument for aid is often reinforced by references to large-scale hunger and starvation in underdeveloped countries, which for obvious reasons provide particularly effective appeal. The extent of starvation in underdeveloped countries is debatable, especially in the face of the rapid increase in population throughout the underdeveloped

---

[1] Massacres such as those of the Ibo in Nigeria, the Chinese in parts of south-east Asia, and the Arabs in Zanzibar also reduced per capita incomes and their rates of growth in these areas. On the basis of the argument for the relief of need, therefore, such massacres could supply grounds for further and increased aid. Perhaps it would be unfair to suggest that the increased aid would in its turn provide grounds for further massacres.

world which, if the word starvation is to be taken literally, is difficult to explain except on very peculiar assumptions. In any case, it is largely irrelevant to foreign aid; much or most of it goes to support government activities entirely unrelated to increased food production or to the means of obtaining additional food.

An appeal for help on grounds of need should appropriately take into account the conduct of the recipient governments and populations of the recipient countries. As we have just noted, recipient governments often pursue policies which reduce current income and the prospect of its rate of increase, thereby necessarily increasing their need for aid. Moreover, the conduct and mores of the population are often uncongenial to material advance or inconsistent with it. In such conditions aid must be irrelevant and ineffective because it cannot substantially improve living standards or their rate of advance.

If relief of need is the purpose of aid there must be certain prerequisites of effective policy: these include first of all an examination of where the funds go, in the sense of which particular groups benefit; second, there must be some assessment of differences in living standards between donors and recipients and also between different actual and prospective recipients; and third, examination is required of the conduct both of the governments and the populations in actual and prospective recipient countries.

If it is thought that the relief of need in the recipient countries is the primary object of aid, transfer of capital for this purpose is inappropriate. As we have already noted, capital is usually more productive in the developed countries. Thus, if it were invested there and the return on it transferred to the underdeveloped countries, the latter could receive more goods and services for the relief of their needs than when the capital is so transferred.

In the advocacy of aid since about the mid-1960s, relief of need has gained in prominence compared to the development of the recipients. This change of emphasis is a shift from a basis which could at least be called quasi-intellectual to one which is more frankly emotional. An appeal directed primarily to the emotions tends to be more strident than one directed at least ostensibly to reason. It is therefore not surprising that an increasingly strident note has crept into the advocacy of aid in recent years. The shift of emphasis from development to need may reflect a certain loss of confidence on the part of its advocates, in aid as an instrument for development, and in the continued appeal of this particular basis for aid. But the operation of aid has set up various powerful vested interests, emotional, political, administrative and financial. Because of the operation of these interests the partial retreat from the axiomatic acceptance of aid as an allegedly necessary and effective agent of development has brought about not a re-examination of the case for it but a search for a new principal ground for its advocacy.

Population problems as ground for aid. The rapid increase in population, coupled with allegedly severe population pressure, resulting in extreme poverty and widespread starvation, is said to present special problems and needs in the underdeveloped world calling for aid from richer countries. It is also often suggested that these problems invalidate comparisons with the past experience of now developed countries, and also undermine the relevance of personal faculties and attitudes as agents of material progress. The subject matter of this subsection overlaps to some extent with that of the immediately preceding one, but we will deal with it here separately because of the special importance attached to this range of issues in current discussion and because of the complexity of these matters. These considerations also seem to warrant a digression on certain relationships between the material achievement and progress of the population, its numbers, and its aptitudes and attitudes.

Acceleration of growth of population in underdeveloped countries does not by itself provide a valid argument for aid. It reflects a fall in mortality and longer life expectation, and thus an improvement in living conditions. It is debatable to what extent people would reduce the number of their children if they had access to more sophisticated methods of preventing conception.[1] But even now there is no reason why they cannot reduce the number of children they have, and they will certainly do so if they value higher living standards for themselves and their children more than the possession of children. Altogether, it is not clear how acceleration of population growth provides an argument for aid.

However, this rapid growth of population in the underdeveloped world figures prominently in the advocacy of aid, in which it is often suggested that it is the main cause of hunger and starvation; for obvious reasons references to starvation and hunger have special appeal in this advocacy. (In passing it may be noted here that there is something of a

---

[1] There are various reasons for believing that a large proportion of the populations of Africa and Asia will not practise contraception for at least another generation. Some of these reasons are acknowledged, albeit briefly and inadequately, in the Pearson Report (pp. 197–8).

paradox in the often expressed concern that the peoples of under-developed countries live at subsistence level and indeed under permanent threat of starvation, which is then coupled with expressions of alarm at the huge increase in their numbers.)[1]

The situation, however, is plainly not that there is not enough food for the subsistence of the existing population or populations. If this were the position there could be no growth in numbers, much less a huge increase. If there is starvation in some underdeveloped countries this must mean that part of the population cannot fend for itself, either because it lacks the ability to do so or because it is prevented from doing so by institutional factors, such as organised barriers to entry into wage employment or restrictions on access to land. Apart from occasional *ad hoc* emergency measures foreign aid is irrelevant to the relief of starvation. As we have argued, it benefits primarily the better-off sections of the populations in the recipient countries, and these sections are certainly not threatened by starvation. And it leaves very largely unaffected the poorest and most backward groups – both the poorest sections of the urban and rural proletariat and also the primitive tribal and aboriginal societies – who are most exposed to famine. And the combination of an overall sufficiency of food, together with the presence – alleged or real – of starvation, also invites the question why international redistribution is advocated when domestic redistribution is not undertaken to the extent that starvation is avoided; which incidentally raises the further point that in such circumstances, where domestic redistribution is not undertaken to the extent of relieving starvation, international redistribution is unlikely to reach the poorest groups, as it is channelled through the governments of these countries.

Finally, much of aid – probably the bulk of it – directly finances, or at least supports at one remove, activities which neither produce food nor the wherewithal to purchase it. Familiar examples of the sort of projects that aid goes to finance or to support include state subsidised airlines, steel complexes, heavy engineering works, and prestige projects of all kinds.[2] By encouraging diversion of domestic resources into these activi-

---

[1] The unquestioning condemnations in the west of high birth rates in the under-developed countries is yet another example of the subconscious patronising attitude of the spokesmen for aid in the west, in that they rarely consider to what extent these high birth rates reflect preferences and decisions on the part of the parents in these countries.

[2] The substantial military expenditure of many recipients of aid directed primarily against other aid recipients or for the suppression of secessionist movements in their own countries presents familiar anomalies which have some bearing on the alleged relevance of aid for the relief of suffering and hunger, but it would not be profitable to explore this complex issue here.

ties foreign aid reduces food supplies in the recipient countries and thus exacerbates the plight of the poorest groups. This effect is especially pronounced when these activities are carried out at such heavy loss that the domestic resources engaged in them have a negative productivity.

Thus the acceleration of population growth does not present a valid argument for aid. Moreover, routine foreign aid (as distinct from special emergency measures) is irrelevant to starvation in the underdeveloped world and may indeed aggravate it.

This may be a convenient place to examine certain aspects of the relationship between population pressure, population growth, personal motivations, and living standards. Population pressure clearly does not explain much or most of the poverty of the underdeveloped world. Most of Africa, Latin America, and south-east Asia, as well as parts of south Asia, are sparsely populated. Some of the poorest groups live in areas which are largely empty; and moreover the numbers of these groups are often stagnant. The extensive areas at their disposal have not helped them to emerge from their primitive conditions, even where the land is cultivable without the injection of significant capital. Indeed, large areas of these regions are substantially underpopulated in the sense that the population density is too low to permit the provision of simple health or transport facilities. Conversely, some of the most advanced areas of the underdeveloped world (as well as, of course, some of the most prosperous areas of the developed world) are very densely populated.

The relationship between population density and living standards cannot be examined usefully without consideration of people's economic aptitudes and attitudes, which are inseparably linked to economic achievement. This relationship is clear from the wide differences in prosperity and progress of different ethnic groups within the same country which can be observed in both underdeveloped and developed countries and which are especially pronounced in the former. And these differences are present also both when the different groups are indigeneous and when they are immigrant.

Population growth, material progress and motivation are also clearly interrelated, with motivation the decisive independent variable. The decisive character of motivation is clear from the consideration already noted that people can always choose to have fewer children if they prefer higher conventionally measured living standards. The decisive importance of motivation is suggested also by the connection between the fall in birth rates and the improvement in living standards which has often been observed in certain stages of material advance. The causality or functional relationship in this sequence is not one of a reduction in the birth rate as cause of an improvement in living standards or in general economic achievement, but one in which both developments reflect a change in outlook and motivation, notably an increased interest in living standards. Reduction in the rate of population growth represents a change of a rate of change which cannot by itself (that is, unless it is a concomitant of other changes) effect appreciable improvement in general living standards over a few years or even decades, and cannot therefore be regarded appropriately as a cause of such improvement over these periods.[1]

Thus, neither acceleration of population growth nor population pressure is a significant independent cause of the poverty of the underdeveloped world. They are dependent variables or effects rather than independent variables or causes since there is extreme poverty even in the absence of high population density or substantial population growth; and conversely there is often increasing prosperity and progress in underdeveloped countries even where population is dense and is increasing rapidly.

Aid as a moral duty. Foreign aid is often advocated as if it were the discharge of a moral duty to help the poor. But the analogy with moral obligation fails. Foreign aid is taxpayer's money compulsorily collected; it is outside the area of volition and choice. Indeed, contributors not only have no choice but quite generally do not even know they are contributing.

It is sometimes urged that in a democracy taxpayers do have a choice, which restores the moral element in foreign aid. This objection is superficial. The taxpayer has to contribute to foreign aid whether he likes it or not and whether he has voted in its favour or against it.

The moral obligation to help the less fortunate cannot be discharged by entities such as governments. It can be discharged only by persons who are prepared to impoverish themselves and weaken their material

---

[1] Mr John Hajnal has examined the marriage and fertility patterns of a number of societies in a highly important article, 'European Marriage Patterns in Perspective: The Uniqueness of the European Pattern', in D. V. Glass and D. E. C. Eversley (eds), *Population in History*, London, 1965. Mr Hajnal shows that the societies of Europe since the eighteenth century, and their lineal descendants in America and Australasia, represented until very recently the only documented examples of societies with an appreciable proportion of the population unmarried until well after puberty and with fertility rates significantly below fecundity rates.

position relative to others in order to help their poorer fellow men. Those wishing to help underdeveloped countries can easily write a cheque in favour of the governments or missions, schools or hospitals operating there.

There are also other differences between foreign aid and voluntary charity. Voluntary action can be readily directed to the specific needs of persons or groups. It sets up possibilities of adjustment to specific requirements and circumstances, which increases the effectiveness of charity. Foreign aid on the other hand is distributed to governments, not to persons or voluntary organisations.

Recognition of the basic difference between foreign aid and voluntary charity is also of considerable political consequence. Most people in underdeveloped countries do not know that their countries receive aid, nor can they reason out the differences between foreign aid and voluntary charity. But those people in the recipient countries who know about foreign aid generally and rightly sense a fundamental difference between voluntary charity and taxpayers' money compulsorily collected; and they accordingly suspect statements that foreign aid is motivated by humanitarian sentiments.

The argument from indebtedness. It has come to be suggested that foreign aid is necessary to enable underdeveloped countries to service the subsidised loans (concessionary finance) under earlier foreign aid arrangements. This argument, which as we have already noted implies that more aid is to be given because the earlier aid proved unproductive, is given some support in the Pearson Report. This sequence implies a vicious circle of indebtedness: concessionary finance used unproductively leads to indebtedness which is then used as an argument for further concessionary finance. Such a vicious circle of aid and indebtedness seems much more real than the widely publicised vicious circle of poverty and stagnation. Moreover, if grants, that is completely free gifts, are used unproductively, the resulting situation can also be used to advocate further grants or subsidised loans. For instance, the grants may be used to erect expensive structures or institutions the costly maintenance of which could then be said to require external support.

To argue for more aid to meet the indebtedness contracted under aid granted in the past is an example of the axiomatic approach from which it follows that either progress or retrogression, success or failure, can be urged as a ground for further aid.

Aid and political strategy. Foreign aid is sometimes justified, especially in American discussions, on two political grounds: first, that it represents a valuable instrument of western political strategy in keeping the underdeveloped countries out of the Soviet bloc; and second, that by promoting the development of poor countries, and thus reducing the extent of the international differences in income, it prevents the emergence of a politically explosive situation and thus helps to preserve world peace.

To deal with these two arguments in turn: the first is in curious contrast to those based on moral and humanitarian grounds. But it is similar to them in that it too is insubstantial.

(i) The argument assumes that foreign aid serves rapidly and appreciably to raise living standards. It assumes further that an inclination to accept communism depends largely on the standard of living. Neither of these assumptions is valid.

(ii) With few exceptions foreign aid promotes centralised and closely controlled economies. Its operation, therefore, tends to favour and strengthen governments which lean towards the Soviet bloc.

(iii) Beneficiaries in this area, as in others, are apt to resent the donors.[1] Because of this resentment they often find it emotionally necessary to assert their independence of the donor, a reaction which in the context of foreign aid may well be politically useful also, both for domestic and for external reasons.[2] This kind of resentment is often noted in general literature but is rarely referred to by supporters of foreign aid. And this resentment is at times exacerbated by a patronising attitude on the part of the donors to those in receipt of sustained external help, an attitude which in spite of disclaimers is often present and not unexpectedly so.

Various influences make it especially likely that recipients of foreign aid should react unfavourably to the providers of these gifts. The transfer of taxpayers' money to foreign governments arouses suspicions of sinister motives, notably of political domination. Disclaimers of such motives and emphasis on humanitarian grounds are apt to strengthen these suspicions. Foreign aid is also often regarded in recipient countries

[1] In an address in Madras in January 1970, Mr M. R. Masani, former mayor of Bombay, quoted an eastern saying which has some truth in it without being generally true, and which is apposite in the context of the political implications of foreign aid. 'Why do you hate me so much? I never tried to do anything for you.'

[2] In domestic policies this reaction in large measure reflects recognition that articulate elements in the population resent the donors. In foreign policy assertion of independence in usually an obvious advantage, or even a necessity, especially for governments who are weak at home and abroad.

as an instrument for forcing them to purchase what would otherwise be unsaleable. Further, many people in the recipient countries consider aid as an admission of guilt on the part of the donors, as partial restitution for past wrongs. This view is fashionable and vocal in the under-developed countries, where it is widely put about that their material backwardness is a result of western exploitation. And it is an opinion reinforced by those feelings of guilt in western society towards under-developed countries, feelings which, as we have already noted, are quite consistent with a patronising attitude towards them.

The uncritical methods of allocation of western aid, particularly American and British aid, in contrast to the more purposeful and selec-tive allocation of Soviet aid, have reinforced some of these adverse political reactions. Its allocation ranges from the indiscriminate (in the sense of its disregard of the political interests of the donors), which arouses suspicion because it is so baffling, to the placatory, which achieves the opposite result to that intended because a hostile response on the part of the recipient country will be more likely to secure a con-tinuation of aid.

In recent years there has been a growing tendency for recipient governments to lay down the conditions for the acceptance of aid, or even to threaten to refuse it altogether, a tendency paralleled by the increasingly placatory attitude of the donor countries. For instance, a dispatch to the *Financial Times* of 17 July 1970, reporting on a meeting of the Aid to India consortium, stated that 'aid givers are coming to realise that *they have no choice* but to accept India as it is without sermonising.'[1] The thought that the aid givers have the choice of with-holding aid has apparently not occurred to the members of the consort-ium or to the author of the dispatch[2]. Indeed, not only is this possibility not considered, but there have been instances of donor countries repeatedly requesting poor countries not to refuse their aid.[3]

For these and other reasons it is not surprising that many govern-ments receiving aid have pursued policies hostile to western donors whom they have opposed, embarrassed and thwarted to the best of their ability. Leaders and spokesmen of many recipient governments have been violently and explicitly abusive to donor countries: examples in

[1] My italics.
[2] Disregard of the policies of the recipient governments and of conditions in recipient countries lies behind certain paradoxical results and implications of the advocacy and flow of aid, some of which we have noted earlier in this essay, especially in the context of the relief of need.
[3] Examples in recent years include Ceylon and Burma.

recent years include Algeria, Ghana, India, Indonesia, Tanzania, the United Arab Republic and Zambia.[1]

(iv) If foreign aid were to serve as an instrument of political strategy it would have to be allocated much more selectively than it is at present. Its allocation would also have to be divorced from pressures from commercial interests in donor countries.

The second argument, that aid prevents the emergence of a politically explosive situation and thus helps to preserve world peace, and particularly the security of the richer nations, has come into prominence in recent years in public discussions on foreign aid. This influentially canvassed argument is again insubstantial. First, and once again, it prejudges the results of aid in taking for granted that it promotes the development of the recipients. But it is also open to more fundamental objections. Governments do not go to war because their countries are poor: the two world wars, for instance, were initiated by the more advanced countries and fought out among them. Moreover, with the important exception of China, which is one of the very few underdeveloped countries not receiving aid from anybody,[2] the military and economic resources of poor countries are meagre (indeed the paucity of their resources is central to the advocacy of aid) so that these countries cannot possibly represent a military threat to the developed countries.[3] Indeed, since it is only technically relatively advanced countries which can represent a substantial threat to other advanced countries, the proponents of this particular argument, if they believe that aid promotes material and technical development, should logically argue against foreign aid to underdeveloped countries.

Thus, considerations of political strategy do not provide substantial arguments for the present foreign aid policy of the western donors.

Aid, the balance of payments and trade barriers. The last argument for aid to be considered here is the curious suggestion, often put forward in Great Britain, that foreign aid promotes exports and thus helps the balance of payments. This argument is the reverse of the truth. The

[1] The Tashkent Conference in January 1966 provides a notable confirmation of the ineffectiveness of foreign aid as an instrument of western political strategy. The governments of India and Pakistan asked the Soviet prime minister to mediate between them over the Kashmir dispute, though the two countries had for years been receiving large amounts of American aid.

[2] In the past China has received massive aid from the Soviet Union, a country with which it is now on unfriendly terms.

[3] Whatever political power the underdeveloped countries possess derives largely from political developments and dissensions in the west, the extent and outcome of which are unrelated to the level of income in poor countries.

argument says that exports are bought with aid; but this amounts to giving away the exports themselves, so that accordingly they contribute nothing to the balance of payments. And as exports have an import content and also diminish domestic supplies, exports which are given away aggravate the external payments problem and thereby increase the corresponding need for deflation of home demand.[1] This argument for aid is analogous to urging a shopkeeper to have his till rifled, on the ground that he will benefit if part of the money is spent in his shop.

If on the other hand the suggestion refers to the provision of shelter in external markets through tied aid, it implies that it is a subsidy to British exporters, which is not what is usually understood by aid.

In assessing the impact of foreign aid on the payments position and on the material progress of donor countries, it should be remembered that private foreign investment in the most productive areas of the world has in recent years been severely restricted by the governments of the United States and Britain, while the flow of official aid to the underdeveloped world has continued. These restrictions were imposed because of payments difficulties, which were certainly aggravated and indeed partly caused by foreign aid. It may be noted in parenthesis that these restrictions necessarily retard the material progress of the developed world, which in turn damages the long-term economic prospects of the underdeveloped world, through adverse effects on the cost of their imports, the market for their exports, and the world supply of capital.

In contrast to the argument that aid benefits the donor countries by assisting their balance of payments there is the argument that it should be given to offset the adverse effects on underdeveloped countries of the trade barriers erected by the developed countries.

The underdeveloped world benefits considerably from the presence of developed countries. Though it is true to say that these benefits would be greater in the absence of trade barriers, how significant these barriers are as obstacles to the progress of underdeveloped countries is a matter of some dispute. But foreign aid lessens the prospects of the reduction or elimination of these barriers. As we have already noted in this essay,

[1] It is sometimes suggested that aid promotes the long-term development of the recipients, to the ultimate benefit of the balance of payments of the donors. This objection is insubstantial. First, it prejudges the effects of aid. Second, it ignores the more productive alternative uses of the funds, some of which are noted later in this subsection. Third, even if it did promote the long-term development of the recipients, there is no assurance whatever that this would result in greater expenditure on the exports of the donors.

the flow of aid obstructs the emergence and diminishes the effectiveness of political opposition to these barriers within donor countries and possibly also within recipient countries.

19   *Potentialities of Aid*

Where the basic personal, social and political prerequisites of material progress are present, capital required for development will normally either be generated locally or will be available from abroad on commercial terms, either to the government or to the private sector or to both. There may however be exceptional political circumstances outside the control of the government where this may not be so. Taiwan in the early 1950s may have presented such an exceptional case. The population of that country certainly possesses the personal faculties and attitudes required for material progress and the internal social and political conditions were also not prohibitive. But it was then widely believed that Taiwan would shortly be taken over by the People's Republic of China. In the conditions of the times this apprehension led to a crisis of confidence which obstructed investment and enterprise. This crisis of confidence was probably alleviated by the flow of American aid, which was regarded as evidence that the country would not be taken over by China in the near future, and which thus restored confidence. The inflow of American aid was also accompanied by major changes in the domestic economic policy of Taiwan, notably the removal of some of the more restrictive economic controls and the withdrawal of the government from direct participation in certain economic activities. It is said that in this particular instance American influence was partly responsible for these changes, and the granting of aid facilitated the exercise of this influence. The material progress of Taiwan since the early 1950s has indeed been remarkable, though not more so than that of Hong Kong and Japan. Aid to Taiwan was stopped in 1964.

The success of Marshall Aid is often quoted as an example of the effectiveness of foreign aid. But the analogy between Marshall Aid and the aid programmes for underdeveloped countries is false. The economies of western Europe had to be *restored*, while those of the present recipients have to be *developed*. The peoples of western Europe had the faculties, motivations and institutions favourable to development for centuries before the second world war. Hence the rapid return to prosperity in western Europe and the termination of Marshall Aid after four years,[1] in contrast to the economic plight of India and of many other recipients of aid after a much longer period. And it is highly probable, especially in the light of the subsequent material progress of western Europe, that it would have recovered without Marshall Aid, though less rapidly.

The effect of the large inflow of gifts into Israel since 1948 was in some ways similar to that of Marshall Aid. The population already possessed the faculties and motivations appropriate to successful development. The country was, however, exceedingly short of capital, especially working capital, which the gifts supplied. The gifts received by Israel are of course not foreign aid as the term is usually understood, since they are gifts by private persons and groups, not intergovernmental grants of taxpayers' money.

Even apart from these exceptional instances, foreign aid unquestionably augments resources in the recipient countries. We have, however, argued that the inflow of resources is accompanied by other repercussions which are apt to offset or more than offset the favourable effects of additional resources. Nevertheless, the benefits from the inflow of resources can exceed the unfavourable repercussions. But this can happen only if the other preconditions of development are already present. And even in these conditions the question still remains why the capital should not be sought on commercial terms but received in the form of external doles, with the political and economic disadvantages which usually attend this course of action. Commercial terms would be more expensive. But, as we have already argued, both the capital and the technical assistance are likely to be much more productive than when they are supplied gratis or on subsidised terms.

Recognition of the limitations of foreign aid still leaves open the question of how far its operation could be improved: assuming that it continues to be supplied, how could its damaging effects be minimised and its possible benefits increased? There seems to be much scope for improvement in several directions.

First, the criteria of its allocation could be drastically revised. It could be allocated much more selectively than it is at present, to favour governments which within their human, administrative and financial resources try to perform the essential and difficult tasks of government and at the same time refrain from close control of the economy. In

---

[1] Over this short period, West Germany had to absorb millions of refugees, among whom there were disproportionate numbers of old people and children, as well as to deliver substantial reparations to the Soviet Union.

other words it could favour governments which try to govern rather than to plan. By the same token it could be withheld from governments which pursue policies which plainly retard the material progress of their countries; policies which, moreover, exacerbate the problems and difficulties both of other aid recipients and often also of the donors. Such criteria would promote relatively liberal economic systems in the recipient countries, minimise coercion, and favour material progress, especially the improvement of living standards. It would probably also reduce political tension in the recipient countries.

The criteria proposed in the foregoing paragraph assume, of course, that the purpose of aid is the improvement of the material conditions of the population of the recipient countries. But these criteria will be unacceptable if the purpose is the different one of the pursuit of political objectives such as the promotion of closely controlled economies and societies or the increase in the resources and power of the international organisations.

Second, much more thought could be given to prevent the inflow of aid from biasing the development of recipient countries in directions based on inappropriate external prototypes. Preference could be given to governments interested more in improving the roads and extending external contacts than in opening western-type universities or in creating heavy engineering works or steel complexes.[1]

Third, there would be various practical advantages (some of which are related) in the untying of aid, that is in not insisting that it should be spent in particular donor countries. Untying of aid would practically eliminate the element of subsidy to exporters in donor countries and thus clearly measure the cost to the donors and the subsidy to the recipients; it would divorce the flow of aid from pressure by commercial, academic and administrative interests for whom foreign aid often presents sheltered markets or agreeable jobs; it would considerably allay the widely prevalent suspicion that foreign aid is a means of forcing un-saleable commodities on to the recipients; and it would simplify the administration of aid in the donor countries.

The suggestion that aid should be untied should not be confused with the suggestion that it should be channelled through the inter-national agencies. This latter suggestion, now so widely publicised, would almost certainly produce extremely wasteful results. If aid were

---

[1] What matters in this context is the pattern of the overall policy of the recipient government, not the productivity or even the wider usefulness of specific projects financed by aid, as such finance normally sets free domestic resources which can be used for other purposes.

distributed in this way all connection between the supplier of aid and the recipient would be severed, with the result that expenditure financed from aid would be scrutinised even less carefully than it is at present.[1] The interest of the supplier of capital in its use tends to increase the effectiveness of its deployment. These likely results are apart from wider political implications of the substantial increase in the resources and power of the international agencies which would accrue to them if they were responsible for the allocation of foreign aid.

It may be objected that the adoption of the criteria proposed in this section for the allocation of aid would amount to unwarranted and unacceptable interference in the domestic policies of the recipients. This objection is spurious on at least two grounds. First, foreign aid necessarily impinges on the domestic policies of the recipients, as is obvious on reflection and is clear from various arguments set out in this essay. Second, foreign aid represents gifts of scarce capital. The demand for aid always and necessarily exceeds the amount available, which is therefore inevitably rationed. Aid to one recipient not only diminishes the resources of the donors, but also reduces the aid available to others. And if aid is used ineffectively by some recipients, aggregate future requirements will be increased. Thus the donors have an inescapable interest in the use to which aid is put and therefore should appropriately concern themselves with the economic policies of the recipients. And other aid recipients have an analogous interest. If some recipient governments pursue policies which obviously damage the development prospects of their countries they may affect adversely, twice over, the prospects of other poor countries receiving aid: first, by enhancing the unpopularity of the aid programmes within the donor countries; and secondly, by increasing their own future requirements.

However, it is unlikely that aid will be reformed along the lines suggested in this section. But even if it were, foreign aid, which does not and cannot affect favourably the principal determinants of development, is unlikely to be a major instrument, let alone an indispensable instrument, for the material progress of poor countries.

[1] This is an instance of the more general point that the further removed is the tax payer from the spending agency the less effective is his control over the expenditure of the funds.

APPENDIX TO PART A: SPECIFIC ARGUMENTS FOR PLANNING[1]

Most contemporary discussion treats the case for comprehensive planning as self-evident. Arguments are advanced occasionally which at any rate seem to be based on technical reasoning or to have specific content. These are usually addressed to more specialised audiences than is the axiomatic treatment of this subject, and they are therefore examined more appropriately in this appendix, which is addressed primarily to the specialist reader, than in the text of the essay. The most widely publicised of these arguments are that planning is required to increase saving and investment; to develop manufacturing industry, especially locally produced capital goods (heavy industry); to make up for the lack of entrepreneurial ability in the population; or to secure external economies.

Raising the level of saving and investment. The most familiar of the quasi-technical arguments for comprehensive central planning is the need to increase saving and investment, sometimes termed compulsory saving. This influential argument is irrelevant. First, much of planning is not designed even ostensibly to increase the rates of saving or of investment. This applies for instance to the licensing of commercial and industrial activity. Indeed, major constituent elements of comprehensive planning constrict saving and investment. Examples include the restrictions on the operation and expansion of organised industrial enterprises, or the restrictions on the inflow and deployment of foreign capital. These policies are general in countries where comprehensive planning is the official policy. Second, saving and investment can be promoted by fiscal and financial policies as well as by various measures designed to promote institutional change without comprehensive planning. To take only the most obvious examples, they can be increased by a budget surplus or by incentives to private saving.

Quite apart from the irrelevance of this argument there is also the wider issue of the justification of compulsory saving. The case for such a policy is no stronger than it is for conscription of labour. If the population shares the opinion of the government about the value of the prospective return on the proposed investment expenditure, the government could finance it from loans issued on market terms, without controls, special taxation, or inflation. Enforced removal by taxation of people's earnings or savings for the ostensible purpose of a future increment in the flow of income is in principle no different from the conscription of labour.

---

[1] This appendix is detailed, and in parts technical; the general reader will lose little by omitting it.

Moreover, the reduction of consumption is certain and immediate, while any future increase in income is speculative and uncertain.

The relationship between investment expenditure and economic development is complex and uncertain. It is often assumed that the material progress of poor countries depends primarily or even wholly upon the level of investment expenditure. But this is superficial. It is not legitimate to assume that an investment programme promotes development without enquiring into its returns and wider repercussions. Discussions on development often assume a high rate of return on total investment expenditure. An anticipated high return might be a criterion for the assessment of the merits of particular projects. But to take such a return for granted confuses an assumption with a criterion. This issue is sufficiently important to justify a digression.

The merits of an investment programme can be assessed properly only after estimating prospective returns or the cost in terms of alternative use of resources. Further, the repercussions of both the collection and the expenditure of the funds must also be taken into account as far as they are ascertainable. Moreover, the return needs to be assessed in terms of an increase in the flow of total income, especially of goods and services which make up the standard of living. The expansion of particular sectors of the economy does not indicate general economic advance.

In current parlance all expenditure of money other than on current consumption or current government services has come to be termed investment and regarded as productive of income. An investment fetish has emerged which has served spuriously to justify all sorts of expenditures and policies regardless of cost, return and other repercussions. This approach needs to be questioned on several different grounds.

Even large-scale investment need not bring about an increase in income.

(i) The personal faculties, motivations and social institutions of underdeveloped countries may be uncongenial to material progress. Investment will be unproductive without the necessary cooperant factors or resources both in the form of the required supplies of labour and in the wider sense of the appropriate motivations and institutional setting. And except in unusual conditions investment will not by itself promote or generate the necessary cooperant or complementary resources.

(ii) The distinction between investment and consumption is in practice largely arbitrary. This arbitrariness, which is particularly pertinent in poor countries, bears on the assumed merits of investment as an instrument for economic development. In underdeveloped countries especially it is consumption, not investment, which often serves to increase the productive capacity of resources, especially of people. Without consumption, the productive capacity of human beings would clearly be nil. Thus the real question is the comparative effect of different patterns of expenditure on the level and growth of income. Moreover, the prospect of improved consumption is often an incentive to higher economic performance, as is recognised in the concept of incentive or inducement goods. The higher economic performance thus promoted often takes the form of additional effort or a decision to produce for sale rather than for subsistence. It may also take the form of additional direct investment in agriculture at the expense of leisure. In these circumstances consumption and investment are complementary. Such a relationship is quite usual in the early stages of economic development.

The imprecise nature of the distinction between consumption and investment is underlined by the arbitrariness of the distinction between capital goods and consumer durables. Major components of the capital stock and of gross investment, notably houses and some other types of buildings, are more appropriately seen as items on which income is spent, that is as consumer durables rather than as instruments for raising future income. They are more akin to a dependent rather than to an independent variable in any functional relationship between investment and material progress. These forms of investment expenditure often represent a substantial proportion of total gross investment.

Conversely many products conventionally classed as consumer goods are more nearly akin to productive capital goods in their effects on economic development, that is as instruments for increasing the flow of future income, either because they serve as incentive goods or because they increase the effectiveness of effort, maintain the health of people and domestic animals, or prevent deterioration of crops and perishable goods. Familiar examples include textiles, hardware (containers, torches, bicycles, sewing machines, simple tools) and insecticides. This range of commodities, and the repercussions of their use, are important in many poor countries. These commodities often represent an appreciable proportion of total cash expenditure and of imports; and they often substantially promote the spread of production for the market. Thus if their supply is curtailed to promote investment this may retard rather than advance economic development.

(iii) Both public and private investment decisions may be unsuccessful in that the return is less than expected or may even be negative. Such hazards are inherent in investment decisions. The risks are less likely to be assessed carefully if expenditure termed investment is regarded as productive *per se*. The risk of failure will be particularly pronounced, and investment least likely to be productive, when those who determine its volume and direction have no direct interest in its productive deployment, because they do not bear the cost nor do they enjoy the return. The interest of the supplier of capital in the costs and returns is a major influence in the productivity of investment.

Again, publicly directed funds cannot usually be geared so closely to consumer demand or to the supply of cooperant resources (that is to market conditions) as can private investment, which is one reason why investment expenditure does not necessarily enlarge the stock of income-yielding capital. When the funds are supplied gratis from abroad they are especially likely to be wasted. Moreover, even if investment expenditure does increase output compared to some alternative uses of resources, no increase in present or future living standards will follow unless the output is related to consumer demand.

(iv) The collection of resources for government financed or sponsored investment often has a substantial disincentive effect on saving, effort and enterprise, because of the taxation or controls imposed for this purpose. These disincentive effects can easily offset, or more than offset, the potential increase in income from investment. The contribution of investment to development is a net factor, after allowing for the repercussions of both the collection and the expenditure of the funds. These repercussions include not only a diminution of resources in activities or sectors from which they have been transferred, but also the consequences of their collection on the incentive to save, invest, undertake risk, incur effort and produce for sale. Yet many discussions on planning consider government development outlay as a simple addition to resources, regardless of the provenance of the funds or the repercussions of their collection.

This approach is in part an example of the practice of economics without costs, that is a treatment which ignores the alternative uses of resources absorbed by one activity. In part, the approach is also an instance of identifying the government with the country as a whole. This treatment regards resources accruing to the government as national gain, and resources forfeited by it as national loss. For instance, when citizens of a country succeed in evading the exchange controls and sell currency to foreign buyers direct, instead of selling them to the representatives of the exchange control, this is often described as national loss. In fact what has happened is that some private citizens have succeeded in keeping some of their resources outside the control of the government.

The desire to achieve a specified level of investment expenditure may serve as a real or ostensible ground for the imposition of a variety of controls which often impede the growth of income. This result is especially likely when the controls restrict occupational or geographical mobility; when they restrict external economic contacts; when they exacerbate political tension; when they divert energy from economic life to political activity; and when they engender a feeling of insecurity which affects adversely domestic saving and investment and promotes the export of capital. All of these are likely concomitants of extensive controls in underdeveloped countries. These repercussions reinforce the more familiar effects of controls on incentives or on the allocation of resources.

(v) Preoccupation with the level of investment expenditure has led to a neglect of major factors affecting development, such as the emergence of the exchange economy, the establishment of suitable institutional arrangements, the advance of technical knowledge, and the extension of interregional contacts. These influences and developments can bring about significant changes in attitudes and mores and often result also in the emergence of new wants, methods of production and the introduction of new crops. Such developments can obviously greatly improve productivity and resources even without net capital formation. The occurrence of such developments can be significantly affected by the costs and repercussions of a major investment programme. The repercussions may be favourable or adverse. Government action is often indispensable for the promotion of favourable developments in this area. These potentialities tend to be neglected and obscured by preoccupation with the level of conventional investment expenditure. For instance this preoccupation leads to overemphasis on physical plant and corresponding neglect of the possible development of human resources.[1]

These are among the reasons why a large-scale investment programme need not promote the material advance of poor countries and may retard it compared to a less ambitious programme.

The problems of assessing the likely results of an investment programme are logically distinct from the problems of ascertaining its results. In practice the two sets of problems are often interrelated and present simultaneously. When investment expenditure is generally assumed to be productive, or more precisely when any expenditure termed investment is so regarded, objective assessment of the returns on investment or of the wider results of the programme is especially unlikely.

There are often many difficulties in ascertaining even *ex post* the returns let alone the wider merits of a substantial investment programme. The difficulties include of course the problems presented by the simultaneous operation of countless influences affecting economic phenomena, and the time lag in the response of producers and consumers to changes in conditions and in variables. All of these problems are especially acute when the performance of a whole economy is considered and related to the operation of specific variables.

It is sometimes suggested or implied that investment expenditure

[1] The considerations listed in (ii) and (v) set up a presumption in favour of a higher productivity of private compared to public investment expenditure within the same broad field. This consideration as well as several other arguments in this appendix do not bear on the investment required for the familiar governmental tasks noted in the text of this essay. They are relevant primarily to the investment expenditure undertaken outside this extensive field, usually in the belief that all investment expenditure as such promotes development.

results in a virtually simultaneous increase in income. But this is plainly unwarranted. Investment can be productive only if it increases income by more than the cost of the assets, a matter which can be established only after a period of years depending on the length of life of the assets.[1]

The difficulties of assessing the merits and ascertaining the results of major investment programmes in poor countries are exacerbated by the presence of major types of capital and capital formation which often elude observation and measurement, and which are often disregarded in discussions both in the literature and in conventional statistics. Much the most important of these categories is represented by cultivated agricultural properties. Others include livestock, simple structures and various types of equipment and traders' stocks. Many conceptual and statistical problems of the measurement of capital are thrown into relief when these types of capital are considered, especially agricultural properties.

Capital formation represented by an increase in these assets is quantitatively and qualitatively important in underdeveloped countries. It is significant quantitatively because of the relative importance of agriculture and its ancillary activities in the economy; and it is important qualitatively because of the role of this kind of capital formation in the transition from subsistence production to a market economy. And the stock of some of these types of capital, especially agricultural properties, can often be enlarged or their productivity improved by the application of effort without monetary investment.

These neglected categories of capital formation are generally affected by government policy, including public finance and the imposition of controls. If these categories are ignored the repercussions from government policy on them are necessarily also overlooked. Accordingly policy cannot be designed to maximise favourable results on productive capital formation. Adverse results on the volume and productivity of these categories of capital formation and on the growth of income are especially likely when all money expenditure conventionally and often arbitrarily termed investment is regarded as productive; and when consumption is complementary and not competitive with these neglected categories of capital formation. Both these conditions are widely present in the underdeveloped world: the former as a result of current fashion, and the latter as a general feature of emerging economies.

This lengthy discussion can be summed up briefly. The accumulation of capital is often a powerful instrument of material advance. But the notion that investment expenditure is practically decisive in increasing the productive capacity required for development is at best an over-

---

[1] The belief in the expansion of income concurrently with the investment expenditure is an inappropriate application of Keynesian employment theory (where the emphasis is on investment as an instrument for increasing monetary demand) to development policy (where the emphasis is on investment as an instrument for increasing the productivity of resources).

simplification and more often is simply unwarranted in that it does not reflect the facts.[1] Investment is too general and vague a concept or category to furnish worthwhile criteria for development policy.[2] Before it can serve even as partial criterion for this purpose it is necessary to examine in detail the methods and the repercussions of an investment programme, including the repercussions of different methods of the collection of funds. The ideas that expenditure termed investment is productive, and that an increase in the volume of monetary saving and investment is necessary and possibly sufficient for material advance, have caused enormous waste throughout the underdeveloped world. And. in any case central planning is not required for increased saving and investment and is much more likely to obstruct than promote productive saving and investment.

Promotion of manufacturing industry. The second major quasi-technical or specific argument for comprehensive central planning suggests that this policy is necessary to accelerate the development of manufacturing industry, which is assumed to be indispensable for economic advance.[3] This argument is again irrelevant: the development of manufacturing industry does not depend on comprehensive central planning; and development does not depend on the enlargement of the manufacturing sector.

The development of manufacturing industry has often occurred without state assistance. Again, it has often been promoted by tariffs or other subsidies without central planning in the currently accepted sense of the term. Indeed until well into the twentieth century state assistance to manufacturing industry was not linked to proposals for central planning. It is thus plain that comprehensive central planning is not necessary for the promotion of manufacturing industry.

The relationship between the level of economic development and the relative importance of manufacturing industry is much less clearcut than is often suggested in current discussions. It is broadly true that richer countries are on the whole more highly industrialised than poor countries,

[1] It is sometimes said that any expenditure which increases productivity is investment. It has even been seriously suggested that any development or occurrence which increases productivity is a form of investment. On this usage, a change in attitudes or habits is a form of investment. Such tautological use of the term underlines its very limited value for operational purposes. Almost any type of expenditure or event favoured by its advocate can be termed investment by assuming or asserting that it will increase productivity at some unspecified time in the future.

[2] Early recognition of the limitations of investment expenditure as a factor in material progress is to be found in a paper by Sir Alec Cairncross, 'The Place of Capital in Economic Progress', in L. H. Dupriez (ed.), *Economic Progress*, Louvain, 1955. Sir Alec Cairncross' pioneer essay is republished in *Factors in Economic Development*, London, 1962.

[3] We shall note here only the most widely publicised general ideas about the need for the promotion of manufacturing activity in poor countries. More specific arguments are at times adduced in various contexts. Some of the more influential of these ideas, put forward in the literature of UNCTAD, are examined in essay 6.

though there are many countries where the proportion of the occupied population in manufacturing industry is lower and in agriculture higher (New Zealand, Canada, Denmark) than in other countries where incomes per head are lower (Belgium, Great Britain, Hong Kong, among others). However, the familiar references to these correlations confuse a statistical correlation with a cause-and-effect relationship. Both the comparative wealth and the higher degree of industrialisation of rich countries reflect the possession of valuable resources, including skills and experience. Thus both phenomena are primarily dependent variables of other influences. The crude suggestion that there is a cause-and-effect relationship between the growth of manufacturing industry and economic advance is analogous to suggesting that because there are more hairdressers, insurance agents and television sets in richer countries than in poor countries, the encouragement of these activities would increase the wealth of poor countries. Indeed, this argument for industrialisation, as somebody once said, is analogous to the suggestion that smoking expensive cigars will make people rich as it is rich people who smoke expensive cigars.

Moreover, in so far as the percentage of people employed in the service industries compared to manufacturing is higher in rich countries than in poor countries (at least according to the conventional statistics), advocates of accelerated industrialisation ought appropriately to propose the accelerated development of service industries.

Finally, the currently advanced industrialised countries were already prosperous while still predominantly agricultural, with far higher incomes than those envisaged for poor countries for decades ahead.

Much of the discussion in this field is confused by a tendency to focus on particular activities or sectors. The output of these activities or sectors is treated as somehow constituting an equivalent net addition to total output. This treatment ignores cost in terms of alternative uses of resources and also the economic demand for the output. To have to subsidise a particular economic activity yielding a saleable output sets up a presumption that the resources would be more productive elsewhere in the economy. All sorts of activities would not emerge without government support or comprehensive central planning, but it does not follow that their emergence would represent either an efficient use of resources or that it would promote economic progress. The same considerations apply to the advocacy of state sponsored import substitution.

A variant of the argument for accelerated industrialisation advocates the establishment of capital goods industries, which are regarded as necessary for material progress, while central planning is regarded as necessary for the development of these industries.

The prior establishment locally of capital goods industries is not a prerequisite of the economic advance of particular countries. There are many highly advanced countries which were already very prosperous before they had local capital goods industries. Indeed there are many rich countries which even now do not produce their own capital goods.

The suggestion that underdeveloped countries have to develop their own capital goods industries as a precondition of development reflects an attempt to follow the strategy of Soviet economic policy. That policy was not designed to promote high living standards but to pursue quite different aims of policy. Moreover it was carried out in conditions radically different from those which prevail in the underdeveloped countries where this prototype is being accepted. The arguments which are used in support of the need to develop capital goods industries in these countries rarely mention costs in terms of alternative use of resources, or the demand for the output, or the effects of the programme on living standards.

The heavy industry programmes of many underdeveloped countries have yielded no worthwhile returns and have often yielded nil or negative returns. They have also served to divert resources from urgently needed consumer goods, including incentive goods. And they have diverted resources and attention from government expenditure on basic services and from potentially productive but politically unfashionable activities, such as service industries, including tourist development. These projects have also often saddled the country with organisations which cannot be effectively manned by local personnel.

Like the term investment, industrialisation is too vague to serve either as useful criterion for policy or as index of material progress, or indeed as a subject for discussion. The term is often used interchangeably to denote the long-term growth of manufacturing industry; a policy of subsidised manufacturing; or the general modernisation of economic activity and of the surrounding society. Indeed the term is meaningless unless it is made clear in which of these senses it is employed.

Certain remarks may be made here in parentheses, remarks which bear both on accelerated industrialisation and on wider issues of development policy. There are various reasons why in many poor countries a large measure of continued reliance on agriculture, notably on agricultural production for sale, is likely to represent the most effective deployment of resources for the promotion of higher living standards. One reason is the familiar argument based on comparative costs. Another, less familiar, reason is that production of cash crops is less of a break with traditional methods of production than subsidised or enforced industrialisation. Agriculture has been the principal occupation in most of these countries for centuries or even millennia. Thus in the production of cash crops the difficulties of the adjustment of attitudes and institutions in the course of the transition from subsistence production to an exchange or money economy are not compounded by the need to have to acquire at the same time knowledge of entirely new methods and techniques of production.

After some time spent on the cultivation of cash crops, people find it easier to get used to the ways, attitudes and institutions appropriate to a money economy. This greater familiarity with the money economy facilitates effective industrialisation. In these conditions of transition from a subsistence to a money economy, conditions widely prevalent in poor countries, production of cash crops and effective industrialisation are thus complementary through time. The unfavourable contrast often drawn between agriculture and manufacturing, to the detriment of the former, is an example of a time-less, unhistorical approach to economic development, an approach which is inappropriate to the historical development of societies.

Compensating for lack of enterprise. Yet another argument put forward for comprehensive central planning instances the alleged absence of constructive entrepreneurial talent in poor countries, and particularly an inability on the part of the population to take a long-term view in investment. The question immediately arises how and whence the government can secure the talent (including business inclination) if there is none in the society.

In fact, in many poor countries there is much entrepreneurial ability, although it shows itself in ways appropriate to these societies, which are different from those in advanced countries. Entrepreneurship manifests itself in the establishment and in the operation of comparatively small trading and transport enterprises and of agricultural properties producing cash crops. The presence, significance and manifestations of these types of entrepreneurship in underdeveloped countries are overlooked by observers who judge these matters largely on the basis of contemporary western experience.

As we have already noted, important categories of investment in agriculture are generally ignored in discussions on investment in under-developed countries and are excluded from conventional statistics. Some of these categories of investment, especially the establishment and oper-ation of properties of tree crops, plainly reflect an ability to take a long-term view.

It is true that there are societies in which there is little entrepreneurial talent. Its absence reflects a society in which faculties, attitudes and institutions are unfavourable to material advance. It is not clear whence the government would secure entrepreneurship in these conditions. And for reasons noted in the text comprehensive planning is more likely to obstruct the emergence of entrepreneurship than to encourage it.

Provision of external economies. Yet another argument for central planning suggests that it is required to secure the benefits of so-called external economies, sometimes known as spillover benefits. These are economies which arise in the productive process but the total benefits of which do not accrue to the individual enterprises which generate them and which are therefore not fully taken into account in the decisions of particular enterprises.

This argument for comprehensive planning begs the question. Activities promoted by central planning imply a transfer of resources to certain uses and a corresponding diminution of activity and of external economies elsewhere in the economy. There is a net benefit only if the emergence and growth of activities promoted by the policy yield goods and services and external economies which exceed in value those lost elsewhere through the diversion of resources, allowing also for the various other repercussions of the transfer of resources. It is improbable that there will be any significant net economies, let alone economies sufficient to outweigh the wider costs and implications of the policy. The very special and exceptional circumstances required to satisfy this condition would need to be specified in detail; this is not usually undertaken in the literature on the subject.

3 The Economics of Resentment: Colonialism and Underdevelopment[1]

1 Colonial Status and Material Progress

Over the last few decades, especially since the first world war and to an even greater extent since the second, statements and suggestions have abounded in publications, both in underdeveloped countries and in the west, asserting that the masses in underdeveloped countries are greatly concerned with their poverty, and alleging also that both in these countries and in the west it is widely recognised that the west has caused the poverty of the underdeveloped world, especially through various forms of colonialism.[2]

It is in fact very doubtful how widespread these sentiments are in poor countries. Some familiarity with several of these countries suggests to me that the great majority of people know little about such matters, do not compare their lot with that of the population of distant countries, and do not ascribe any of their problems to present or past actions of western countries. The great majority are concerned with their own daily lives; in Africa and Asia at any rate the vast majority normally know and care little about politics beyond the tribal or village level. But there are many vocal and politically influential people both in underdeveloped countries and in the west who have effectively canvassed the notion of western responsibility for the poverty of the former. They have secured wide publicity and considerable political acceptance for this view, as well as for the related notions that the masses in underdeveloped countries both resent international income differences and attribute them to exploitation by the west.

The readiness of articulate opinion in the west to accept the claims of these vocal groups to represent the general opinion of the peoples of the underdeveloped world, enhances the political effectiveness of these groups and lends spurious plausibility to their claim to represent mass opinion. But their political success does not substantiate either the

[1] The original version of this essay appeared in the *Journal of Contemporary History*, January 1969.
[2] The essay examines various arguments on the economic effects of colonial status; it does not deal with wider questions of the merits of colonial rule.

allegation of western responsibility or their pretension to represent mass opinion; political effectiveness has little to do with objective assessment.

I shall argue first that it is untrue that the west has caused the poverty of the underdeveloped world, whether through colonialism or otherwise. I shall then examine other, somewhat more speculative issues, and try to identify groups and sections in both rich and poor countries who stand to gain from acceptance of the idea of western responsibility for the poverty of underdeveloped countries, and to examine the reasons for their success in propagating this idea, especially in the west.

General Principle Fourteen of the first United Nations Conference on Trade and Development (UNCTAD) provides a convenient starting point for the discussion.

Complete decolonisation, in compliance with the United Nations Declaration on the Granting of Independence to Colonial Countries and Peoples and the liquidation of the remnants of colonialism in all its forms, is a necessary condition for economic development and the exercise of sovereign rights over natural resources.

Leaving aside for the moment questions of meaning and interpretation of colonialism (especially 'colonialism in all its forms'), it is untrue to say that colonial status is incompatible with material progress, and that its removal is a necessary condition of economic development. Some of the richest countries were colonies in their earlier history, notably the United States, Canada, Australia and New Zealand; and these countries were already prosperous while they were still colonies.

Nor has colonial status precluded the material advance, from extremely primitive conditions, of the African and Asian territories which became colonies in the nineteenth century. Many of these territories made rapid economic progress between the second half of the nineteenth century, when they became colonies, and the middle of the twentieth century, when most of them became independent.

In essay 1 we presented some statistics of this progress. We noted also that statistics by themselves cannot convey the far-reaching and pervasive changes which have taken place in some of these areas. The impact of these changes has often set up considerable strains because of personal, social and political difficulties of adjustment to rapid change, especially the adjustment of attitudes and of social institutions. Many of the social and political problems of ex-colonial countries reflect difficulties of rapid and uneven advance, not those of stagnation and retrogression.

Thus UNCTAD General Principle Fourteen, that colonial status and economic progress are incompatible, is patently untrue. Yet it has been formally and solemnly announced, published and publicised by a United Nations conference made possible by the financial and moral support of the western governments. But emphatic announcements do not turn into sense what is immediately demonstrable as non-sense.

Although, as we have seen, it is untrue that colonial status is incompatible with material advance, the question whether colonial status has promoted material progress cannot be settled or demonstrated so conclusively, for the answer to that question depends in part on what political regimes would otherwise have prevailed in the colonial areas of Africa and Asia, and also on the assumed effects of their policies on economic development. However, it is highly probable that over the last century or so the establishment of colonial rule in Africa and Asia has promoted, and not retarded, material progress. With relatively little coercion, or even interference in the lives of the great majority of the people, the colonial governments established law and order, safeguarded private property and contractual relations, organised basic transport and health services, and introduced some modern financial and legal institutions. This environment also promoted the establishment or extension of external contacts, which in turn encouraged the inflow of external resources, notably administrative, commercial and technical skills as well as capital. These contacts also acquainted the population with new wants, crops, commodities and methods of cultivation, and served to establish new markets for local produce and to open new sources of supply of a wide range of commodities. These changes engendered a new outlook on material advance and on the means of securing it: for good or evil these contacts promoted the erosion of the traditional values, objectives, attitudes and customs obstructing material advance.

It is unlikely (though this cannot be proved conclusively) that in the absence of colonial rule the social, political and economic environment in colonial Africa and Asia would have been more congenial to material progress. Indeed it was the presence of conditions unfavourable to material progress, especially the frequency of civil and tribal war and the prevalence of slavery, which led in most instances to the establishment of colonial rule. While it is not true that colonialism brought about poverty, there is some truth in the notion that poverty brought about colonialism.

The presumption that colonial rule has promoted rather than retarded economic development over the last hundred years is supported by the material backwardness of some independent states compared to ex-colonies in the same region, such as Ethiopia and Liberia compared to Uganda and Ghana.

2 Colonialism as Exploitation?

The notion that colonial rule has precluded or at least retarded economic advance derives from several sources, or more precisely is compounded of several distinct but related ideas.

The first of these is the allegedly exploitative nature of political colonialism or imperialism. While the concepts of exploitation, colonialism and imperialism are all ambiguous, their broad meaning is fairly clear in the political and economic literature of the twentieth century. The notion of exploitation does not usually refer to plunder of the type which often accompanied military conquest before the nineteenth century, nor even to taxation of the colonies for the benefit of the metropolitan country. The alleged exploitation refers primarily to the conquest of countries in order to secure markets for capital and commodities, supposedly necessitated by the otherwise inevitable decline (or even disappearance) of the rate of profit, and by the related need to find outlets for commodities unsaleable at home because of the insufficiency of the purchasing power of the exploited masses. Well-known exponents of this view include J.A. Hobson, H.N. Brailsford, Leonard Woolf, and, above all, Lenin.

Lenin's *Imperialism: the Highest Stage of Capitalism*, a work of negligible intellectual quality but vast political consequence, has been enormously influential in both developed and underdeveloped countries, especially among the millions who may be termed vicarious readers, or readers by proxy – those who have not read the book but know of its contents only by hearsay. The book is far inferior to many writings of Marx and Engels, and also to some of Lenin's other works. The principal reason for its influence is that the author made himself master of a huge country which, partly through him, has become a world power and has pervasively affected the course of contemporary history.

The Leninist thesis seems to explain the reasons for the nineteenth-century European expansion into Africa and Asia, while simultaneously explaining away the failure of the major Marxist prophecies of falling real wages, declining profits and ever-deepening crises. This latter aspect of the thesis of economic imperialism has obvious appeal to Marxists.

The obvious and familiar defects of the ideology of economic imperialism and colonial exploitation, especially in its Leninist version, include the following, among others: until the first world war (the period covered by this literature) the great bulk of capital exports from the advanced countries did not go to colonies but to independent countries, mostly to other advanced countries; several of the richest countries were indeed not exporters but importers of capital; Great Britain, the leading colonial power, pursued an open-door, free trade policy in its colonies. Further, most of this literature does not ask the obvious question: how could extremely poor people (or indeed materially primitive people as in Africa) pay for the capital and the commodities forced on them by capitalists in search of profits?[1]

The insubstantial nature of the thesis of imperialist exploitation has not diminished its political effectiveness. Numerous examples of this influence can be found in the writings of African and Asian politicians. For instance they abound in the writings of Dr Nkrumah, who until his downfall was one of the most influential African leaders and whose utterances were widely quoted and much respected not only in Africa but also in the west. Here are some characteristic observations:

Thus all the imperialists, without exception, evolved the means, their colonial policies, to satisfy the ends, the exploitation of the subject territories, for the aggrandisement of the metropolitan countries. They were all rapacious; they all subserved the needs of the subject lands to their own demands; they all circumscribed human rights and liberties; they all repressed and despoiled, degraded and oppressed. They took our lands, our lives, our resources and our dignity. Without exception, they left us nothing but our resentment. . . . It was when they had gone and we were faced with the stark realities, as in Ghana on the morrow of our independence, that the destitution of the land after long years of colonial rule was brought sharply home to us.[2]

[1] These points and other criticisms of the Leninist thesis are familiar. Attention may however be drawn to Dr R.J. Hammond's illuminating article, 'Economic Imperialism, sidelights on a stereotype', *Journal of Economic History*, December 1961.

[2] Kwame Nkrumah, *Africa Must Unite*, London, 1963, p. xiii. The sentiments reflected in these utterances of Dr Nkrumah (typical of those of countless Asian, African and Latin American spokesmen) may be interpreted as expressions of envy or of resentment, a distinction interesting in certain contexts but not relevant to our argument. An extensive discussion of envy and of its role in the relations between developed and underdeveloped countries will be found in Professor Helmut Schoeck's important and perceptive study, *Envy*, London, 1969.

These remarks, politically effective as they were and still often are, ignore first of all the extreme backwardness of pre-colonial sub-Saharan Africa. For instance, with unimportant exceptions,[1] there were no schools in sub-Saharan Africa, next to no literacy, practically no roads or even paths, and little peaceful contact between different tribes. Africans still depend largely on communications constructed by foreigners.

These characteristic remarks of Dr Nkrumah's ignore also the very rapid progress of many of the areas with which the west established contact; and also the fact that Great Britain, the principal colonising power, pursued a free trade, open-door policy. Indeed they simply bear no relation to reality.[2]

3 *Colonialism and Sovereignty*

A more recent and less familiar but nevertheless influential argument, rather different from the Leninist thesis, suggests that political colonialism has retarded the economic progress of the colonies by depriving them of the economic benefits of a sovereign national state. This view is clearly implied in some of the writings of Professor Gunnar Myrdal. He writes:

From one point of view, the most important effect of colonialism was related to the negative fact that the dependent nation was deprived of effective nationhood and had no government of its own which could feel the urge to take protective and fomenting measures in order to promote the balanced growth of the national economy. Lack of political independence meant the absence of a unifying and integrating purpose for the collectivity. . . .The political independence they have won for themselves, or are now winning, is their most precious asset: the national state.[3]

Such suggestions overstate the potentialities of state power as an instrument of economic progress. Inappropriate government policy can retard material progress or even obstruct it altogether, especially when a government cannot maintain law and order or when it establishes extensive and close control over economic life. But there is no reason

[1] There were a handful of missionary schools established by European and American missionaries which antedated formal establishment of colonial rule, and in the Moslem areas around the fringes of the Sahara there were some Koranic schools. There was also a modest amount of literacy among Swahili-speaking people on the coast of East Africa in contact with the Arab world; there was however no literacy in the interior of Africa.

[2] These defects and some other shortcomings of the Leninist position are discussed in essay 4.

[3] Gunnar Myrdal, *Development and Underdevelopment*, Cairo, 1956, pp. 54, 59.

believe that the conduct of sovereign governments would have been ore favourable to economic development over the relevant period than nat of the colonial regimes. The contrary is strongly suggested by the experience of the independent countries in the former colonial regions of Africa and Asia in both the nineteenth and the twentieth centuries.

Professor Myrdal and his followers frequently blame colonial regimes for failure to pursue active economic development policies, especially in undertaking comprehensive central planning, which these writers regard as a prerequisite of economic advance. We have already shown, however, that central planning is certainly not necessary for material progress and that it is much more likely to retard it than to promote it.

A variant of the foregoing argument criticises the colonial regimes for their failure to assist by tariffs or other forms of subsidy certain specific activities, especially manufacturing industry, or the local production of capital goods. Quite apart from the question of the ability and willingness of a hypothetically independent government to have encouraged these activities, the development of subsidised manufacturing or of capital goods industries is more likely to retard than to advance economic development in the sense of a general rise in living standards. This consideration applies particularly to Africa and Asia in the nineteenth and early twentieth centuries, where the promotion of these activities would have required heavy subsidisation at the expense of the rest of the economy.

4 A Legacy of Colonialism

Colonial status may well irritate or even humiliate certain sections of the population. But it does not follow that this status obstructs material advance. To suggest this is to overstate the significance of political forms and rights as determinants of economic attainment or material progress. There is, however, a range of issues which bears on colonial status and economic development and which is rarely discussed in this context.

In the concluding years of colonial rule, especially between the mid-1930s and the mid-1950s, policies were introduced in many colonies, notably in British Africa, which have left a fateful legacy in their wake. A wide range of economic controls was introduced, including the establishment of state trading monopolies; extensive licensing of industrial and commercial enterprises, as well as of imports, exports, and foreign exchange; and the creation of many state-owned and operated enterprises, including state-supported and operated so-called coope atives. The introduction of state monopolies over all agricultural export produced by Africans was particularly important, since it gave govern- ments close and direct control over the livelihood of the producers, and has served as a powerful source of patronage and finance for the rulers.

The state agricultural export monopolies in Burma and in East and West Africa have withheld from producers a very large proportion of the sales proceeds, totalling hundreds of millions of pounds over little more than a decade. This policy has had far-reaching political, social and economic results. Indeed, the political and economic history of these countries since the second world war cannot be understood without reference to these export monopolies, which were, incidentally, operated in a manner diametrically contrary to specific official guarantees given at the time of their establishment.

These policies have created tightly controlled economies in which people's lives and activities and the alternatives open to them as producers, consumers and traders (outside subsistence production) are largely determined by the government. Indeed the ready-made frame- work of a *dirigiste* if not a totalitarian state was erected for the incoming governments of the newly independent countries.

These policies have been prompted by intellectual fashion and by political, administrative and commercial pressures quite unrelated to the promotion of material advance. As we have already noted at length in essay 2, such policies are much more likely to inhibit economic development, especially a rise in living standards, than to promote it.[1]

It is conjectural how far such policies would have been introduced without colonial rule. The most articulate and influential contemporary critics of colonialism welcome them and indeed criticise governments for not having introduced them earlier. It is probable that their intro- duction would have been attempted in the last twenty years, in part with the help of the international agencies, even without colonial rule. But it is doubtful whether they could have been introduced so widely and effectively without the administrative resources of the colonial

---

[1] The most articulate critics of colonial regimes have emphatically advocated strictly controlled economies in underdeveloped countries. It is therefore appropriate to re- capitulate succinctly why such a policy obstructs economic development in these societies. These reasons include restriction of external contacts and of occupational and geographical mobility; curtailment of the supply of incentive goods; restriction of the establishment of new enterprises and the accumulation and productive deployment of capital; exacerbation of political tension; and diversion of energy and ambition from economic to political life.

governments and in the absence of the examples they set. The establishment of these close economic controls and their far-reaching political and social implications has proved a major legacy of the colonial regimes.

5 Interpretations of Political and Economic Colonialism

Discussions on colonialism and underdevelopment often refer to various types of colonialism. UNCTAD General Principle Fourteen quoted above is one of many examples.

Although political colonialism has many manifestations, the concept does have some definite meaning. A colonial government is not sovereign: it has to accept the instructions of the metropolitan government. In recent usage, however, colonialism has come to be applied to situations or relations without these political elements. The term has largely lost identifiable meaning and has become a term of abuse of institutions, policies, governments, relationships, groups and individuals disliked by the speaker or writer, especially of technically or materially successful countries, organisations or groups. Two expressions or types of usage may be appropriately discussed here, namely economic colonialism and neo-colonialism.

The term economic colonialism is now widely used to refer to economic relationships between relatively more and relatively less prosperous countries, regions and groups, including economic relations within a country, as for instance between the north and the south in the United States or between West and East Pakistan. This usage, which is especially prominent in the recent literature of the economics of resentment, in effect identifies colonial status with relative poverty and thereby deprives the former term of its usual and particular meaning.

At times economic colonialism is used with more readily identifiable (although rarely exact) connotations or implications. For example, it is often suggested that economic relations between groups and areas differing in prosperity are quasi-colonial in that they are biased in favour of the richer group whose members secure most of the benefits of the relationship, usually because of successful manipulation of market conditions. This approach fails to distinguish between low incomes and prices reflecting an abundance of supply (either of labour or of commodities) relative to demand on the one hand, and monopolistic action designed to affect market conditions on the other, a distinction which is essential both for elementary analysis and for policy. Differences in wealth or in technical or commercial sophistication cannot confer effective monopolistic power, which requires centralised decision-making or concerted action by members of a group and also effective restriction on entry. These conditions are not present in the situation usually discussed in the literature of economic colonialism, which does not attempt to identify or analyse the special conditions in which members of a more prosperous group or region can manipulate market conditions to their own advantage.

Political independence is now often alleged to be unreal without economic independence; and the alleged lack of economic independence of many former colonies, as of other underdeveloped countries, is supposed to represent another category of colonialism, related to the other concepts and ideas examined in the preceding section.

Unlike political independence or sovereignty, economic independence is an ambiguous term. The most plausible interpretation would be that of solvency, that is, the ability of a country to pay for the goods and services it uses without recourse to external grants and subsidised loans. Another possible interpretation would be the ability to withstand adverse changes in external conditions without substantial dislocation. However, the literature of economic colonialism interprets economic independence quite differently, mainly because it has been so deeply influenced by Marxist-Leninist literature.

In this literature any country in which there is substantial private foreign investment is regarded as economically dependent, since the return on such capital is seen as a form of exploitation which would not be tolerated by a truly independent country. This politically effective argument has no basis in logic or empirical evidence.

The presence of certain activities, especially manufacturing industry or the production of capital goods (heavy industry), is often canvassed as a criterion of economic independence. Large-scale development of domestic capital goods industries, explicitly in order to achieve economic independence, has been a prominent objective and component of Indian economic planning since the mid-1950s. The pursuit of this policy, largely regardless of the cost and the methods of the process or of the demand for the output, has been a major factor in India's dependence since about 1960 on large-scale external doles of food and foreign exchange. Somewhat similar results have accompanied the pursuit of so-called economic independence in a number of other underdeveloped countries, especially in Africa.

6 *Neo-Colonialism*

Neo-colonialism, which also figures prominently in current discussion, including the UNCTAD literature, is another exceedingly vague concept.

Dr Nkrumah, a vocal exponent of the alleged dangers of so-called neo-colonialism, writes as follows on this subject:

... our problems are made more vexed by the devices of neo-colonialists. ... The greatest danger at present facing Africa is neo-colonialism, and its major instrument, balkanisation. The latter term is particularly appropriate to describe the breaking up of Africa into small, weak states. . . .[1]

In fact, the division of Africa into small states reflects the age-old presence and multiplicity of diverse ethnic groups and tribal societies, a multiplicity perpetuated by the virtual absence of man-made communications; and the demands of these groups for political independence, which has become more intense as the stakes in the fight for political power rise with the enlargement and enhancement of the powers of government. The economic effects of the division of an area into a number of independent states depend on the policies pursued by their governments. It is notable that even quite small countries have often progressed rapidly, as for instance Hong Kong and Israel, or are even among the most prosperous in the world, as Switzerland, New Zealand and Holland. But in any case the process of political subdivision in Africa reflects local pressures and forces, as seen in the attempts of Biafra and Katanga to secure independence.

The failure of Dr Nkrumah, as of other writers, to provide the term 'neo-colonialism' with intelligible meaning is the more remarkable because of the importance assigned to the concept. His *Neo-Colonialism*[2] discusses the concept at great length, but interprets it largely as the operations of large foreign-owned corporations in underdeveloped countries, whose profits are said to reflect the exploitation of the local populations. This interpretation is in effect simply an application of the Marxist-Leninist idea of the exploitative nature of any return on private capital.

In recent years the term neo-colonialism has been introduced into discussions on foreign aid in three contexts. First, to protest against the imposition of conditions in the granting of intergovernmental aid; second, in support of the demand that aid should not be tied to

[1] *Africa Must Unite*, pp. xv, 173.
[2] London, 1965.

purchases of specific commodities or from specific sources; third, especially in support of multilateral aid, on the ground that bilateral aid involves dangers of neo-colonialism. Whatever the merits of these arguments, the term neo-colonialism obscures rather than illuminates the issues.

7 Alleged Causes of Backwardness

The principal consistent theme of the literature of colonialism, economic colonialism, or neo-colonialism, is the explicitly alleged or clearly implied responsibility of external, especially western, forces and influences for the material backwardness and poverty of the former colonies, and more generally of all underdeveloped countries. Although this notion is plainly untrue (indeed the reverse of the truth), it has a powerful political and emotional appeal. To use a felicitous phrase of Jacques Barzun's, the idea enables people to achieve 'the desired status of victim'. It is emotionally comforting to be told that external factors explain the failure to achieve specified goals, including material prosperity.

The idea that external factors are behind the material backwardness of underdeveloped countries is closely interwoven with the notion that the incomes of individuals and groups are somehow extracted from others, rather than being a return for services rendered by themselves and their resources. This notion has a long and disastrous history. It has often been prominent in the economics and politics of envy and resentment, and has frequently been a major influence in the persecution and expulsion of ethnic minorities, particularly those which have achieved prosperity from poverty – Jews in Europe, Levantines and Indians in Africa, Chinese in south-east Asia.

Whilst this notion and the sentiments behind it long antedate Marxist-Leninist writings, this literature, particularly in its Leninist version, has greatly promoted the spread and influence of the idea that the progress of the developed countries has been achieved at the expense of the underdeveloped world; that the wealth of the former has been extracted from the latter; and that the underdeveloped world is in fact an economic colony, or group of economic colonies, of industrial countries. In this literature private property incomes, notably return on private capital, imply exploitation; and service industries are generally regarded as unproductive. And as earnings of expatriate capital, and of expatriate companies and traders, are important in many underdeveloped countries,

...ing to this literature they are exploited and in a state of economic
...ction.

...hese ideas represent an extension of the concept of the exploitation
...the proletariat from the domestic to the international sphere, with
...e population of the underdeveloped countries (most of whom are
...n fact subsistence agriculturalists) somehow identified with a domestic
industrial proletariat.

The unfounded nature of these allegations is made especially clear
by the prosperity of rich countries such as, say, Canada, Australia,
Japan, Switzerland and Scandinavia which has quite obviously not been
extracted from the underdeveloped world, with much or most of which,
including the poorest parts, they have until recently had few economic
contacts. Most of the rich countries which have contacts with underdeveloped countries were already, when they first contacted these
countries, materially far more advanced than the latter, sometimes even
than the same countries are now. It is also relevant, especially in the
context of this essay, that on the eve of colonisation material conditions
were extremely primitive in the colonial regions, especially in sub-
Saharan Africa and south-east Asia.

In many underdeveloped countries the idea that poverty has external
causes is strengthened by important elements of the traditional culture,
notably the belief in the power of extraneous, especially supernatural,
forces over the destinies of individuals or groups, and by a paternalistic
and authoritarian tradition which encourages the belief that one is not
responsible for one's lot.

Certain contemporary influences operate in the same direction. Men
are said to be created equal. Yet the underdeveloped countries are
poorer than the developed countries. To many people this situation
suggests the operation of fortuitous or unjust external forces; and the
suggestion is reinforced by more specifically political factors. Before
independence the local politicians in many colonies attributed the
poverty and technical backwardness of their countries to their colonial
status, notably to alleged exploitation by the metropolitan powers, an
attribution which was spuriously reinforced by the presence in the
country of expatriates with higher incomes than those of the local
population. The politicians thus aroused unwarranted expectations of
the prosperity which would follow the attainment of independence.
Since the political or even physical survival of the political leaders in
many underdeveloped countries may depend on their ability to explain
away the disappointment of these expectations, their easiest course is

to invoke external responsibility, particularly in view of the abser
effective local opposition parties and the continued presence of relat.
well-to-do foreigners. Allegations of external responsibility also di
attention from the real factors behind material poverty and from t
difficulties of removing them. Moreover, the alleged need to comba
adverse or sinister external political and economic forces can also be
cited to justify the introduction of policies and measures for extensive
state control over the economy, and is therefore welcome to local
politicians, administrators, and those intellectuals who favour such
policies. As so often happens, vague and insubstantial notions serve to
evoke definite emotions and to promote specific policies.

In the west also there are influential political, administrative, intellectual and financial interests which favour the idea of western responsibility
for the poverty of underdeveloped countries. Policies supported by these
groups include government-to-government aid; the extension of the
activities of international agencies; the extension of economic controls
and of redistributive (progressive) taxation from the national to the international or supra-national level in order to standardise conditions
internationally; and, less obviously but none the less substantially, the
enlargement of state control over the economies of underdeveloped
countries. These policies create numerous lucrative opportunities and
influential positions for politicians, administrators, academics and
businessmen, and also promote political and social conditions in underdeveloped countries favoured by many of these people in advanced
countries.

The charge of western responsibility for the poverty of underdeveloped
countries also engenders or strengthens feelings of guilt in the western
world which promotes the flow of foreign aid. Many people in the west
wish to reduce the stature and influence of the west to the advantage
of the international organisations and agencies and, ostensibly at any
rate, for the benefit of the underdeveloped countries. Any increase in
the influence of these countries is welcome, not only to their own politicians, civil servants, consultants and advisers, but also to those groups
and individuals in developed countries who support world government
by means of the international agencies. All stand to gain from the
emergence or extension of feelings of guilt in the west promoted by
belief in western responsibility for the poverty of the underdeveloped
world.

The notion that the incomes and wealth of persons, groups and
countries are extracted from others rather than earned for resources

⊃lied, often lends effective support to the argument that possessors
⊐igh incomes or substantial wealth are not entitled to them and should
deprived of them. Thus those who wish to promote policies of
⊃nfiscation at home find it useful first to secure acceptance on the
⊐aternational plane of the idea that relatively high incomes are generally
extracted rather than earned. Acceptance of this idea subsequently
facilitates its transfer to the domestic sphere.

Certain passages from a recent book by Professor Peter Townsend
illustrate exceptionally well the argument that domestic and international differences in incomes are basically analogous, notably in that
the prosperity of the rich has been achieved at the expense of the poor.

I argued that the poverty of deprived *nations* is comprehensible only
if we attribute it substantially to the existence of a system of international
social stratification, a hierarchy of societies with vastly different resources
in which the wealth of some is linked historically and contemporaneously
to the poverty of others. This system operated crudely in the era of
colonial domination, and continues to operate today, though more subtly,
through systems of trade, education, political relations, military alliances
and industrial corporations. A wealthy society which deprives a poor
country of resources may simultaneously deprive its own poor classes
through maldistribution of those additional resources.[1]

The differences in material prosperity between developed and underdeveloped countries has nothing to do with colonialism or with 'a
system of international social stratification'. The greater prosperity of
the societies of the developed countries reflects the presence there of
more productive resources, especially human resources. And these
resources in the developed countries have contributed greatly to such
material progress as has been achieved in the underdeveloped world.
Thus, the allegations on this subject in the passage just quoted are the
opposite of the truth.

8 *The Helpful and the Helpless*

The belief in western responsibility for the poverty of the underdeveloped
world might have proved much less effective but for certain further,
deep-seated factors.

Many, perhaps most humanitarians and social reformers, and

[1] Peter Townsend, 'Measures and Explanations of Poverty in High Income and Low
Income Countries: The Problems of Operationalizing the Concepts of Development,
Class and Poverty' (*sic*), in Peter Townsend (ed.), *The Concept of Poverty*, London,
1971, pp. 41–2.

especially the most vocal and influential of their number, seem prim
interested in groups which can be declared or classified as helpless.

We are familiar with the emotional dependence of psychoanalysts
their patients, of teachers on their pupils, and of priests on sinners.
similar relationship often exists between social reformers and thos
groups whose condition they ostensibly seek to ameliorate. Humanitarians and social reformers particularly need people who can be
classified plausibly as helpless victims of causes and conditions beyond
their control. And the classification of groups as helpless then actually
promotes their helplessness, thus serving the psychological, political
and financial aims of the classifiers.[1]

Many of these reformers, particularly the most vocal, seem much less
interested in groups which cannot readily be classified as helpless even
if they have to face formidable obstacles and difficulties and even if
they are actually victims of political hostility. Indeed, self-reliant
groups and individuals who are savagely persecuted, such as the
Indian and Levantine minorities in Africa, or the Chinese immigrants
in south-east Asia, are often viewed with indifference or even disfavour
by the most vocal and influential contemporary social reformers and
historians.

The practice of considering the peoples of the underdeveloped world
as victims of external factors, especially of various types of colonialism,
is an example of environmental determinism, the belief in the overriding
power of the environment over personal decision and responsibility.
This belief again has strong emotional appeal and enjoys the support
of powerful vested interests. The supposed helplessness of people in
face of their environment serves as a basis for the advocacy of far-
reaching policies for moulding the social environment, as well as the
activities and attitudes of the alleged victims themselves. Those who
have diagnosed the condition of the so-called victims as one of helplessness then claim the ability and the right to frame and execute these
policies.

Although the massive and influential activity of social reformers,
especially in the international field, is relatively recent, the need of
reformers for helpless groups has long been recognised. Lord Bristol
is supposed to have said in the eighteenth century: 'Il me faut absolu-
ment des malheureux pour en faire des heureux.' This remark epitomises

---

[1] The potentialities of classification as an instrument of political and social strategy
are examined in a perceptive article by Professor T. S. Szasz, 'The Psychiatric Classification of Behavior: a Strategy of Personal Constraint', in Leonard D. Eron (ed.), The
Classification of Behavior Disorders, Chicago, 1966.

of the sentiment behind the literature on both underdevelopment
olonialism.

he suggestion of the helplessness of people discourages the emer-
ce or development of self-reliance and of personal provision for the
ure. This suggestion of helplessness is also linked to that of external
esponsibility for the material poverty of the underdeveloped world
which promotes or facilitates a whole range of policies adverse to
material progress, including the establishment of extensive state controls
over economic activity, especially over external economic relations; and
the imposition of restrictions on the activities of foreign and of ethnic
and linguistic minorities, and often also the confiscation of their assets
and the expulsion of these groups. These policies have seriously
damaged the development prospects of poor countries, because of the
importance of external contacts and of the activities of minority groups
as agents of material progress.

4 Marxism and the Underdeveloped Countries[1]

1 Pertinent Elements of Marxism

The founding fathers of Marxism[2] did not concern themselves much with what is now called the underdeveloped world, and their remarks on the subject are ambivalent. Marx accused the metropolitan countries of plundering the colonies but he also regarded them as a progressive force in promoting modernisation. And, as we shall see later, the Communist Manifesto pays eloquent, perhaps even extravagant tribute to the potentiality of capitalism in promoting social and economic change in backward societies. In later Marxist literature the underdeveloped countries are prominently discussed as victims of exploitation and imperialism, and as natural allies of communist countries. The subject was a major concern of Lenin's and it was largely through his writings that Marxist ideas were transmitted to the underdeveloped world. His writings reveal little of the intellectual insight of Marx or Engels. As his principal ideas on this subject are familiar, and are readily accessible in one small book, *Imperialism: The Highest Stage of Capitalism*, I need not summarise them. In spite of glaring defects – indeed utter intellectual inadequacy – the Leninist extension of the Marxist analysis has gained enormous influence not only in underdeveloped countries but also in the worldwide discussion of their economies. It is therefore useful to indicate some prominent features of current discussion which, whatever their intellectual origins, reflect the Marxist-Leninist analysis.

In Marxism-Leninism, ownership of the means of production by a communist government is necessary for freedom and material progress.

[1] The original version of this essay appeared in Milorad M. Drachkovitch (ed.), *Marxist Ideology in the Contemporary World – Its Appeals and Paradoxes*, Stanford, 1966.

[2] Marxism, Marxism-Leninism, Leninism and communism are closely related but not identical concepts. I shall use Marxism largely to refer to general Marxist ideas; Marxism-Leninism to Lenin's extension of these ideas; Leninism to specifically Leninist ideas; and communism chiefly to political, practical and organisational matters. The distinctions are at times imprecise but this imprecision does not affect the substantive argument.

general idea, applicable both to developed and underdeveloped
.itries, is familiar. I shall not discuss it, but confine myself to some
jor ideas of Marxism-Leninism which apply specifically to the under-
.veloped world.

First, that the underdeveloped world is not only desperately poor but
stagnant or even retrogressing; this notion is the current version of the
doctrine of the ever-increasing misery of the proletariat. Second, that
the exploitation of underdeveloped by developed countries is a major
cause of this poverty; this is the current version of the doctrine of the
exploitation of the proletariat. Third, that political independence or
freedom is meaningless without economic independence; this is an
extension of the suggestion that political freedom and representative
government are meaningless under capitalism. Fourth, that comprehensive development planning is indispensable for economic advance in
underdeveloped countries and especially for the industrialisation required
for material progress. Though reflecting Marxism-Leninism less
directly, this last point nevertheless owes much to the recognition of the
political possibilities of economic planning (as exemplified in Soviet
experience), and also to the emphasis on the industrial proletariat in
communist literature and strategy. The key role of industrialisation
was urged before Marxism-Leninism, but this ideology has powerfully
reinforced it, especially in the context of underdeveloped countries,
and has firmly identified it with the distinctive methods and policies of
Marxism-Leninism.

2 External Exploitation

The late Paul A. Baran, Professor of Economics at Stanford University,
was a well-known exponent of Marxism-Leninism. According to him,
capitalism has caused the misery and stagnation of the underdeveloped
world.

It is in the underdeveloped world that the central, overriding fact
of our epoch becomes manifest to the naked eye: the capitalist system,
once a mighty engine of economic development, has turned into a no
less formidable hurdle to human advancement . . . there [in the underdeveloped world] the difference is between abysmal squalor and decent
existence, between the misery of hopelessness and the exhilaration of progress, between life and death for hundreds of millions of people. . . . A socialist transformation of the advanced west would not only open to its own
peoples the road to unprecedented economic, social and cultural progress,

it would at the same time enable the peoples of the underdevel
countries to overcome rapidly their present condition of poverty
stagnation.[1]

In fact, as we have seen, there has been substantial material progress
in most of the underdeveloped world since the end of the nineteenth
century; much of this advance, though by no means all of it, is reflected
in longer life expectation. In many areas material advance has been
extremely rapid. For instance, the millions of acres under cash crops in
West Africa and south-east Asia, notably cocoa, groundnuts, kola nuts
and rubber, were established in a few decades after about 1890. Most of
this acreage is owned and operated by the local population. The emergence of these crops has transformed the living conditions of a large
section of the population in these areas.[2]

Material progress in these areas has largely come about as a result
of contacts established by the more advanced countries, where attitudes
and institutions have over centuries been adapted to a money economy.
Sudden exposure to a vastly different and materially successful economic
system has created extreme problems of adjustment of values, attitudes,
customs and institutions in these societies, many of which had under-
gone little change for centuries. The impact of rapid change on
materially very backward peoples has not only created acute problems,
but (as I shall argue later) has also helped to prepare the ground for the
support of ideas, notably Marxism-Leninism, which paradoxically deny
the presence of economic growth.

Of course, even in the areas of the underdeveloped world which have
progressed substantially over, say, the last hundred years, incomes are
still relatively low (though not as low as often urged, since the conventional statistics tend greatly to understate their level) because of a late
start from a very low level. And there are also large groups which have
progressed relatively little, such as some tribal populations of Africa
or the desert peoples and aborigines in various parts of the world; and
over large areas of rural Asia total output has increased relatively slowly.
But the material backwardness and relatively slow progress of these
groups – largely subsistence producers with few or no external commercial contacts – are plainly unrelated to capitalism, market forces, or
exploitation by more advanced countries, since they are largely outside

[1] *The Political Economy of Growth*, New York, 1957, pp. 249–50.
[2] Some details are presented in essay 1.

‎‌bit of these forces and influences.[1] Their poverty reflects the ‎‌.ce of capacities, attitudes and institutions favourable to material ‎‌,ress.

Interpretation of Imperialism

Marxist-Leninist literature attributes the poverty of underdeveloped countries largely to exploitation by the advanced countries, especially by colonial powers – the extension, as we have just noted, of the doctrine of the exploitation of the proletariat. This idea is present in many publications on economic conditions in Africa and Asia. It is the principal theme of the writings of Dr Nkrumah, whom we have already quoted in essay 3. This Leninist influence is especially clear in his pamphlet *Towards Colonial Freedom*, first published in book form in 1962, several years after he became president of Ghana. Here is a typical passage:

The growth of the national liberation movement in the colonies reveals: (1) The contradiction among the various foreign groups and the colonial imperialist powers in their struggle for sources of raw materials and for territories. In this sense imperialism and colonialism become the export of capital to sources of raw materials, the frenzied and heartless struggle for monopolist possession of these sources, the struggle for a redivision of the already divided world – a struggle waged with particular fury by new financial groups and powers seeking newer territories and colonies against the old groups and powers which cling tightly to that which they have grabbed. (2) The contradictions between the handful of ruling 'civilised' nations and the millions of colonial peoples of the world. In this sense imperialism is the most degrading exploitation and the most inhuman oppression of the millions of peoples living in the colonies. The purpose of this exploitation and oppression is to squeeze out superprofits. . . . The theory of the national liberation movement in colonial countries proceeds from [certain] fundamental theses: (1) The dominance of finance capital in the advanced capitalist countries; the export of capital to the sources of raw materials (imperialism) and the omnipotence of a financial oligarchy (finance capital) reveal the character of monopolist capital which quickens the revolt of the intelligentsia and the workingclass elements of the colonies against imperialism and brings them to the

---

[1] Throughout the underdeveloped world, then, the most backward areas are those outside the market system, with few or no external contacts. Yet Baran writes: 'The dilemma that the majority of mankind faces today is either to liberate itself from both [monopoly and capitalism] or to be cut down by them to the size of the crippling clogs [sic].' *The Political Economy of Growth*, p. 248.

national liberation movement as their only salvation. (2) The incre
the export of capital to the colonies; the extension of 'spheres of influ
and colonial possessions until they embrace the whole world; the trans
mation of capitalism into a world system of financial enslavement a
colonial oppression and exploitation of a vast majority of the populatie
of the earth by a handful of the so-called 'civilised' nations.[1]

These remarks bear no relation to reality, for reasons already indicated
in essay 3. They ignore the extreme backwardness of Africa in the nineteenth century, the advance of the areas in contact with the west, and
the free trade, open-door policy of Great Britain, the principal colonising
power.

A rather different account of the experience of Ghana under colonial
rule was provided by the representative of Liberia at the United Nations,
on the accession of Ghana to the United Nations as a sovereign state.
He said then:

The remarkable development of the state of Ghana while it was under
guardianship provides a unique example of what can be accomplished
through the processes of mutual cooperation and good will among
peoples.[2]

4 Political and Economic Independence

The suggestion, now widely accepted, that political independence is
meaningless without economic independence reflects the Marxist idea
that outside communism neither freedom nor democracy is real. The
emphasis on economic independence at times serves obvious political
purposes: the promotion of a closed and therefore more readily control-
lable economy in preference to one with many diverse and dispersed
external contacts; the orientation of the remaining external contacts
towards communist countries; and the diversion of attention from
domestic problems. Moreover, in orthodox Marxism-Leninism, any
return on private capital denotes exploitation, and service industries are
regarded as unproductive; thus if foreign capital in poor countries earns
a positive return, or foreigners in service industries, including traders,
earn incomes from these unproductive activities, the local population
by definition is exploited, and this would not be tolerated in truly
independent countries.

[1] *Towards Colonial Freedom*, London, 1962, pp. 38–40.
[2] Speech to the General Assembly, 8 March 1957.

I. Potekhin, a leading Soviet authority on African economic matters, wrote extensively on western responsibility for African poverty. The following passage is characteristic:

The economic essence of colonialism, whatever form it takes, consists in exporting a part of a colony's national income to the metropolitan country without return imports of an equivalent value. This explains why metropolitan countries made such big strides in their economic development during the last century while colonies lagged behind.... Why is there little capital in Africa? The reply is evident. A considerable part of the national income which is supposed to make up the accumulation fund and to serve as the material basis of progress is exported outside Africa without any equivalent.[1]

These remarks are again wholly unrelated to reality. There are no dividend and interest payments or other remittances abroad from much of Africa and none from the poorest parts. When such payments occur they represent returns on resources supplied from abroad and not payments extracted from the local population. The prosperity of the west has been generated by its own population and not achieved at the expense of Africa or of other underdeveloped countries. As we have already noted in other contexts, the western countries were already materially much more advanced than the underdeveloped countries, particularly Africa, when they established contact with the latter in the eighteenth and nineteenth centuries. And there are many developed countries now, including some of the richest, which have few economic contacts with the underdeveloped world.

If the operation of foreign-owned enterprises and the presence of expatriate personnel in underdeveloped countries denote exploitation of the local population, it can be said that the poverty of these countries shows that they have experienced too little rather than too much exploitation. This conclusion, incidentally, is clearly implicit in some perceptive but often ignored passages of the Communist Manifesto:

The bourgeoisie, by the rapid improvement of all instruments of production, by the immensely facilitated means of communication, draws all, even the most barbarian, nations into civilisation. The cheap prices of its commodities are the heavy artillery with which it batters down all Chinese walls....

The poverty of underdeveloped countries, especially in Africa, is often regarded by current Marxist-Leninist literature as evidence or

[1] *Problems of Economic Independence of African Countries*, Moscow, 1962, pp. 14–51.

effect of lack of economic independence. Academician Potekhin suppli
a convenient formulation of this view, and of the conditions which i
this view are necessary for economic independence:

The aim is to close all the channels through which national income is
leaking out of Africa. The governments of many African countries have
already tackled this problem. Let us enumerate some of the principal
measures directed towards the elimination of 'financial haemorrhage':
nationalisation of enterprises belonging to foreign companies; compulsory
reinvestment of a part of foreign companies' profits; higher taxation of
profits; establishment of national banks and insurance companies; setting
up of their own maritime shipping and air fleet; and state control over
exports, imports and foreign exchange transactions. Little has been done
so far, and this is quite understandable as the majority of African countries
won political independence just two or three years ago. . . . There is a
question pertaining to both aspects of our problem: which is to be pre-
ferred – private capitalist enterprise or the setting up of state-owned
establishments? To our mind, the latter has every advantage as compared
to private enterprises. Briefly, these advantages are reduced to the
following: the establishment of state-owned enterprises ensures an
incomparably higher rate of economic development than private enterprise; it is the most reliable way of closing the channels for the leakage of
national income abroad and the surest means of eliminating the dominance
of foreign monopolies. Taking into account the extreme weakness of
private national capital in nearly all the countries of the continent, it
should be admitted that it is only the setting up of a state-owned sector in
the economy that will ensure economic independence in a short space of
time.[1]

Detailed examination of these sentiments is not necessary here. It will
be noted that foreign enterprise is identified with monopoly; state
ownership is identified with rapid development; there is no reference
to the relationship between economic development, consumer demand
and living standards; and there is no mention of costs, including the
cost of securing capital.

The usual interpretation of the term economic colonialism in Marxist-
Leninist and related literature has certain very definite and specific
political implications. Any country in which foreign private capital
earns a positive return or where foreigners are engaged in service
industries is an economic colony; and conversely any country whose
citizens have investments abroad, or who perform services there, is
economic imperialist or neo-colonialist. Afro-Asian spokesmen constantly

[1] *Ibid.*, pp. 15-7.

state that the independence of their countries is not secure while colonialism in any form survives. While this is often only a convenient slogan to divert attention from domestic difficulties, notably continued poverty, it is also a reflection of the messianic nature of Marxism-Leninism and anti-colonialism. A messianic creed is never victorious until it has conquered all internal and external enemies within sight; the history of the French Revolution is a familiar example. If the current interpretation of economic or neo-colonialism prevails, then decolonisation is not complete until all foreign private capital in poor countries has been liquidated and all foreign enterprises and activities terminated. Moreover, as the people are not deemed really free and truly independent except under a communist government, complete decolonisation requires the establishment of such governments throughout the underdeveloped world. Much current opinion, including influential opinion, regards the operation of private foreign companies in underdeveloped countries as an instance of economic colonialism or neo-colonialism. This interpretation lends special interest to the UNCTAD resolution, quoted in essay 3, on the liquidation of colonialism in all its forms as necessary for economic development.

5 Prerequisites of Progress

Until such time as the means of production are owned by the communist state, Marxism-Leninism regards comprehensive central planning as essential for development.

Baran writes:

The establishment of a socialist planned economy is an essential, indeed indispensable, condition for the attainment of economic and social progress in underdeveloped countries.[1]

In this literature, comprehensive central planning is deemed necessary for economic advance generally and in particular for the promotion of manufacturing, especially the production of capital goods, which in turn are required for economic progress and independence. For instance, according to Potekhin:

To develop mining and consumer goods industries, machine tools and equipment are required. Who is to supply them? The industrially developed western countries would like to reserve the monopoly in

[1] *The Political Economy of Growth*, p. 261.

delivering machinery to African countries. . . . 'Balanced industrialisation' entails the setting up of an industry putting out the means of production.[1]

I shall not discuss these contentions in detail but simply note a few relevant points.[2] Neither the level of prosperity, nor the rate of development, nor the rate of capital formation, nor the subsequent development of manufacturing, depend on the prior establishment of a national or local capital goods industry. Nor is the development of manufacturing industry generally a necessary condition either of prosperity or of economic development. The richer countries are usually (but by no means invariably) the more industrialised ones largely because the higher rate of development and the presence of manufacturing industries reflect their possession of valuable resources (including capital, skill, attitudes and experience); the presence of manufacturing is not simply the cause of the prosperity. Again, there are many highly developed and rich agricultural regions in the world, and conversely, relatively poor industrial areas. And the rich and industrially advanced countries were already relatively prosperous while still predominantly agricultural, far richer than many of the present poor countries.

In the planning literature, especially in recent Marxist-Leninist literature, economic advance is usually defined without reference to general living standards but primarily in terms of industrial development, notably of capital goods industries, or in terms of the performance of some other particular sector. The advocates of large-scale industrialisation, and especially of the massive development of heavy industries, hardly ever refer to prices, incomes, cost, demand or standard of living. They are not mentioned in the passages already quoted.

There are obvious political motives behind the insistence on comprehensive planning: the establishment of a socialist or communist government is much easier once close and comprehensive economic controls have been established. And such governments are more likely to support other communist governments. Marxist-Leninist literature has traditionally regarded the industrial proletariat as the vanguard of the revolution and the recruiting ground for the most active, reliable and effective party members; and it has also regarded the industrial sector as most readily subject to effective political control. Its emphasis on industrialisation seems to derive largely from such political motives;

[1] *Problems of Economic Independence of African Countries*, p. 10.
[2] Some of these points have already been instanced in the appendix to essay 2.

this is suggested by the absence from the literature of the sophisticated or popular arguments for industrialisation found in the economic textbooks or the popular non-Marxist literature.

More recently Marxist-Leninist literature has shown much greater interest in the development of agriculture, as long as this is part of development planning. This shift of emphasis seems to derive in part from the realisation that in many areas, notably Africa and much of Asia, the industrial proletariat is, and will remain for many years, negligible, and also from the realisation that without a sizeable agricultural surplus, not yet available in many poor countries, industrialisation would be politically inexpedient. Moreover, the possibility of close control over agricultural producers through government-organised cooperative societies, state trading companies and government export monopolies has also come to be recognised. By these and similar devices it is possible even with rudimentary administrative machinery to control closely the pattern of agricultural production for sale, the prices and incomes received by the producers, and the use of the agricultural surplus; and it is also possible to prevent the emergence of a prosperous or independent peasant population, or of a trading class or a bourgeoisie. In communist literature on agricultural development the adoption of one or more of these devices (in addition to the expropriation of landlords which is axiomatic) is prominent; without such measures agricultural development is regarded as a colonial-type development incompatible with economic independence.

6 Policy Prescriptions of Marxism-Leninism

The views about underdeveloped countries and the policy prescriptions for their progress described here as Marxist-Leninist have in fact · become the current orthodoxy in this field. Whatever the exact process of their intellectual derivation, these views are widely and frequently expounded by well-known writers not regarded as Marxist or Leninist. As we have noted, the current development literature dwells on the alleged ever-widening discrepancy of incomes and living standards between rich and poor countries and the starvation or near-starvation in the latter, in much the same way as orthodox Marxism stresses the gulf between oppressor and oppressed and the ever-increasing misery of the proletariat.

For instance, Professor Gunnar Myrdal often alleges an ever-widening international inequality and refers to western Europe, North America and Australasia as the upper class of countries, and to the rest of the world as underprivileged:

The trend is actually towards greater world inequality. It is, in fact, the richer countries that are advancing while the poorer ones, with the large populations, are stagnating or progressing much more slowly. . . . For mankind as a whole there has actually been no progress at all [*sic*]. I have chosen to focus attention on one particular aspect of the international situation, namely the very large and steadily increasing economic inequalities as between developed and underdeveloped countries. . . . These inequalities and their tendency to grow are flagrant realitities.[1]

He writes subsequently:

The larger part of the rest of mankind forms in this sense a lower class of nations . . . in contrast to the upper class of advanced countries. As a matter of fact, and considering their actual levels of living, the term 'proletariat' would be more appropriate in such an international comparison than it ever was or, anyhow, is now within any of the advanced nations. The 'great awakening' in the backward nations is slowly also creating among them the class consciousness without which a social conglomeration is amorphous and unintegrated.[2]

As noted elsewhere in this volume, the assertions of an ever-widening inequality are in part meaningless, in part oversimplified, in part untrue and in general unsubstantiated.[3]

The policy prescription based on this description or diagnosis closely reflects Marxist-Leninist ideas, or indeed the practice in the Soviet Union. In particular, it generally issues in an axiomatic insistence on central planning as indispensable to material progress.

The pervasive influence of Marxism-Leninism, even on professed critics of communism, is neatly illustrated in a book entitled *Africa and the Communist World*:

The 'demonstration effect' of Soviet economic growth most certainly had a profound impact on the thinking of the leaders of nationalist movements in backward areas. But to be impressed [by Soviet growth] does not necessarily mean to be converted. Obviously, one need not be a very orthodox 'Marxist-Leninist' or a particularly heterodox 'bourgeois

[1] *An International Economy*, p. 318.
[2] Professor Myrdal adds (p. 319) that he regards effective combination by the underprivileged countries as most important, to increase their bargaining power, to raise their standard of living, and to promote world integration and democracy. These ideas are developed further in his *Development and Underdevelopment*, Cairo, 1956, *passim*.
[3] See essay 1.

economist' in order to agree with the following baldly stated propositions: (1) a rapid increase in the rate of economic growth in backward countries, which is indispensable in order to break out of the vicious circle of near stagnation, calls for a marked increase in the saving-investment effort; (2) economic development is bound to involve industrialisation at a rather early stage, and also, before long, a relatively rapid growth of domestic capital goods industries coming both in response to and as an added stimulant of the accelerated pace of overall expansion; (3) the availability of a sufficiently large volume of foreign investment and sufficiently extensive foreign trade connections cannot always be taken for granted; (4) since superior productive technology in developed countries represents both a challenge and a threat, the new state would have to intervene more actively to promote and protect economic development than was necessary in older industrialised countries during comparable periods of their history.[1]

In this passage, items (1) and (2) are demonstrably and obviously untrue, (3) is irrelevant and (4) is an obvious *non sequitur*. It would seem that, contrary to what they say, these writers have been both impressed and converted.

7 *Appeal of Marxism-Leninism*

How can we account for the pervasive influence and appeal of Marxism-Leninism? First, Marxism-Leninism is an intellectual structure, comprising method, analysis and empirical observation, which claims to explain the operation and prospects of society. Second, it is also a secular messianic faith or creed which covers all aspects of life and which promises salvation on earth but in the indefinite future, that is, salvation here but not now. Third, it is a programme for political action. The threefold aspect of Marxism and Marxism-Leninism as an intellectual structure, a messianic creed, and a political programme should always be remembered in assessing its appeal.

Marx and Engels revealed some unusual insights over a wide and diverse area which have undoubtedly contributed to its intellectual appeal. These include the explicit recognition (by Engels in *Anti-Dühring*) of the massive technical progress of Europe in the fourteenth and fifteenth centuries; the habitual treatment of phenomena as part of a process; the assessment of developments and policies in terms of their effects on the total situation; and the interest in both micro- and

[1] Alexander Erlich and Christian R. Sonne, 'The Soviet Union: Economic Activity', in Z. Brzezinski (ed.), *Africa and the Communist World*, Stanford, 1963, pp. 54–5.

macroeconomics. In spite of these merits, Marxism-Leninism as an intellectual structure exhibits major shortcomings. The system abounds in internal inconsistencies and its most specific and explicit predictions have been refuted by events. The attempts to rationalise the internal contradictions and explain away the unsuccessful predictions are unconvincing and even unedifying.

However, the main reason for the appeal of Marxism-Leninism derives from the creed, and from the political successes of Marxist parties and governments. The attraction of a messianic, all-embracing, secular religion promising salvation on earth but in the future is obvious, and especially powerful at times of rapid erosion of traditional values and beliefs. The emphasis on the future is attractive in part because promises cannot be checked against performance, but also because of its appeal to selflessness, that is with its concern with the future against the present. The adherents also feel that they belong to a movement which is destined to achieve victory, that they are active participants in the march of history; the faith successfully combines a suggestion of freedom with predestination – freedom is the recognition of necessity. The doctrine of exploitation has an obvious appeal through its suggestion that poverty is the result of oppression and is removable by human action. Then there is the quasi-scientific appeal of a system working with a few apparently clearly defined variables and establishing grand functional relationships. The presence of a logical structure, however defective, has enhanced the attractiveness of Marxism as a messianic faith by making its acceptance intellectually more respectable than that of other types of messianism. The Marxist faith also helps to integrate the intellectuals and the masses, bridging the void which has arisen with the decay of religion and the remoteness of contemporary philosophy and art from the great majority of people.

Marxist parties, moreover, have gained control in several countries, including two of the most powerful, and this has evident appeal. *On ne juge pas les vainqueurs.* This applies notably in the social sciences, especially economics, where there has always been an ambivalence between the advancement of knowledge and the promotion of policy. Marxism-Leninism has been politically successful; and those who do not distinguish between political results and scientific achievement are particularly prone to accept its intellectual claims.

It is of course not new to accept ideas because of the political or military successes of their advocates rather than the analytical or empirical bases of the ideas. But in the twentieth century this phenom-

:non has become conspicuous, notably among intellectuals who like to be thought immune from such influences. And when the political and military success of the advocates of an ideology is allied with political or emotional appeal of its constituent elements, then its acceptance is often entirely unrelated to intellectual merit. For instance, the appeal and acceptance of Lenin's notions on imperialism reflect clearly the operation of these influences.

It is often suggested that the extensive feelings of guilt in the west have served to increase the appeal of Marxism-Leninism, particularly in Anglo-Saxon countries. There is an association here but the direction of the causal or functional relationship is not clear. It may run as much from the acceptance of Marxism to the emergence of feelings of guilt as in the other direction. For instance, the notion that the west has caused the poverty of the underdeveloped world may reflect naïve acceptance and expansion of Marxist ideas of exploitation and of the unproductive nature of services. But it is also possible that a feeling of guilt, derived from a variety of influences, has facilitated uncritical acceptance of the Marxist idea of exploitation.

8 *Special Appeal in Poor Countries*

It is no surprise, therefore, to find that throughout the under-developed world public opinion on economic matters is pervaded by Marxism-Leninism. This has come about through the operation and interaction of various influences: the same factors responsible for its appeal to the west, just noted, are even more attractive; the implicit or explicit suggestion that external forces account for the poverty of the underdeveloped world; the political and military successes of Marxist parties and governments; the pursuit of comprehensive economic planning in the Soviet Union, particularly the large-scale development of capital goods industries; the socialist influence in the international flow of ideas and information; and the impact of rapid change brought about by greatly extended contacts with advanced economies.

The doctrine of exploitation has always been a major factor in the appeal of Marxism. Leninism has helped to extend this on a world scale, with obvious appeal to the political and intellectual leaders in under-developed countries. There is no need to enlarge on the connection between this doctrine of exploitation and the allegations of the results of colonialism and neo-colonialism.

Although it may be said to be implicit in state ownership of the means of production under the dictatorship of the proletariat, economic planning as such does not figure in pre-1917 Marxist-Leninist literature. For various reasons, however, it has become an integral part of communist economic policy. Its influence and appeal again derive from a number of interrelated factors which are substantially similar to the factors behind the appeal of Marxism-Leninism in general, such as the record of the Soviet Union, the appeal of social engineering, and the advantages which some influential groups expect to derive from concentration of power.[1] These factors, and other related influences in the appeal of comprehensive planning, have already been considered in essay 2.

This appeal is especially strong for politicians and intellectuals, since it implies massive concentration of power in the hands of the government. These groups believe that they can and should closely control the rest of society, a belief even stronger in underdeveloped countries than elsewhere, because there these groups feel so much superior to the rest of the community.

Close and intensive government control of much of economic and social life promotes political polarisation, and in this way presents distinct opportunities and advantages for a revolutionary ideology and party. These opportunities are greatest where the mass of the people are traditionally unconcerned with politics, at least beyond the village level. Virtually throughout the underdeveloped world the vast majority have never known elected government or majority rule, and have not participated in politics but concerned themselves only with the tasks of their daily lives. The rulers or governments in their turn, while not elective, usually have had little impact on the lives of the great majority of people. A well-organised, vocal, articulate and often well-armed movement, even if numerically small, can readily exploit such a situation and establish a totalitarian society relatively easily. Both communist ideology and practice ensure that the communist party should benefit most from the potentialities of such a situation.

Much of the appeal of the Soviet experience derives from its interpretation by both Soviet and western writers. These interpretations emphasise the growth of industrial capacity and military power without reference to consumer demand, cost, or welfare, either in terms of human lives (including the mass famines of the 1930s), standard of living, or

---

[1] The attraction in this context of social engineering and of ostensibly conscious control over social evolution has often been noted. For instance, the point is discussed in F.A.Hayek, 'The Intellectuals and Socialism', in George B. de Huszar (ed.), *The Intellectuals*, Glencoe, 1960, p. 377.

of personal freedom; and without reference either to such relevant ~~~ters as the comparatively advanced nature of pre-revolutionary ~~~ussia (as reflected in a sizeable agricultural surplus and a relatively ~~~igh literacy rate compared to the underdeveloped world), or the ~~~ountry's rapid industrialisation before 1914, or to the development of many underdeveloped countries which have progressed rapidly without massive government coercion. Nor do these interpretations usually examine the meaning or limitations of Soviet statistics.

This interpretation of Soviet experience in turn reflects the strong socialist influence in the media of mass communications; this influence is particularly strong in international communication and especially in intellectual contacts between the west and the underdeveloped countries, which are practically confined to opponents of the market system. The situation, noted in a somewhat different context by Professor Hayek, applies overwhelmingly to the intellectual contacts between the west and the underdeveloped countries:

In no other field has the predominant influence of the socialist intellectuals been felt more strongly during the last hundred years than in the contacts between different national civilisations. . . . It is this which mainly accounts for the extraordinary spectacle that for generations the supposedly 'capitalist' west has been lending its moral and material support almost exclusively to those ideological movements in the countries farther east which aimed at undermining western civilisation; and that at the same time the information which the western public has obtained about events in central and eastern Europe has almost inevitably been coloured by a socialist bias.[1]

Many parts of the underdeveloped world have experienced rapid and uneven changes (uneven in that they affect some aspects of life more than others) in recent decades, largely through contact with more advanced economies. The resulting strains and problems of adjustment are particularly acute for the intellectuals, who have to face not only the sudden erosion or disappearance of traditional beliefs and values but often a conflict of loyalties and an alienation from the rest of the community. Throughout the underdeveloped world the western-educated or semi-educated intellectuals, though they feel much superior to the rest of the community are yet desperately anxious to belong to it. The gap is perhaps widest in the African tribal communities but it is also wide and deep throughout Asia. The strains are much enhanced by the clashes of loyalties which such people often experience when traditional

[1] *Ibid.*, p. 375.

and tribal custom or family ties conflict with obligations imposed modern legal systems. The attractions of an all-embracing, pervasi secular, materialistic faith are readily understandable in such condition It offers a haven to people who have lost their moorings. Perhaps eve more important, it offers the prospect of reunification with the rest or the community.[1]

Other consequences of rapid change are relevant here. Such changes invariably result in appreciable shifts in the relative economic and social position of individuals and groups. Price changes always affect adversely some groups in the community; the advance of the market economy undermines the position and authority of traditional leaders; so do various political developments resulting from external contacts. Such changes present ample opportunity for grievances, particularly when their causes cannot be ascribed to natural phenomena but at the same time are not clearly understood. For these reasons the hazards of an exchange economy, although far less acute than those of a subsistence economy, are much less readily accepted, particularly when the impact of a money economy has been rapid and discontinuous. Such developments present considerable opportunities to a party ready and resolved to exploit all grievances.[2] The breach of continuity with the past is pronounced even when the rapid advance is by the production of cash crops, which is closely related to people's traditional activities and pursuits. It is much more pronounced under rapid industrialisation and urbanisation, a consideration which may partly account for communist advocacy of such policies.

9 Debasement of the Language

In recent decades several prominent writers, among them Karl Kraus, George Orwell, Jacques Barzun and Richard M. Weaver, have perceptively discussed what they have recognised as a debasement of (or

---

[1] These points have again often been noted. There is a perceptive discussion of the conflict of loyalties facing the westernised intellectuals in underdeveloped countries and of their alienation from the rest of society by Prabhakar Padhye, 'The Intellectual in Modern Asia', in de Huszar (ed.), *The Intellectuals*. Mr Padhye emphasises the attraction to alienated intellectuals of the secure and legitimate place which they hope for in a communist-planned society. Substantially the same point is made by Czeslaw Milosz in *The Captive Mind*, London, 1953, in the context of eastern Europe.

These considerations are distinct from the appeal to intellectuals of the prospect of increased power in a planned society, an appeal which these considerations reinforce.

[2] The determination of the communists to do so is known in a general way but for its full appreciation it is necessary to read the literature, notably Marx's *Address to the Communist League of Germany*, 1850, and the principal writings of Lenin before 1917.

vhat George Orwell calls an abuse of) the language, in the sense of an increasing use of vague or meaningless terminology.[1] Marxist-Leninist literature has both promoted and exploited this debasement, by systematic reliance on vague general terms whose interpretation can be varied in different circumstances and adapted to the pursuit of specific political goals, by the use of terms in a manner divorced from their accepted meaning, and by ceaseless repetition of demonstrably untrue statements. Such practices are particularly effective in underdeveloped countries where a critical approach to the printed word or to political discussion is even less developed than in the west.

The debasement of the language has gone to such lengths in both popular and academic writing in development economics that words have lost their meaning. How otherwise is it possible for Baran who, it will be recalled, was Professor of Economics at Stanford University, to write thus:

To the dead weight of stagnation characteristic of pre-industrial society was added the entire restrictive impact of monopoly capitalism. The economic surplus appropriated in lavish amounts by monopolistic concerns in backward countries is not employed for productive purposes. It is neither plowed back into their own enterprises, nor does it serve to develop others.[2]

The statement is obviously untrue because extensive agricultural, mineral, commercial and industrial complexes have been built up throughout the underdeveloped world with reinvested profits. Such utterances are, however, characteristic of the writings of Professor Baran, and also generally of Marxist-Leninist literature in this field, which in this area have been highly influential. The overwhelming concern with the pursuit of political aims, and the consequent subordination of intellectual activity to this purpose, has brought it about that the Marxist-Leninist writings on underdeveloped countries have more often than not obscured the scene rather than illuminated it.

Systematic discussion becomes impossible if widely different

[1] The writings of Orwell, Barzun and Weaver, though less well known than they should be, are at least reasonably accessible. Herbert Luthy's penetrating discussion on this subject is not available in English. His essay, 'Fragmente zu einem Instrumentarium des geistigen Terors', published in 1945 in Switzerland and included in a recent collection of essays, *Nach dem Untergang des Abendlandes*, Cologne and Berlin, 1964, is a powerful discussion of the far-reaching consequences of the decay of the language and of its systematic exploitation in communist writings. The disrupting effect of the decay of the language was a major theme of the essays and plays of Karl Kraus, who was writing in Vienna in the early part of the twentieth century.

[2] *The Political Economy of Growth*, p. 177.

meanings are attributed to the same expression or if palpably untru statements and readily demonstrable falsehoods are deemed admissible because of their contribution to political purpose; the passages quoted from Baran and Potekhin are a few among countless examples. Indeed, such writings exemplify what amounts to a destruction of the language. Marxism-Leninism accepts and indeed promotes any misuse of the language if it contributes to the ultimate political goal. It has thereby exacerbated the difficulties of serious study or discussion of economic development.

5 Asian Vistas[1]

In 1968 Professor Gunnar Myrdal published *Asian Drama*, a book of well over one million words, on which he had been working with an international team of collaborators since 1957. The principal theme of this massive work is Professor Myrdal's insistence on the necessity of radical transformation of man and society throughout south Asia by means of government action. The text of this essay focuses on Professor Myrdal's central theme, but it reviews also some major supporting themes. Some other themes of these three large volumes, less closely related to the main theme, are also notable, especially for economists and for others interested in the state of development economics, and these are examined in the appendix to this essay. They have been placed there in order not to divert attention from the main themes.

1 *Mainsprings of Progress*

What very largely determines economic progress in underdeveloped countries is the people who live there. Though we usually speak of underdeveloped countries, economies or nations, these entities consist of people, whose material wants the economy has to satisfy, and whose faculties, motivations and institutions substantially determine its performance. But in these respects the great majority of peoples in underdeveloped countries differ from the great majority of those in the developed world. Grudging, incomplete but nevertheless clear recognition of these simple truths – offensive as they are to influential political, intellectual and emotional interests – is a major feature of Professor Myrdal's mammoth survey of south Asia from Pakistan to the Philippines, as will be clear from the passages quoted in subsequent sections of this essay.

Another significant contribution is Professor Myrdal's insistence on the uselessness of some of the models, methods of approach and major

[1] Gunnar Myrdal, *Asian Drama: An Inquiry into the Poverty of Nations*, London, 1968. This essay has not been published before, except for a few paragraphs in the *Spectator* of 9 January 1969 under the title 'The Million Word Pamphlet'.

concepts which dominate the current literature on economic development, such as the frequent use of capital-output ratios (the ratio between the stock of capital and total output, or between changes in these aggregates); surplus labour (the volume of rural labour supposedly removable without loss of output); and shadow prices (notional equilibrium prices for guiding planning decisions). On these points one can readily agree with Professor Myrdal; the concepts and variables prominent in the theoretical development literature, and widely employed in development planning throughout the underdeveloped world, are largely unrelated to the personal and social determinants of development. They are chosen for their susceptibility to formal, especially to quasi-mathematical treatment, rather than for their relevance to development.[1]

Professor Myrdal correctly notes that reliance on these methods conduces to neglect of the major determinants of development. Indeed, in this context one can go much further than does Professor Myrdal. It is a corollary of this neglect that the impact of policy on these determinants will also be overlooked. For instance, trade and exchange controls, introduced to promote development by operating on the volume and allocation of domestic spending, in practice also influence the volume and nature of external contacts, occupational and geographical mobility within the country, the supply of incentive goods, the position and prospects of the various ethnic groups within a country, the character and intensity of political conflicts, and the direction of people's energies. These other repercussions are almost certain to be more important than the direct impact of the controls.

Among Professor Myrdal's other useful observations are his recognition that Marx has had a pervasive influence in current development literature; and also that many liberals share with Marxists the unfounded belief in economic organisation and technical processes as primary causes of economic development and social phenomena generally, in contrast .to the allegedly derivative nature of motivations, values and institutions. Professor Myrdal rightly criticises this approach, the irrelevance of which is patent in south Asia. He also notes that throughout this region, and especially in India and Pakistan, the increase in state control over economic life in recent years has benefited primarily

---

[1] The comprehensive, methodical and effective criticism of currently fashionable development models in appendix 3 by Professor Streeten is the best part of the book. The concept of surplus agricultural labour (a basic assumption of much south Asian planning) and attempts to measure its extent by casual observation and against western ideas about working habits, are also effectively dismissed in chapter 21 and appendix 6.

better-off people – politicians, administrators, industrialists, and the more articulate villagers. Such an outcome was to be expected because of the wide differences in political effectiveness between various social and occupational groups.

Professor Myrdal also rightly notes the effects of climate on economic performance, and he points to its comparative neglect in the development literature. But he himself nowhere attempts to reconcile his recognition of the adverse effects of tropical climate with his emphasis on inequality, colonialism, and entrenched social interests, as alleged major causes of backwardness.[1]

2 Reinterpretation of Planning

Professor Myrdal's main message is the need for a thoroughgoing transformation of man and society throughout south Asia, if necessary by coercion. He considers coercion justified because of the urgent need for more rapid material progress, which may require compulsion unlimited both in time and intensity.

This drastic message emerges in the following way. According to Professor Myrdal, extreme poverty, stagnation and even retrogression characterise south Asia, which contains one-quarter of the world's population; there are also wide inequalities in wealth, income and status between persons and groups;[2] and the relation between poverty and stagnation and of both these to inequality reflect what he terms 'generally operative circular cumulative causation' in economic and social life, so that in the absence of politically organised countermeasures social and economic influences and trends reinforce themselves. Poverty, according to Professor Myrdal, not only inhibits the accumulation of capital but also perpetuates values and institutions which obstruct

[1] The comparative neglect of climate in much current writing is plainly indefensible in view of the obvious concentration of material backwardness outside the temperate zone, and more especially in the tropics. Professor Myrdal observes that references to high civilisations in the tropics in the past are irrelevant to the issues currently discussed in development economics. He recognises that the aptitudes required for economic progress differ in pre-industrial and more nearly modern conditions, and that the effects of climate on economic performance and thus on differences in performance are likely to be more important in more nearly modern conditions. It may be added that the material achievements and successes of past civilisations were largely in the nature of the creation of outstanding monuments and works of art rather than general, diffuse, material achievement. Finally, in some regions where there were high civilisations in the past climatic changes seem to have recurred adverse to economic progress.

[2] Professor Myrdal practically always refers to inequality when discussing differences in incomes and wealth. The implications of this practice, which he shares with most economists, are considered in essay 1.

progress. He argues that inequality of status and wealth represses people, removes incentives, inhibits a rise in productivity, and obstructs the emergence and effectiveness of policies which might improve the situation, notably policies described by Professor Myrdal as rational planning.

Backwardness, the argument runs, accounts also for the persistence of ethnic, linguistic and other cultural differences within countries. These various differences both inhibit material advance and retard that national consolidation which would unify markets and facilitate planning. Colonialism has often aggravated the situation by generating and perpetuating the attitudes, institutions and social structures inimical to progress.

Professor Myrdal regards comprehensive planning as indispensable for the promotion of higher incomes.[1] Moreover, planning is also desirable in itself primarily in order to promote national consolidation, which Professor Myrdal again considers as necessary for higher incomes, and as desirable in itself. Thus in his terminology the case for central planning is both an independent and a derived value premise.

Professor Myrdal considers pursuit of higher per capita incomes as the objective and criterion of rational government policy. The pursuit of this aim requires fundamental changes in people's modes of conduct, attitudes and institutions, together with large-scale removal or far-reaching reduction of cultural, ethnic and linguistic differences as well as of inequalities of wealth, income and status. These massive changes can be brought about only through comprehensive central planning.

The current development literature usually interprets planning as actual or attempted state control of the economy outside subsistence agriculture. It has never been made clear why such a policy should promote economic development in the sense of raising general living standards. Professor Myrdal now recognises that central planning in this sense is insufficient for material progress. Hence his revolutionary interpretation of central planning as a policy for the forcible remoulding of man and society. The book is thus a landmark in its clear reinterpretation and extension of central planning from attempted state control to attempted compulsory transformation of man and society. I shall quote from Professor Myrdal's book at length to illustrate his thesis. This will show the significance of the new departure and should forestall objections that the quotations are out of context.

---

[1] I shall follow Professor Myrdal in using interchangeably the terms planning, central planning, comprehensive planning and comprehensive central planning.

. the success of planning for development requires a readiness to place obligations on people in *all* social strata to a much greater extent than is now done in any of the south Asian countries. It requires, in addition, rigorous enforcement of obligations, in which compulsion plays a strategic role. . . . Under present south Asian conditions development cannot be achieved without much more social discipline than the prevailing interpretation of democracy in the region permits.[1]

. . . there is little hope in south Asia for rapid development without greater social discipline. To begin with, in the absence of more discipline – which will not appear without regulations backed by compulsion – all measures for rural uplift will be largely ineffective.[2]

In so far as these other valuations [which retard development] clash with the modernisation ideals, they act as *inhibitions* when held by members of government and by those who participate in shaping and carrying out government policies. They account for the hesitancy and the half-heartedness in making and executing plans. When present *only* among the majority of the people who are not active participants in policy formation and execution, these conflicting valuations act as *obstacles*. . . . They must either be overcome by policy measures that constitute a rational plan or be circumvented, if planning as an expression of the modernisation ideals is to forge ahead. . . . The distinction in this study between 'inhibitions' and 'obstacles' is a somewhat simplifying abstract model though we believe it represents a realistic approach. It envisages a government and its entourage as the active subject in planning, and the rest of the people as the relatively passive objects of the policies emerging from planning.[3]

In such a national community the barriers of caste, colour, religion, ethnic origin, culture, language, and provincial loyalties would be broken down, and property and education would not be so unequally distributed as to represent social monopolies. A nation with marked social and economic equality, high social as well as spatial mobility, and firm allegiance of the whole population to the national community is visualised.[4]

The central and essential theme of Professor Myrdal's argument is clear, although at times it is obscured by vague, meandering or

---

[1] p. 67. Professor Myrdal's italics.
[2] p. 895. Professor Myrdal's italics.
[3] pp. 72–3. The words 'inhibitions' and 'obstacles' are italicised by Professor Myrdal, the word 'only' by me.
[4] p. 60.

contradictory exposition. It is that planning must not only control th economy, but remake people and society: personal conduct and socia. attitudes are to be restructured in the interest, or at least the declared interest, of higher per capita incomes.

Professor Myrdal deplores what he calls the gradualist approach in the region:

...the adherence to the gradualist approach to this extent and in this manner in spite of the common recognition of the need for revolutionary change must, of course, be explained by the social situation in these countries, especially the innumerable inhibitions and obstacles that rational planning meets.[1]

The use of the expression common recognition is paradoxical particularly as Professor Myrdal often notes that the people at large do not support such policies. Common recognition thus refers to a relatively small number of vocal and influential people.

Instead of gradual change rapid and thoroughgoing transformation is required:

The bigger and more rapid change ordinarily must be attained by resolutely altering the institutions within which people live and work. ... But institutions can ordinarily be changed only by resort to *what in the region is called compulsion* – putting obligations on people and supporting them by force.[2]

It is not only in south Asia that such policies are called compulsion; this is precisely what they are, and would be called by that name wherever they were pursued.

Time and again Professor Myrdal quotes with approval official Indian documents on the necessity of remoulding institutions so that they contribute to the 'realisation of wider and deeper social values'. In this context he writes:

But the prospects of breaking down the barriers to development in the south Asian countries would be quite different if in a country like India, for example, the government were really determined to change the prevailing attitudes and institutions and had the courage to take the necessary steps and accept their consequences. These would include the effective abolition of caste, prescribed by the constitution [of India], and measures, accepted in principle, that would increase mobility and equality, such as effective land reform and tenancy legislation; a rational policy

[1] p. 116.
[2] pp. 115–6. My italics.

for husbandry, even if it required the killing of many half-starved cows ... in general, enactment and enforcement, not only of fiscal, but also of all other obligations on people that are required for development.[1]

Like many writers on development economics, Professor Myrdal often refers to the reform and modernisation of sectors, activities, beliefs and institutions. But what is actually under discussion is not the reform and modernisation of this sector or that activity, but of the people engaged in them; not of beliefs and values, but of those who hold them; and not the institutions but of those who participate in them. The subjects of the transformation are people, that is persons and groups of persons, not abstract entities such as activities or sectors. Professor Myrdal does not explain how this modernisation through transformation and standardisation is to be brought about beyond insisting that the governments must be given sufficient power to carry out these policies. He does not say how people are to be transformed, by what specific policies and with what resources.

As we have just noted, Professor Myrdal is apt to refer to sectors, activities and institutions rather than to people. When, however, he does turn his attention to the people, whose welfare his drastic policies are supposed to promote, the tenor of these references does not suggest either sympathy or respect. Thus he writes:

The prevailing attitudes and patterns of individual performance in life and at work are from the development point of view deficient in various respects: low levels of work discipline, punctuality and orderliness; superstitious beliefs and irrational outlook; lack of alertness, adaptability, ambition, and general readiness for change and experiment; contempt for manual work; submissiveness to authority and exploitation; low aptitude for cooperation; low standards of personal hygiene; and so on.[2]

These remarks may to some extent explain both Professor Myrdal's readiness to resort to drastic policies and his lack of concern with the effects of these policies on the population at large, matters which we shall come to consider in this essay.

3 Transformation of Man and Society

Professor Myrdal envisages a thoroughgoing and compulsory transformation of individuals and societies throughout south Asia. He notes

[1] pp. 1909–10.
[2] p. 1862.

a wide range of mores, modes of conduct, attitudes, institutions and phenomena which need to be radically modified or even eliminated in so far as, in his view, they inhibit material progress. Nearly the whole range of human conduct is involved. Within his comprehensive purview of reform there are three broad areas which can be distinguished for purposes of exposition: first, personal and cultural modes of conduct, values and mores; second, ethnic and linguistic differences; third, economic differences, especially in income and wealth. These areas are related and to some extent overlap. However, the imprecision of the distinctions does not affect the substantive argument.

Conduct and mores. The first category includes such diverse elements of conduct and culture as reluctance to take animal life; belief in the efficacy of occult and supernatural forces; objection to women working outside the home; refusal to practise contraception; high preference for leisure or for non-manual work; acceptance of the caste system; the prestige of a contemplative over an active life; acceptance of things as they are; and many others.

Professor Myrdal is ambivalent about the strength and depth of the mores inhibiting material progress. At times he suggests that they are no more than habits and conventions, perpetuated by the influence of colonialism, inertia and vested interests. Accordingly, 'what is needed is *merely* the eradication of the ballast of irrational beliefs and related valuations'.[1] At other times he suggests that some of these mores and attitudes are deep and strong. This latter interpretation is implicit in the frequent references to the necessity for compulsion. Professor Myrdal wonders

...whether people will change in the way development requires: and whether all these changes will happen rapidly enough, without a deliberate reformation of popular religion that would drive out superstitious beliefs and elevate in their place the cherished rites, philosophical thoughts, and general moral precepts accepted by most of the intellectuals.[2]

It is certainly misleading to imply, as Professor Myrdal does, that the beliefs, modes of conduct and institutions most harmful to material advance in south Asia are mere social conventions reinforced by vested interests and readily removable in the pursuit of higher incomes. For

[1] p. 105. My italics.
[2] p. 109. Professor Myrdal does not specify these 'cherished rites' of the intellectual. In the context of the discussion, they seem to be primarily proposals for compulsory transformation and standardisation of human beings.

instance, what vested interests could benefit from the reluctance to take animal life, or the refusal to kill cattle, or the people's preference for leisure or for contemplation against an active life? Some of the beliefs and attitudes which obstruct material progress in south Asia are most ancient. The worship of cows in India, for example, goes back about three thousand years, and reflects the unwavering attachment of the Aryans to these animals, a feeling which pervades the culture of much of rural India. The inviolability of sentient animal life reflects the belief that nature is a continuum, without sharp distinction between man and the rest of the organic universe, and that man should live with nature rather than harness it to his purpose.

The widely prevalent and readily observable torpor and inertia of the population of the Indian subcontinent reflect to some extent the debilitating climate, which not only affects people's energies directly but may also have contributed to the persistence of mores and institutions adverse to material progress. In parts of his book Professor Myrdal explicitly notes the effects of climate on economic performance, but generally he ignores it when referring to the causes of material backwardness and the agencies and potentialities of change.

The effects of caste on material progress are, in fact, ambiguous. Caste obstructs social, occupational and geographical mobility; on the other hand it has for centuries been a cohesive force in Hindu society and has probably held in check the forces of anarchy.[1] Caste is certainly deeply and inextricably interwoven with other elements of the culture of rural India, including marriage, and could not be coercively eliminated without destroying the society over much of India.

As already noted, Professor Myrdal's position is ambivalent about the strength of these obstacles to material progress. He almost certainly greatly underestimates the depth, intensity and tenacity of some of the beliefs and attitudes he censures. This underestimation in part reflects the unhistorical approach of the book. It is a corollary of this neglect of the history of the region that the book is without the basis of worthwhile assessment of the depth and strength of the beliefs, attitudes and institutions of south Asia.

This unhistorical approach partly explains Professor Myrdal's exaggerated belief in the possibilities of state action to modify those mores and attitudes of which he disapproves, although the over-emphasis may perhaps also reflect a desire to make out a case for granting

---

[1] It was seen as a cohesive force by the late J. S. Furnivall, a writer often quoted by Professor Myrdal, but without mention of this point.

extensive powers to the state. At times Professor Myrdal advances curious arguments in support of his occasional optimism about the likely results of central planning:

The attention drawn to development as an end will tend to incline people increasingly to attach a positive independent value, not only to rises in levels of living – itself a novel valuation to many people in a backward, stagnating country – but to a change upwards in all other conditions in the social system, including attitudes and institutions.[1]

This is another unsubstantiated assertion. In practice the suggestion is more nearly the opposite of the truth. For instance, in India the enactment of the ban on the slaughter of cattle (not only of cows) in Uttar Pradesh, the largest Indian state, coincided with the inception of the Second Five-Year Plan.

Another major theme of the book is the need to abolish discrimination in social life and personal conduct. This objective is unattainable and indeed inconceivable. All human relations involve discrimination, though different people discriminate for different purposes and on different criteria. Absence of discrimination on one count usually involves discrimination on another criterion. In south Asia discrimination on the basis of religion, colour, race and language is practically general throughout society. Colour feeling is especially strong in India and Pakistan.[2]

Social discrimination – the selection of associates, including mates, on the basis of consistent criteria – is general not only among human beings, but also among higher animals; it is less clearly present among lower animals. In human societies adoption of consistent criteria for the basis of association is often an indication or presumption of a large measure of shared background and experience. A common background and experience is a condition of the cohesion of society or of groups. This may explain why those who wish to replace societies by an inert standardised mass are so violently opposed to discrimination in the sense just outlined. Insistence on ethnic and linguistic uniformity and on absence of discrimination inside state boundaries reflects Professor Myrdal's predilection for a society in which there are no differences or

---

[1] p. 1883.
[2] A detailed and perceptive discussion of the antiquity and intensity of discrimination on the basis of colour in India will be found in two books by Mr Nirad C. Chaudhuri, *The Autobiography of an Unknown Indian*, London, 1951, and *The Continent of Circe*, London, 1965; another book by an Indian which notes the intensity of colour feeling in south Asia is Prakash Tandon, *Punjabi Century 1857–1947*, London, 1961.

distinctions except between the all-powerful government and the homogeneous subject mass.

We may note an important paradox here. The thrust of the argument throughout Professor Myrdal's book is ostensibly directed against differentiation and discrimination. It is in fact directed only against the types of differentiation and discrimination which are practised by ordinary people and which reflect their background, inclinations and preferences. On the other hand, it favours the preferences of politically articulate and effective groups. Thus he consistently and sharply discriminates against the values held by the majority of people.

Ethnic and linguistic differences. Professor Myrdal envisages substantial reduction or even elimination of ethnic or linguistic differences and loyalties. He objects to these differences because they increase the difficulties of central planning and also stand in the way of national consolidation, both of which he regards as necessary instruments for material progress besides being desirable in their own right. He also thinks that these differences restrict the size of markets.

But very large numbers of people, probably the great majority of the population of south Asia, are strongly attached to their ethnic and linguistic traits and identities, and would find it impossible to divest themselves of these traits. It would, for instance, be impossible for the Chinese, Indian and Malay communities of Malaysia to do so. Attempted elimination of these differences would present difficulties which are certain to be formidable and which would probably be insurmountable.

Most of the present state boundaries of south Asia are recent and arbitrary. Their location may serve the purposes of some governments, and they may be convenient as a starting point for central planning. But these countries are not nation states in the accepted sense of the term.[1] The boundaries often encompass diverse ethnic groups which do not regard the other groups as part of the same nation or society. This is obvious between the different communities in Malaysia and Indonesia but is substantially true of many other countries. The effective expulsion of Indians from Burma and the treatment of the Chinese in Indonesia underlines this point. Moreover, the boundaries are not only arbitrary, they are also shifting. For instance, Singapore broke loose from Malaysia in 1966. Was Malaysia a nation state before Singapore became independent? Or did Singapore become a nation state overnight?

[1] The Concise Oxford Dictionary defines nation as a distinct race or people having common descent, language, history, or political institutions.

Nor do the existing so-called nation states of south Asia represent even single national markets. They are broken up partly by large distances and poor communications whose effects are reinforced at times by the physical separation of different parts (Pakistan, Indonesia, Malaysia and to some extent India). This is quite apart from differences in the requirements and consumption patterns of the different ethnic and cultural groups within the state boundaries.

Ethnic uniformity within a country need not be a condition or even an agent of material progress. Ethnic differences and the associated cultural differences often lead to new ideas and methods, set up comparisons, and thus promote material advance. And attachment to certain elements of an ethnic tradition and the related cultural tradition is often a dynamic force because it is one of the ingredients of purpose and meaning in people's lives. But even if ethnic and linguistic uniformity were an agent in material progress, this would not warrant either the exercise of compulsion over unwilling populations, or the acceptance of the present arbitrary and accidental frontiers.

The different and often mutually antagonistic ethnic and linguistic groups within the boundaries of the so-called nation states of south Asia have been distinct for centuries or even millennia. These antagonisms have already been exacerbated by the extension of state power, a connection which is indeed noted by Professor Myrdal himself.[1] The tension would be much increased if enlargement of state power were used to support systematic attempts to eliminate strongly felt ethnic and linguistic differences.

Income, wealth and status. The same predilection for uniformity is evident in the third major sphere in which Professor Myrdal envisages enforced large-scale transformation, namely the economic sphere. Professor Myrdal generally regards differences in income and wealth as indefensible, abnormal, irrational and adverse to material progress. As already noted, he habitually refers to economic differences as inequalities. And he regards inequality as inequitable, thereby equating economic differences with inequity.

Professor Myrdal frequently implies that higher incomes are usually the result of privilege or exploitation; that they have somehow been extracted from the rest of the population; and that economic activity is a kind of zero sum game in which incomes earned by some are lost by

[1] For instance, pp. 382, 898.

ıers. At times he even manages to imply that it is reprehensible for
me groups to have emerged from the surrounding poverty.

Indeed, Professor Myrdal is obsessed with differences in material
conditions. Income difference even between urban and rural areas,
or between different districts, are noted at great length and with
disfavour. Professor Myrdal does not usually examine either the meaning of the data, or the conditions and factors behind these differences.

In south Asia, as elsewhere, incomes are not usually extracted from
other people. There, as elsewhere, they are received for activities
performed and for resources supplied. Higher incomes reflect primarily
such abilities and aptitudes as readiness to perceive and exploit economic
opportunity, capacity to work hard, and willingness to save and invest.[1]

This suggestion that differences in incomes are inequitable or even
downright unjust implies that peoples' faculties, motivations, living
conditions and requirements are identical; and when groups of people
are being compared the suggestion also implies that there are no differences in age composition. This approach assumes that people are somehow made of the same basic stuff and that the only real and significant
differences between them are differences in income. It follows that
simply by virtue of being born they are entitled to substantially identical
incomes; that differences in income are both abnormal and reprehensible
and at the same time readily rectifiable. But peoples' faculties, motivations, interests, living conditions and requirements often differ substantially. And these differences are especially pronounced when large
areas and large numbers of people are surveyed.

Professor Myrdal often emphasises the importance of equality of
opportunity as well as equality of wealth and income. But differences
in economic faculties and motivations ensure that equality of opportunity in any worthwhile meaning of the term will ensure differences
in wealth and income. It is possession of the required economic aptitudes,
especially readiness to perceive and exploit economic opportunity,

[1] Many well-to-do people have, of course, benefited from inheritance, which means
that some of their resources were generated by their forbears. This does not affect
the argument of the text. The inheritance of wealth does not mean that it has in any
way been extracted from others; and the suggestion that it is inequitable is, of course, a
value judgment. And the idea that a man has no right to accumulate wealth for the benefit
of his descendants raises widest issues of social policy and of the significance of the
concept of the family. Moreover, it is worth noting that inherited wealth has little or
nothing to do with the largest fortunes in south Asia, such as the Chinese fortunes in
south-east Asia or the recent industrial fortunes in India.

The inheritance of above-average intelligence and good looks confer advantages
analogous to those of material wealth. But like other social reformers Professor Myrdal
does not seem to object to this type of inheritance.

interest in money-making, resourcefulness and sheer hard work, which has enabled the exceedingly poor Chinese immigrants of south-east Asia to outdistance both the indigenous population and the other immigrant groups. The wealth of countless Chinese merchants, miners, planters, contractors and other entrepreneurs in the region owes nothing to official favours or even to the inheritance of wealth (though it may owe much to the inheritance of certain faculties).

Professor Myrdal insists that wealth and status are correlated, and that the rich have a monopoly of political power. These allegations are again simply not true. For instance, in India, especially in the country-side, the status of a relatively poor Brahmin is often higher than that of a prosperous trader of a lower caste. And it is patently untrue that the rich monopolise political power, as is evidenced, for instance, by the treatment of the prosperous Chinese in Indonesia and of the Indians in Burma. This point will be developed at greater length later in this essay.

The allegation that income differences generally retard material advance is unfounded. There is no general reason why the prosperity of some persons, groups or regions should obstruct the advance of others. Differences in incomes are more often a condition of material progress and evidence of its occurrence rather than an obstacle to its realisation. In Asia, as elsewhere, the prospects of material rewards have encouraged millions of people to work hard, save, experiment and invest, often in distant countries. In short, it is not true that differences in incomes inhibit economic development, or that higher incomes are generally extracted from other people, or that they reflect exploitation and privilege, or that they represent political power.

There is, however, a category of incomes in south Asia which does reflect a privileged position. This is represented by the windfalls, often very large, which have accrued to recipients of licences for foreign exchange and imports in India, Pakistan and Ceylon. In the conditions which have prevailed in these countries for the last ten or fifteen years the granting of these licences has often amounted to cash gifts, part of which may have had to be handed back to politicians and civil servants as bribes. But these windfalls do not justify suggestions that the incomes of the well-to-do are generally the result of privilege rather than of economic performance. The windfalls simply reflect one facet of the operation of controls under planning.

Professor Myrdal's strictures against economic differences and well-to-do people invite some obvious questions, the relevance of which xtends beyond south Asia. Why should everybody be entitled to substantially the same income, simply by virtue of being born, and regardless of conduct, motivations, faculties and contributions to the economy? Why should it be inequitable that people who revere animal life, or who do not let women work outside the home, or who do not exert themselves greatly, should have lower incomes than do others who do not impose such constraints on themselves? Or why should it be inequitable that the Chinese in Malaysia and Indonesia, or the Indians in Burma, or the Europeans in south Asia should earn higher incomes than do the indigenous populations, when they work harder, often face great hardships, and incur risks far from their countries of origin?

4 *Hostility to the Prosperous*

Professor Myrdal is generally hostile to the more prosperous and materially successful persons and groups, with the exception of the westernised intellectuals and civil servants. As we have already noted, he often clearly implies that the incomes of the materially successful, especially those of aliens, foreign investors, traders, moneylenders and landowners, have somehow been secured at the expense of the rest of society.

Professor Myrdal's hostility to prosperous people is notable in his references to the economically successful Asian minority groups (whom he sometimes terms oriental aliens), such as the Chinese throughout south-east Asia, or the Indians in Burma. These self-reliant and successful groups, who have achieved prosperity from poverty, have contributed greatly to the material advance of the areas in which they have been allowed to operate, frequently in the face of official hostility. In recent years they have often been subjected to expropriation or expulsion.

There may be various reasons for this distinctly unfavourable attitude towards these groups. Professor Myrdal may dislike them because their achievement refutes the notion of the vicious circle of poverty; or because they are (or were) more prosperous than the rest of the population, which he considers objectionable; or because they are self-reliant and thus not in need of the attention of social reformers; or because in various ways they differ from the indigenous population, and he objects to differences and distinctions; or because they have been subject to expropriation by governments with whose policies Professor Myrdal sympathises.

Professor Myrdal, then, portrays better-off people unsympathetically, as responsible but selfish agents. In contrast, he regards the rest of the population as victims of circumstances, generally of the social environment and especially of the political and economic manipulations of the rich. The less well-off are described as oppressed and underprivileged. This latter term, now so familiar in both academic and popular literature, is a nonsense expression. Privileged people are recipients of special official favours denied to others. Underprivileged is therefore a self-contradiction akin to under-overfed.

5 Compulsory Standardisation and its Implications

As we have seen, in south Asia wholesale compulsion is required for attempted standardisation of people's modes of conduct and mores and of their ethnic, linguistic and cultural condition. And the same applies to attempted standardisation of material conditions, when economic faculties and motivations and physical and social requirements differ. Such policies imply great inequalities of power. And the more deep-seated and pervasive are the differences in faculties, motivations and physical requirements, the more intensive is the compulsion required to standardise conditions, and the greater becomes the inequality of power between rulers and subjects. Such inequalities in power differ radically from differences in incomes, since the former do and the latter do not imply a subject group whose freedom of choice and action can be curtailed – and usually is severely curtailed – by the more powerful group. Yet this inequality, namely that between rulers and their subjects (when the former are engaged in comprehensive planning), is the only difference or distinction between people which Professor Myrdal accepts, and indeed welcomes, as imperative for a rational ordering of society.

Professor Myrdal's insistence on a large measure of standardisation of material conditions reflects certain related and influential notions, some of which we have already had occasion to note: the idea that people are substantially identical in capacities, motivations and requirements and differ only in conventionally measured incomes; that differences in income and wealth obstruct material advance; that these differences reflect primarily the operation of external factors unrelated to personal faculties and motivations; and also that the incomes of better-off people have been secured at the expense of those who are poorer. It follows from these ideas that removal or substantial reduction of differences in income is equitable, relatively easy, probably beneficial to material advance, and certainly not damaging to it. As we have seen, these notions are invalid and so are the conclusions derived from them.

Professor Myrdal envisages that the basic planning decisions for the promotion of material progress and the standardisation of material conditions should be taken by authorities in charge of large areas and populations. His unit is normally a country under one central government, which he terms the national state. As we have seen, this terminology is misleading, since the state boundaries of south Asia do not generally encompass nation states in the accepted sense of the term but distinct groups whose members do not regard each other as belonging to the same community. Professor Myrdal's terminology may reflect an inclination to favour large units of politically powerful or influential entities. At times, however, Professor Myrdal goes beyond the national state as a unit for planning and envisages supernational planning as well.

The insistence on large units has important political implications which are often ignored but which need to be noted. The larger the areas and the greater the number of people subject to one government or planning agency the more diverse are the people and the conditions subject to the same controls; thus the more intense is the coercion required to standardise people and conditions, or even to promote identical objectives. Large size of the basic unit also implies that most of the population is remote from the centre of decision-making. General policies or specific measures which harm even large numbers can therefore always be spuriously justified as allegedly benefiting other distant and unspecified groups. References to decentralised planning do not affect these issues, as they mean only the local execution of decisions taken centrally.

This connection between the size of the basic unit of central planning and the intensity of controls required to achieve standardisation is relevant to the implications of Professor Myrdal's preference for large units. It is also relevant to the contemporary advocacy of world government supported by Professor Myrdal, with the extension of the role of the present international agencies as a first step in that direction. Many advocates of world government, including again Professor Myrdal, envisage substantial reduction of international differences in incomes as one of its major tasks. Because of the very wide differences in the conditions and modes of living of the countless societies in the world, which range from aborigines to highly industrialised societies, attempts to promote a significant measure of international equality in conventional incomes require not only world government but world government with totalitarian powers.

6 *Raising of Income as Ground for Compulsion*

Professor Myrdal specifies a rise in per capita incomes as a major, indeed as an overriding objective both of rational government policy and of rational personal conduct. And he considers that the pursuit of this aim justifies far-reaching coercion.

Professor Myrdal ignores here several fundamental, related problems of the concept of income, and of the costs and methods by which they may be changed. For instance, per capita incomes are reduced by an increase in births and often also by the longer life of children and of old people. Yet, as we have repeatedly noted, many people like to have children, like them to survive, and like to live longer. These considerations are ignored in a treatment which is confined to conventionally measured per capita incomes. Moreover, conventional incomes could be increased by forcing people to work longer hours or to transfer to more lucrative but also more arduous or for some other reason less-preferred occupations. Housewives could be forced to go into paid employment. In fact countless people in rich and poor countries could be compelled to increase their conventional incomes by forcing them to give up working habits, attitudes and beliefs which they cherish. It is bizarre to say the least to describe people as irrational for not trying to maximise conventionally measured incomes. It is an approach which disregards people's own preferences in such matters as life expectation, possession of children, working habits, personal values and social mores, including personal preferences for leisure and contemplation against higher conventional incomes; it also disregards considerations of national security.

The question of alternative objectives is obviously closely related to problems of the concept and interpretation of income. The pursuit of higher incomes as an objective is quite obviously far too vague and open-ended to serve as an overriding aim of policy, especially as basis of a policy involving large-scale compulsion.[1]

Even if compulsion were justified in the pursuit of higher incomes

---

[1] To equate the pursuit of higher incomes with rational conduct, to the neglect of methods and costs of increasing income, is an instance of the confusion of income as an accounting concept of a flow of goods and service with a psychic concept of welfare and satisfaction. This issue is noted at greater length in essay 1.

it is most unlikely to be effective for this purpose in the major contexts envisaged by Professor Myrdal. The exercise of compulsion in these spheres is more likely to inhibit material progress than to promote it. Attempts forcibly to obliterate ethnic, cultural and linguistic identities, which are in any case not major obstacles to material progress, would be strongly resisted. Attempts to remove differences in income and wealth would not meet with the same resistance but they also would encounter considerable difficulties, especially because these differences are generally readily acceptable by most of the population. Thus attempts to eliminate them would certainly provoke political tension as well as widespread feelings of insecurity, which would reinforce other effects of such policies unfavourable to material advance, such as adverse effects on saving, enterprise and work.

Mores and modes of conduct widely prevalent in south Asia are major factors which retard material progress. Attempts to influence these determinants of economic achievement raise complex problems. As we have already suggested, the right to force people to change their values, attitudes and conduct simply in the interests of higher incomes is disputable. And quite apart from the moral issues involved it does not follow that attempts to force people to abandon modes of conduct and values which obstruct material progress would in fact promote progress. When people are not ready to change their beliefs and mores attempts to modify these forcibly are quite likely to obstruct progress further. Such attempts would certainly set up intense resistance and may even bring about active revolt. But even if such a reaction could be overcome the experience might still prove traumatic, and would indeed be likely to reduce many people to the status of a listless, dejected mass, with lives largely without meaning and purpose, with the result that ambition and achievement would appear largely pointless. Such a population would not exhibit the traits required for material advance. If, for instance, an Indian government were to decree compulsory slaughter of much of the cow population this would be seen as an unmitigated disaster by many millions of people.

Religious beliefs and practices have supplied inspiration and dynamism in many cultures. The drive behind material as well as non-material progress may be impeded when such beliefs and practices have to be forcibly abandoned. Such results may happen when these beliefs and practices disintegrate rapidly even without government pressure. The dynamism behind the phenomenal progress of Japan may well owe much to the partial maintenance of traditional values and beliefs during the process of economic and technical modernisation, which, incidentally, was carried out without coercion.

Large-scale compulsion also goes counter to that uncoercive liberation of mind which can serve both as an instrument and an objective of material advance. Uncoercive liberation of the mind is especially important in south Asia because of the long authoritarian tradition of that region which has subjected people both to political authority and to that of traditional custom. It may be noted here that the age-old acceptance of authority in south Asia differs substantially from the subjection of people to their rulers envisaged by Professor Myrdal. The traditional system was more personal and had in it a much larger voluntary element. It practically never involved large-scale attempts coercively to transform people's conduct and values.

Except in certain very restricted and special conditions (not examined by Professor Myrdal) there is an inherent contradiction in the idea of a rise in general living standards engineered by compulsion, that is against the will of the supposed beneficiaries.[1] It is pertinent to recall what Sir Arthur Lewis wrote in 1955: 'The advantage of economic growth is not that wealth increases happiness, but that it increases the range of human choice.'[2]

By contrast, voluntary changes of modes of conduct or institutions do not involve these disadvantages and contradictions. If people voluntarily give up their beliefs and modes of conduct to secure material advantages, this implies that they value more what they receive than what they have given up. The change, therefore, will not produce a resentful people. Throughout the underdeveloped world there are many examples of large-scale voluntary adjustment to new opportunities. For instance, external contacts, especially commercial contacts, have brought about great changes in attitudes and habits in many poor countries. There is no certainty that the emergence of new opportunities will bring about such changes, though it is notable that when external contacts are widely dispersed and reach large numbers of people, voluntary changes in attitude are frequent. But the uncertainty does not provide either a moral justification for the exercise of compulsion, nor does it in itself invalidate the foregoing analysis of the likely implications and results of its exercise. It may be noted parenthetically that efficient performance of the extensive range of well-recognised

[1] It seems necessary to insist here that the argument in the text is in no way inconsistent with recognition of an extensive range of necessary governmental tasks. This point is examined at length in essay 2.

[2] *The Theory of Economic Growth*, Homewood, Ill., 1955, p. 420.

and essential governmental tasks usually contributes substantially to the voluntary transformation of mores and modes of conduct harmful to material progress. The preoccupation with comprehensive planning has in fact inhibited the efficient performance of these essential functions of government.

Professor Myrdal's far-reaching and drastic suggestions are unlikely to be carried out. But the substantial movement in the direction envisaged by him which has already taken place, primarily through the imposition of close economic controls, has been generally harmful to material progress. The planning policies of south Asia reinforce the authoritarian traditions of those societies and thereby discourage experimentation, self-reliance and provision for the future. The controls restrict internal mobility and external contacts and thereby retard the modernisation of people's minds. They enlarge and intensify the power of politicians and civil servants over the people, which in turn provokes and increases political tension. In such situations energy and ambition are transferred from economic activity to political life. These various results of the politicisation of economic life are evident in south Asia from West Pakistan to Indonesia. And even if these controls brought about an increase in total output, which is most unlikely, this would be unrelated to consumer demands and thus to living standards. Indeed, as we have already noted, there is a large element of self-contradiction in suggestions for large-scale compulsion to improve living conditions.

7 Comprehensive Planning : Objectives and Corollaries

Like most other advocates of comprehensive planning Professor Myrdal simply assumes and asserts that this policy will improve general living standards. But he does not explain why people's material condition will be improved by the overriding of their decisions, the attempted removal of their ethnic or cultural identities, or the attempted compulsory transformation of their mores and conduct. Whether as an instrument for attempted remoulding of man and society, or as a system of state control of the economy, comprehensive planning implies large-scale state control of economic and social life. This result is a central and inescapable corollary of Professor Myrdal's system. Any rise in living standards is at best a doubtful, and more nearly a highly improbable or even impossible, result of the policy.

Certain aspects of Professor Myrdal's treatment suggest he may be more interested in this inevitable corollary of his proposals rather than in the improbable rise in living standards. Thus, while a rise in living standards is an explicit objective of Professor Myrdal's proposals, he refers to 'the difficult problem of how to squeeze and twist consumption so as to provide for development.'[1] Simultaneous insistence on higher living standards and on a reduction of consumption is a frequent theme of Professor Myrdal's writings, without any attempt to resolve the contradiction.[2]

The same conclusion is also suggested by Professor Myrdal's commendations of the economic achievements of the Soviet Union and communist China. Few readers of Professor Myrdal's book would suspect that after half a century of severe hardship and mass coercion living standards in the Soviet Union are extremely low – almost unimaginably so by western standards – in housing, clothing and consumer durables. (To give but two examples: the number of motor cars per thousand people in the Soviet Union is certainly less than one-half of the corresponding figure for *non-whites* in South Africa, and probably as little as one-quarter; another example is provided by the following episode: in September 1970 three men were sentenced in Moscow to terms of imprisonment of three, four and ten years for profitable black-market trading in second-hand clothes and chewing gum bought from western tourists. The leader of the 'gang', who received the ten-year sentence, was a university student in economics.) It is also an inescapable fact that ordinary, politically unexposed people have to be forcibly prevented from leaving the country. Like many other current commentators on Soviet-type economic systems, Professor Myrdal does not examine living standards in these economies, but refers to other criteria entirely unrelated to living standards when commending their achievements.[3] And his commendations of the Soviet system

---

[1] p. 717.

[2] Another instance of this contradiction is noted in the introduction to this volume. It may be that the argument implies that a reduction in current consumption makes possible additional investment and thus higher living standards in the future. However this is not a necessary sequence, especially in underdeveloped countries. For many reasons, some of which are set out in the appendix to essay 2, less jam today does not necessarily imply more jam tomorrow and indeed when brought about by compulsion is likely to imply less jam. If more jam tomorrow were both the likely result of the additional investment and were also valued by the population, the government could finance the expenditure from loans without inflationary creation of money.

[3] Professor Myrdal repeatedly and explicitly commends the rapid industrial expansion in the Soviet Union. More surprisingly, he also suggests that under the Soviet system it is still possible '. . . by and large, to maintain a fairly adequate level of nutrition' (p. 1918). Whether the level of nutrition in the Soviet Union of large numbers of the population, including the millions in labour camps, can be described as fairly adequate

contrast with his disregard of the rapid material progress and rise in general living standards in many other countries, as for instance Japan and Hong Kong, which are not mentioned in this context.

8 Provenance of Resources and the Role of the Intellectuals

Extensive remoulding of personal and social life and standardisation of material conditions in south Asia would require vast resources of personnel and money, and possibly specific equipment. Professor Myrdal does not discuss the provenance either of the required personnel or the physical and financial resources. They are certainly not available locally. Some of the personnel, as well as the finance and equipment, may come from abroad. But even then the resources would be unlikely to be sufficient for the forcible modernisation of people and society, though they may help to establish or maintain in power governments favoured by the supplying countries. In any event, the likely provenance of the required resources ought to be specified.

Although Professor Myrdal does not specify the personnel required for his ambitious policies, he clearly implies that it must come from among the ranks of westernised politicians, administrators and intellectuals. However, throughout south Asia these groups are weak both in numbers and in the popular respect and support they command. The intellectuals, so highly regarded by Professor Myrdal, are notably weak on both counts. These groups, especially the intellectuals, are unlikely to retain power in south Asia for long, even with external help, least of all the large-scale power called for by Professor Myrdal's objectives. They are likely to be confined to the role of court theologians, interpreting and developing the official ideology and rationalising and explaining official policy.

If such massive concentration of power does emerge in south Asia, it is likely to be in the hands of party administrators, or of the military,

is necessarily a subjective judgment. Professor Myrdal does not observe that whatever the (doubtful) validity of his remark, it can apply only to those who have survived the famines.

He also sees the system as expressing human solidarity (p. 687), as well as a radical egalitarianism (p. 1363). He quotes with approval the view of Mr K. M. Panikkar that the Soviet Five-Year Plans converted a semi-colonial economy into one of the leading industrial nations of the world, and that communist China promoted economic betterment of the country (p. 727). He also refers to an American writer who commends simultaneoulsy the west and the Soviet Union on their success in building a modern society (p. 1366). He does not mention the differences either in living standards or in the cost of building what he terms the modern society. There are many other generally favourable references to the Soviet system.

or of representatives of traditional groups, that is, people who know how to manage power or who command substantial local support. Members of the westernised group may help to pave the way for a totalitarian regime through their attempts to iron out differences in culture, beliefs, language, status, wealth and income, and also through their attempts to dissolve the bonding agents of society. But even if their activities eventually led to the emergence of a totalitarian state, they would not rule it.[1]

The claims made by the westernised politicians and intellectuals for the right to remake man and society in south Asia are certainly not modest. Professor Myrdal writes: 'Development plans often explicitly define planning as a comprehensive attempt to reform all unsatisfactory conditions.'[2] This role is one which has hitherto been attributed only to God, and even then only by religious fundamentalists. But Professor Myrdal takes the claim for it seriously.

Altogether, Professor Myrdal strongly sympathises with the westernised intellectuals, whom he regards as the enlightened leaders of progressive Asia. He repeatedly praises their selfless and rational attitudes, their efforts for and devotion to the general good, especially by the promotion of central planning. In general he sees them as possessing faculties superior to the rest of the population. As we have seen, he describes their ideas as 'cherished rites and philosophical thoughts' in contrast to the 'popular religious and superstititious beliefs of the rest of the population'. The westernised intellectuals alone, among the relatively well-to-do, escape Professor Myrdal's strictures.

This distribution of commendation and blame is the wrong way round. Traders, moneylenders, colonial administrators and even landowners have usually improved rather than damaged the material conditions of the local population. It has been the westernised intellectuals who have been largely behind the south Asian planning policies of recent decades which in India, Indonesia and Burma at any rate have inflicted much avoidable hardship on the poorest people. These policies have included such familiar measures as large-scale diversion of resources to costly prestige projects; the neglect of agriculture; the restriction of supplies of cheap consumer goods; the promotion of

---

[1] And if there has to be an extreme concentration of power it is perhaps better in the hands of people who would probably not go to the extremes to which the sense of superiority, self-righteousness and assumption of infallibility is likely to push the intellectuals in underdeveloped countries, perhaps even more than elsewhere. The sense of superiority of the intellectual over his fellow men, and his lack of sympathy for the rest of the population, are especially pronounced in poor countries.

[2] p. 711.

..ion; the introduction and operation of controls, with the attendant .mous windfalls to recipients of licences; and in Burma heavy .cial taxation of farmers.

It is thus inappropriate to single out this class for special commen-..ation, much less to envisage it as either a popular or a suitable instrument for the remaking of man and society in south Asia. Professor Myrdal greatly overrates not only the influence and standing of this class but also the extent and depth of their commitment to western habits and values. His sympathies may have been influenced by the concentration of his contacts with members of this class, and also by their readiness to claim a right and an ability to remould their fellow men, an approach which Professor Myrdal finds congenial.

9 *Planning as an Axiom*

Professor Myrdal treats as axiomatic the case for central planning, whether as extensive state control of economic activity or as a policy to remake man and society. Once a course of action is treated as axiomatically desirable then all subsequent developments can serve as an argument for extending the policy in scope, intensity and duration: progress as evidence of its success and failure as evidence of the need for its reinforcement.

For example Professor Myrdal explicitly notes some of the major deficiencies and adverse results of Indian planning. But he takes it for granted that it must be continued and indeed extended both in scope and in time. Here are a few passages which illustrate this consequence of the axiomatic treatment of the case for planning.

In short, one of the most serious shortcomings of policy in the countries in which comprehensive planning has been undertaken is the failure to plan more ambitiously and on a larger scale. What these countries need is a programme that will induce changes simultaneously in a great number of conditions that hold down their growth.[1]

It is for this reason that *underdeveloped countries cannot rely on a 'gradualist' approach* and that a growing number of economists have come to support the 'big plan'. Backwardness and poverty naturally make it difficult for a country to mobilise enough resources for a big plan, but they are precisely the reason why the plan has to be big in order to be effective.[2]

[1] p. 1205.
[2] p. 1899. Professor Myrdal's italics.

Planning for development must aim, as we have said, at jerking entire social system out of its low-level equilibrium and setting o cumulative process upwards. *There is economy in the big push.* Smal efforts mean waste.[1]

In a similar vein Professor Myrdal quotes Mr T. Mende, formerly a journalist, subsequently on the staff of UNCTAD:

They [the Asian governments] have attacked one problem at a time; I am not condemning them for it, because after all they had no personnel, they had no capital. I think it is important to realise that to create the general dynamism which makes people work wonders – you see sometimes in these communist countries that people do extraordinary things which statistically speaking are not expected of them – it is necessary that they go on attacking all the problems simultaneously and generate this almost superhuman enthusiasm which makes people do extraordinary things. This has not been attempted anywhere in south-east Asia.[2]

Neither Mr Mende nor Professor Myrdal make clear how the resources for these policies are to be provided. But the general sentiment behind these passages is reasonably clear. It is that the communist system achieves economic wonders, in contrast to the economic policies hitherto pursued in south-east Asia. The fact that it is in south-east Asia, especially Malaysia, and not in communist countries, that general living standards have risen in recent decades is ignored by them.

10 The Rural Sector

Professor Myrdal considers differences in income and status especially reprehensible and harmful in the rural sector. Apart from numerous shorter discussions, a chapter the length of a large book is devoted entirely to rural problems. Professor Myrdal takes for granted the case for land reform, a policy which he interprets loosely as redistribution of land in favour of tenants and agricultural labourers by partial or total expropriation of existing landowners. However, land for the land workers is no more self-evident than factories for manual workers or offices for office workers. Professor Myrdal does not make it clear whether the primary objective of land reform is to be greater equality of wealth or an increase in agricultural output or in total national income. These are three quite different objectives.

[1] p. 1901. Professor Myrdal's italics.
[2] pp. 1907–8.

f redistribution of wealth is a primary objective there is, of course, reason to single out landowners for partial confiscation. For this policy the appropriate criterion is total wealth or income, not ownership of land. Many landowners affected by the various land reform measures of south Asia which Professor Myrdal supports are far less well off than are many industrialists, traders or salary earners. The case for expropriating landowners in the pursuit of compulsory redistribution is even weaker in south Asia than elsewhere because there is generally no great landed wealth in the region and no heavy concentration of land ownership.

Nor is it at all clear how land reform would raise agricultural productivity and per capita income.[1] The main causes of rural poverty in south Asia are not lack of status or shortage of land, but low levels of technique, effort and capital, and these in turn largely reflect prevailing attitudes and mores adverse to material advance.

The comparative unimportance both of status and of shortage of land is strongly suggested by the poverty of peasant-owners, as well as of rural tenants and workers, in most of India and Pakistan and also in most of south-east Asia where land is generally abundant and where in many areas cultivable land is a free good. Professor Myrdal explicitly refers to the great poverty of the Malay peasants;[2] yet in Malaysia there is abundant unused but cultivable land.

Professor Myrdal condemns absentee landlords without enquiring why absentee ownership should be harmful in agriculture but not in the ownership of urban property or of joint stock enterprises. In fact absentee ownership often promotes the inflow of urban capital into rural areas. He also criticises share cropping at length for its alleged

---

[1] In India the case for land reform is sometimes supported on the ground that yields per acre on smaller properties are higher than on larger units, so that a break-up of larger properties would increase agricultural output. This argument is superficial. Even if yields of surface units on smaller properties were generally higher than on the larger units – which is, of course, not invariably true – this would not mean that they yield a higher net return for all the resources employed. If the cultivation of smaller properties were generally more economic in this fundamental sense, and their establishment would not encounter other obstacles, one would expect owners of larger units to sell off parts of their properties or rent them out in smaller units.

Academics have sometimes found it tempting to construct models which would 'explain' how land reform could materially promote economic advance. These models involve particular assumptions about the preferences of individuals, the alternative opportunities open to them, and techniques in agriculture. Such models, however, are as relevant to the political proposals for land reform as would be analogous models to 'explain' the expulsions of Indians from Burma, the Chinese from Indonesia, the Asians from East Africa, or, for that matter, the expropriations of the French and Soviet revolutions or the treatment of Jews in national socialist Germany.

[2] p. 382.

disincentive effects on tenants. This familiar criticism is again supe
ficial. It ignores the fact that in practice landlords often bear part of th
costs of running the farm. What is more important, it also fails to ask
why crop-sharing arrangements persist when both parties would gain
by alternative arrangements if share cropping really discouraged effort.[1]

Professor Myrdal freely castigates the landlord-tenant relationship
without making it clear why such a separation of ownership and management should be damaging. He suggests that high rents act as disincent-
ives to tenants, especially in discouraging improvement, investment
and effort, for fear that the rents would be raised. The lack of cogency
of this suggestion is borne out, however, by the fact that peasant-
owners as a group do not perform better in improvement and investment than do tenants on comparable holdings. (If they did, landlords
would have a strong incentive to sell land rather than to rent it.) The
attribution of low levels of investment and productivity to high rents
is further shown to be inappropriate by the presence of prosperous
and enterprising commercial firms in hired premises in cities in underdeveloped countries.

Land reform, which in the usual sense involves the partial or total
confiscation of the land from those who own it, is much more likely to
retard than to promote agricultural progress. It engenders a feeling of
insecurity, discourages investment, and transfers land to less enterprising and resourceful people. Of course, landless workers or tenants will
often propose redistribution of land, especially if it is already equipped.
Who would not accept a free gift?

Professor Myrdal notes the prevalence of high interest rates in the
rural sector. He condemns these without pausing to enquire how far
they reflect scarcity of capital, expectation of inflation, risk of default,
cost of administration and supervision of small loans, or monopoly
position of the lender.[2] Examination of these considerations is necessary
for worthwhile discussion of this subject. Professor Myrdal ignores all
these issues, as well as the effects of inflation both on the income of
lenders and on the burden of agricultural indebtedness.

[1] Professor Steven N.S. Cheung has shown in a careful and illuminating monograph, *The Theory of Share Tenancy* (Chicago, 1969), that share cropping does not lead to inefficient land use, and more generally that under private property rights different contractual arrangements do not imply different efficiencies of land use. Professor Cheung's discussion is supported both by analytical reasoning and by empirical evidence. See also P. K. Bardhan and T.N. Srinivasan, 'Cropsharing Tenancy in Agriculture: A Theoretical and Empirical Analysis', *American Economic Review*, March 1971.

[2] This last factor is the least likely, because there is no organised barrier to entry into moneylending in south Asia.

many parts of south Asia the role of moneylender is much more fundamental than is suggested either by Professor Myrdal or by the familiar, routine condemnations of the moneylender's activities. The moneylender frequently acts as a channel through which urban capital finances agricultural operations and exceptional items of expenditure of the rural population. The moneylender can borrow on his own security from the urban sector and lend to the peasants whom he knows personally. In many underdeveloped countries, including India, the small cultivator cannot borrow from a bank at all. He requires very small individual loans. The security he can offer is difficult to evaluate and verify by substantial organisations, which have to operate according to formal rules. For these reasons the cost of administering and supervising loans to small cultivators, and even more to other members of the rural population, is prohibitive except to lenders who operate informally, who know the borrowers personally, and who are prepared to face considerable risk of default on particular loans. On the other hand, banks will accept deposits from the peasant even though they do not readily lend to him. Thus the establishment of commercial banks in the countryside is apt to channel savings from agriculture to the urban sector.

It might be thought that cooperative credit societies could effectively perform the functions of the moneylender; but this is not usually so in underdeveloped countries. This is chiefly because there are ample opportunities in private economic activity for the available entrepreneurial talent, which is therefore not available cheaply for the management of cooperative societies. If the cooperative societies were economically viable it would not be necessary to subsidise them heavily, as is the case throughout south Asia and elsewhere in the underdeveloped world.[1]

The case for state support of cooperative enterprise is another policy which is taken for granted throughout the book. This case is again far from self-evident.

A cooperative society is a form of business organisation, the capital of which is provided by its suppliers or customers. There is no inherent merit in this form of organisation compared to state, municipal or private enterprise. If this form of organisation is suitable to the conditions of the society, it will survive without systematic state support granted at the expense of the rest of the community. This was the in nineteenth-century England, where the consumers' coop

---

[1] This matter is developed at length in essay 10.

movement progressed rapidly for various social and economic rea[...]
which do not apply in south Asia or probably anywhere in
underdeveloped world.

In south Asia, notably India, the cooperative societies are cooperati[...]
in name only, since their capital is often provided largely or even wholl[...]
from public funds and their operations are supervised or even administered by civil servants. Especially in India, state assistance to the
cooperatives has become very expensive, without specific economic or
social justification. On the other hand, the policy may, of course, have
served unacknowledged political objectives, in that it has created yet
another substantial class of people dependent on the state and its
agencies without being openly in the public sector.

Indeed, the content of Professor Myrdal's very long discussion of
rural problems amounts to little more than the assertion that agricultural backwardness reflects differences in income and wealth and the
operation of vested interests. Professor Myrdal does not examine the
operation either of the more deep-seated determinants of development
in this context, such as human faculties and motivations, nor the operation of the familiar variables of economic analysis. Worthwhile discussion of the determination of output, rents, prices and interest rates is
not possible without a modicum of systematic analysis.[1]

There are major policies in the region which obstruct agricultural progress. These policies are ignored by Professor Myrdal, or
mentioned by him only casually. An incomplete list of these includes
the large-scale diversion of resources into manufacturing, particularly
heavy industry (this is especially true of India); severe restrictions
on the import or even on the local production of cheap incentive goods
(India, Ceylon); restrictive licensing of transport and limitations on
the movement of crops (India); discriminatory heavy taxation on agriculture (Burma); refusal to alienate unused land for private cultivation
and the charging of rents by the authorities on alienated land which
bear no relation to fertility or location (Malaysia); and expulsion of
alien traders (Indonesia and Burma).

11 Expectations from Birth Control

Like many other contemporary observers, Professor Myrdal emphasises
the need for birth control as an instrument for the promotion of living

[1] The institutions of society do indeed affect prices, including rents and wages. They
do so by acting on supply and demand. Their influences cannot be understood without
some economic analysis.

ndards. In this context he does not advocate compulsion as he does
readily over certain other matters. Accordingly, his discussion of
irth control does not in this sense raise quite such fundamental political
and moral issues as some of his other proposals and suggestions. However, the subject is sufficiently prominent in these volumes, and of such
general interest, that it warrants discussion in the text of this essay
rather than in the appendix. The economic argument behind the vigorous advocacy of birth control is not self-evident. In particular it seems
very doubtful whether even extensive adoption of birth control would
bring about an appreciable improvement in living standards in the foreseeable future.

The case for and against birth control can be argued on several
distinct planes. It can be suggested that knowledge of contraception
enlarges people's range of choice in literally vital aspects of human
existence. It can also be legitimately urged that knowledge of contraception may in itself contribute to a change in attitudes, notably
increased interest in material well-being, and a sense of personal
responsibility for the economic position of oneself and one's family, in
other words a voluntary change in attitudes in directions helpful to
material progress. On the other side it can be argued that its widespread
adoption would increase further the sharp break in continuity with the
past, which is already promoted by other contemporary developments.
Sharp discontinuities in personal and social life often cause bewilderment or even outright confusion, as is evident in contemporary life.
Such results in turn often affect material progress unfavourably.
Various other arguments of wide social and political relevance could
be introduced on either side of the controversy. However, examination
of these issues would plainly be outside the scope of the present discussion. We are concerned here only with the effects on per capita incomes
of a significant reduction in the rate of increase in numbers.

The general living standards of a population reflect overall average
real productivity per head. A slowing down of the rate of population growth can affect living standards significantly in only two
conditions: first, if a reduced rate of population increase affects
age composition significantly when productivity per head differs
appreciably between age groups;[1] second, if relatively small changes

[1] Differences in the productivity of different age groups often go hand in hand with
differences in capital requirements. For instance, a relatively high proportion of children
in the population may increase capital requirements per head of the population,
especially for the construction of school buildings. However, the capital formation
represented by their construction, as well as the maintenance and operational costs of

in land and capital per head affect productivity substantially. This la
condition implies steeply falling marginal productivity of labour alon
both the extensive and intensive margins of cultivation. Either or both
such conditions may well exist. But they are not general and their
presence in specific instances would need to be supported by extensive
and detailed empirical evidence.

Moreover, any effect of a reduction in birth rate on the level of income
would be significant only after a long period. Changes in birth rates
refer to changes in rates of change of population which by themselves
can affect appreciably the level of income only over a time span of at
least several decades. As noted in essay 2, there are many authenticated
instances of a simultaneous decline in population growth and an
improvement in material conditions. But the former was not a principal
cause of the latter: both reflected changes in basic determinants of
development, especially changes in attitudes.

Like many other advocates of birth control Professor Myrdal refers
to its potential benefits largely in general, impressionistic terms. It
seems very unlikely that in south Asia reduction in population growth
would significantly improve living standards, much less that it would
lead to improvements comparable to those which would be brought
about by changes in abilities, motivations, institutions or official
policies. Here are some reasons for these suggestions.[1]

Large parts of south Asia, especially south-east Asia, are very
sparsely populated, including areas where the quality and configuration
of the land are not particularly unfavourable to material achievement
and progress. Yet the populations living there have exceedingly low
living standards in the conventional sense, indeed living standards
which are amongst the lowest in the region. Obvious examples include
northern Thailand, Borneo, Sumatra and Burma, but the same applies
also to parts of India and Pakistan.

Examples from other parts of the underdeveloped world, or from
countries which until quite recently were underdeveloped, suggest that

[1] The next two paragraphs restate in the present context parts of the argument of
essay 2, section 18.

schools and teacher's salaries are included in the calculation of the national income, and
hence in that of per capita incomes. Thus the need to satisfy these requirements does
not reduce conventionally measured incomes. But even when some of these items of
expenditure are not included in the measurement of the national income, or in the
standard of living, any net effect from this omission would be small in underdeveloped
countries, including those of south Asia, where a large proportion of children do not
attend school, or attend only for a relatively short period, and where school buildings
are simple and inexpensive structures.

operation of the fundamental determinants of development affect capita incomes and living standards to a far greater extent than do ferences in population density or rates of population increase. examples include experience in the West Indian islands, which are usually regarded as overpopulated but where the economic performance of poor Chinese and Lebanese immigrants usually far exceeds that of the West Indians. And the very rapid progress of such densely populated areas as Japan and Hong Kong also points in the same direction. Such examples could of course be readily multiplied.

Reduction in the rate of growth of numbers is unlikely appreciably to affect per capita incomes and cannot do so in the foreseeable future. Changes in attitudes could do so, and familiarity with contraception may serve as one of the agents in promoting such a change, although such an effect is speculative.[1] But this is a different issue from the question of the likely effects of a change in numbers.

12 *Economic Change in South-East Asia*

In support of his contention that enforced transformation of man and society throughout south Asia is necessary for economic advance, Professor Myrdal insists many times on the basic similarity of conditions throughout the vast region he surveys and in which he explicitly includes south-east Asia. Here are some examples:

There is a similarity in the basic economic conditions of the south Asian countries. . . . Social and economic inequalities are extreme, and are usually most pronounced in the poorest countries. All have endured a long period of stagnation in regard to the larger part of their economies.[2]

. . . we have already noted the lack of vigorous development in south Asia, except perhaps to some extent for the Philippines and lately for Thailand.[3]

Broadly speaking the basic cause [of the low level of intraregional trade] is itself the general lack of economic growth in these countries.[4]

---

[1] We have noted in essay 2, section 18 important observations by Mr J. Hajnal on the uniqueness of the European marriage and fertility patterns which emerged some three centuries ago. Improved knowledge of contraception was clearly not a major agent of this development.
[2] p. 46.
[3] p. 571.
[4] p. 607.

These allegations of stagnation throughout the region are pate
untrue, most evidently so for Malaysia but not only for that coun
Their untruth is plain from the most obvious evidence of the mater
progress of south-east Asia over the last eighty years. For instance, thei
were no rubber estates or smallholdings in south-east Asia before
1890. In fact, the whole economic history of south-east Asia since the
late nineteenth century contradicts several of Professor Myrdal's major
themes and assertions. I shall list only a random and incomplete
selection of these contradictions.

In many parts of that sub-region, especially but not only Malaysia and
Thailand, there has occurred very rapid and pervasive economic
advance, starting from a very low level. This progress refutes Professor
Myrdal's thesis of the vicious circle of poverty and stagnation, a major
theme of this book as of Professor Myrdal's other writings. It also
refutes his allegation that political dependence largely precludes
material advance. Moreover, Malaysia and Thailand are countries
with ethnically and culturally diverse populations. Yet Professor
Myrdal considers ethnical and cultural diversity as a significant obstacle
to material advance. Rapid material progress has thrown into relief
great differences between ethnic groups and persons in such economic
faculties as the willingness and ability to perceive and exploit economic
opportunity, as well as in industry, thrift and general resourcefulness.
These differences are, of course, especially obvious between the Chinese
immigrants into south-east Asia and other ethnic groups.

The originally penniless Chinese immigrants have accumulated vast
wealth in many parts of south-east Asia, often in areas which were
extremely backward when they arrived, so that their incomes were
plainly generated by themselves and not extracted from the local
populations. Moreover, the fact that they outdistanced not only the
local population but also the other immigrant groups is of much interest,
in that it shows the different economic performances of different ethnic
groups. And what adds further interest to the comparison is that, in
Malaysia for instance, the great majority of both the Chinese and the
Indian immigrants came as simple labourers.

The bulk of the acreage under rubber in south-east Asia is under Asian
ownership and has indeed been Asian-owned for decades. A rubber
tree takes six years to mature. The extensive Asian interest in the
industry conclusively refutes the assumption of many outside observers,

:luding Professor Myrdal, that private entrepreneurs in Asia are
nable or unwilling to take a long view.

There is hardly a major argument of Professor Myrdal's which is not
obviously and conclusively refuted by the experience of south-east
Asia over the last eighty years or so. It is refuted also by much of the
experience of the Indian subcontinent, but the evidence from south-east
Asia is especially obvious and clearcut.

13 Wealth, Inequality and Political Power

We have already noted Professor Myrdal's allegations that throughout
south Asia wealth and political power go together, especially that wealth
brings political power. But this is not generally so.

Political power is not necessary for the achievement of wealth. For
instance, in south-east Asia the poor immigrant groups, such as the
Chinese and the Indians in Malaysia, attained considerable prosperity
without political power and often in the face of political disabilities.
In this respect they were in the same position as were the Jews in
Europe and the Nonconformists in Britain.

Still less is it true that wealth is necessary for political power. The
Buddhist priesthood, so powerful in Ceylon and south-east Asia, and
some of the influential civil servants in India and Pakistan, are not rich.

Not only is wealth not necessary for political power, it does not even
assure political power. The relative prosperity of well-to-do Hindus in
Pakistan, of Moslems in India, of Indians in Burma, and of Chinese in
Indonesia, did not bring them political power, or even security. Indeed
their relative prosperity focused resentment on them. Here again there
is some similarity with the experience of the Jews in Europe.[1] Nor has the
great wealth of the Chinese in Malaysia endowed them with political
power. Indeed, this last fact is noted by Professor Myrdal, though he
does not attempt to reconcile the inconsistency.[2]

[1] Success in the pursuit of wealth is indeed rarely correlated with the achievement of
political power. The two objectives generally require different aptitudes. Moreover,
preoccupation with material prosperity not only diverts time and energy away from other
activities but also often stifles the faculties required for the discernment of political
realities.

[2] On this subject Professor Myrdal flatly contradicts himself within two consecutive
sentences. 'A greater Malaysian defence effort would entail larger sacrifices from the
wealthier classes of the population – a prospect they would not greet with enthusiasm;
this is the more important since these classes have a monopoly of political power everywhere except in Singapore. Most of these wealthier people are Chinese; the fact that
they are discriminated against politically cannot increase their enthusiasm to carry heavier
defence burdens' (p. 382).

Thus there is generally no connection between riches and politic power. And where they are connected, the causal relationship i generally very different from that suggested by Professor Myrdal, and indeed is more nearly the opposite of that envisaged by him. Malay sultans and Indian princes are more prosperous than most of their compatriots: political and military power brought them prosperity, not prosperity political power. The same applies often to the beneficiaries of import licensing and foreign exchange licensing in many south Asian countries. Those who, like Professor Myrdal, extol political action and dislike economic success and independent and prosperous people, are especially apt to get any causal relation between riches and power the wrong way round.

Professor Myrdal's preoccupation with political forces as alleged determinants of material achievement leads him to attribute to past colonial rule significant responsibility for the material backwardness of south Asia. He does not attempt to reconcile such suggestions with the extreme backwardness of countries in Asia and elsewhere in the underdeveloped world which have never been colonies.

Professor Myrdal specifically blames colonial rule both for attempting to maintain the *status quo*, that is the existing social organisations and institutions,[1] and also for destroying them.[2] He also argues repeatedly that the construction of an infrastructure is necessary for development. Yet he quotes with approval suggestions that the railways built by colonial powers or financed externally drained the wealth out of these countries by carrying export products.[3] He also instances the concentration of French portfolio investment in French Indo-China on infrastructure projects as an example of the refusal of private capital to finance risky investments.[4]

The causal relationship between poverty and colonial status is generally the reverse of that envisaged by Professor Myrdal. The poverty of some countries resulted in their becoming colonies; their poverty was not caused by their colonial status. Colonial rule generally promoted material advance, especially a rise in living standards.

---

[1] 'Indeed, it was part of colonial policy not to "disturb the natives", but to preserve a tranquil environment for a burgeoning economic activity of primary benefit to the industrialised west' (p. 452).

[2] 'Furthermore, the inherited institutional forms of social organisation [in Burma] were disturbed or destroyed by colonial rule. . . . British rule led to a very rapid and almost complete breakdown of all popular and cooperative activities, except to a minor extent in the smallest unit, the village' (p. 859).

[3] p. 125.

[4] p. 617.

...sides criticism of the metropolitan powers and of the developed ...tries of the west, the treatment is characterised by hostility to ...sperous persons and groups, including hostility to those who started ...ry poor, and by suggestions of their responsibility for the poverty of ...e rest of the society. There are innumerable examples of sneer and ...nnuendo at the expense of all these groups.

With the exception of the civil servants and the intellectuals, the more successful groups are always said to control, dominate or monopolise the activities and sectors in which they are engaged. It would be more appropriate to say that they have initiated, generated or developed them. Further, as we have already noted in a different context, Professor Myrdal generally writes or implies that the incomes of better-off people are gratuitously received or even extracted from the rest of the population rather than earned or produced by the recipients. This presentation may reflect in part the Marxist idea that property incomes imply exploitation and that service industries are unproductive.

14 *Absence of Time Perspective*

Much of the discussion is without a time perspective or dimension. Professor Myrdal frequently, indeed generally, writes or implies that the development of the west began in the eighteenth or even in the nineteenth century.[1] The very long and complex period of economic evolution in the west before the industrial revolution is generally ignored. Professor Myrdal also neglects the history of south Asia before the nineteenth century or sometimes even the history of a country prior to political independence. Yet neither the present position nor the development prospects of India and Pakistan can be appreciated without an understanding of the past. In particular, the tenacity of Hindu beliefs and mores cannot be understood without it.

Professor Myrdal often mentions the differences in what he terms the initial conditions of development between the western world in the eighteenth and nineteenth centuries and the present-day underdeveloped countries. He writes that these initial conditions are much less

[1] For instance, pp. 582, 685–6, 705, 715 and 1942.

An unhistorical approach is evident throughout the book. It is also explicitly acknowledged: 'We realise that the lack of historical depth in our approach restricts our understanding of the social reality we are investigating. This again is due solely to the practical limitations of time, research facilities, and technical competence' (p. 43). These factors may well partly explain the absence of time dimension and the unhistorical approach of the book. But the recognition of these defects does not affect their fundamental character.

favourable to the underdeveloped countries, especially because allegedly less buoyant international trade. But it is misleading to to the situation in eighteenth- and nineteenth-century Europe representing initial conditions in development. By then the west w pervaded by the attitudes and institutions appropriate to an exchang economy and a technical age to a far greater extent than is south Asi today. These attitudes and institutions had emerged gradually over a period of eight centuries. No such secular development has taken place in south Asia, which largely explains the difference in the economic climate of Europe in the eighteenth and nineteenth centuries and that of present-day south Asia. The opportunities afforded by external contacts, especially by international trade and by the availability of more advanced technical knowledge elsewhere, favour south Asia much more than they did the west in the eighteenth and nineteenth centuries for reasons already stated. But these favourable external factors are much less important than the domestic determinants of development.

The absence of the time perspective directly bears on Professor Myrdal's main theme. He does not specify the time horizon he has in mind for the achievement of his reforms. He mostly implies great urgency for radical changes in attitudes; instant reform so to speak. Thus in his treatment both the past and the future are drastically foreshortened.[1] The alleged or implied necessity for immediate and thoroughgoing changes, without specific discussion of their method, cost and feasibility, is characteristic of much contemporary advocacy of drastic policies. The alleged necessity of urgent action serves as justification for the adoption of coercion.

15 Blueprint for the Future

Professor Myrdal's book deals with real and important issues, even immense issues, and not with trivial matters. It is therefore regrettable that in spite of its length and diversity the book is not a treatise on

[1] 'The south Asian countries are in a hurry and need the modern infrastructure in order to mobilise popular support for planning and development. . . . The sense of urgency is logical, given the low economic levels and the rapid and accelerating population increase in these countries' (p. 869). Professor Myrdal also repeatedly quotes Nehru (for instance, pp. 716 and 869) on the necessity for speedy action.

How can it be said that these countries are in a hurry, when the population does not wish to change its ways, as Professor Myrdal himself repeatedly recognises? Once again the treatment of a population as a single personified entity and its identification with the government obscures the fundamental issues and dilemmas.

ie economies of south Asia; both in substance and presentation t is primarily a politicial pamphlet, albeit of well over a million words.

The primary thrust of the pamphlet is a plea for all-powerful government, dedicated to remaking people and society. The secondary thrust, related to the first, is the emphasis on the alleged responsibility of more prosperous persons, groups and countries for the poverty of the rest.

Asian Drama may well become one of those books, like Lenin's *Imperialism* in a related field, which are read by few, but which influence many. Its forbidding size must restrict its readership, even though its price is relatively low and there is also a paperback edition. The sheer bulk of the three volumes, the diversity of the topics, the disjointed treatment, the cumbersome meandering style, the inclusion of a mass of irrelevant material, and the frequent contradictions, must all reduce the number of readers who receive its important message on first-hand reading or on casual perusal. And if readers are likely to be few, re-readers will be fewer still. However, the central argument is sufficiently congenial to important political, administrative and intellectual interests, and sufficiently in tune with the spirit of the age, to make it probable that the message will eventually be received widely, if only indirectly.

That message, as we have said, is for the replacement of human society by a standardised mass, subject to rulers with unlimited power. Such a result is the logical outcome of Professor Myrdal's conception of man and society. By decrying cultural, ethnic, religious and economic differences, and incessantly inveighing against discrimination, he seeks to build a society which is profoundly dehumanised. A society without distinction, differentiation and discrimination, except between subjects and ruler, would be more akin to that of the insects.

Professor Myrdal's practice of regarding poorer people as helpless victims of society is also dehumanising, as it suggests that persons neither have nor should have any choice, control or responsibility in matters which affect their position and prospects. His approach and proposals are examples of the inhumanity of many professed, or should one say professional, humanitarians. He first dehumanises people and then envisages an inhuman destiny for them.

Although the message for a thoroughgoing transformation of man and society by coercive action is drastic, it is, of course, not novel. The Soviet regime has already made the attempt, and in so doing has anticipated Professor Myrdal's major aspirations. That society has been

succinctly described by Mr T. Szamuely in an article in the *Spectato*
on the 50th anniversary of the Bolshevik revolution:

Nothing – no barrier, no law, no institution, no tradition, no association, no property rights, no interest group – stood between him [the individual] and the omnipotent state. The state is the sole employer – that goes without saying. But the state is also the trade union, the pensions board, the arbitration committee, the landlord, the sports manager, the sole educator, the sole newspaper proprietor, the sole publisher, the film producer, the theatre director, the neighbourhood grocer, the hotelier, the Academy of Sciences, the dry cleaner, the youth club. It is the policeman, judge, jury, prosecutor and executioner, all in one. It codifies not only the laws, but the moral standards – and changes them at will. And, as laid down by Lenin, there can be no restraints, no limitations upon the untrammelled power of the state.[1]

In the absence of substantial external intervention a society of this kind is unlikely to emerge in south Asia in the foreseeable future. Without external conquest or large-scale inflow of external resources in support of local governments with totalitarian ambitions, matters are unlikely to be pressed much beyond the present extent of economic planning in south Asia, that is beyond the close control of economic activity outside subsistence agriculture. Such policies will continue to waste resources, inhibit material advance, and inflict hardship. But the results of the policies proposed by Professor Myrdal would be much more serious. Insistence on forcible destruction or erosion of deeply and intensely felt values and beliefs, strongly held attitudes, cherished traditions and distinctions, long practised ways of living and modes of conduct, and respected institutions, as well as of accepted or even desired cultural, social and economic differences, might well bring about total spiritual and moral collapse of the people subjected to such destructive treatment.

---

[1] 'Russia Fifty Years After', *Spectator*, London, 20 October 1967. The possibilities of the emergence of such a society are clearly envisaged in some celebrated passages in Tocqueville's *Ancien Regime*, especially chapters xv–xx. Some less familiar observations in Charles Dickens' last book, published almost exactly a century ago, aptly describe the attitudes and activities of philanthropists with totalitarian leanings (*The Mystery of Edwin Drood*, chapter 6).

APPENDIX: TECHNICAL APPARATUS AND SOME PREOCCUPATIONS
OF THE BOOK

Methodology and terminology. The need for transforming man and society, and the required pursuit of central planning, represents the principal argument of the book. Among the many supporting and related themes, arguments and topics, discussions on methodology are prominent, as they usually are in Professor Myrdal's writings. The main emphasis in this field is his insistence that explicit statement of value premises is necessary and apparently also sufficient to establish objectivity in social study. On the contrary it is neither. Any such statement is irrelevant to the validity of scholarly argument and discussion, which depends on logical consistency and conformity with empirical evidence, which in turn have nothing to do with value premises. Nor does a statement of value premises confer scientific merit, rigour or objectivity on a discussion. Fundamentalist history and theology, Leninist economics and Nazi biology do not become valid if the implicit value premises behind them are made explicit.

Countless examples in this book demonstrate that statement of value premises does not ensure objectivity, rigour or consistency. Some defects of Professor Myrdal's general treatment have already been noted, and a long though still incomplete list of factual misstatements and elementary technical errors is presented later in this appendix. Professor Myrdal's principal value premises, such as rationality, modernisation, equality, nondiscrimination among others, are in any case hopelessly vague or even meaningless. And his treatment of them is inconsistent and self-contradictory in that his interpretation of the concepts shifts and in that several of the concepts are mutually incompatible as objectives of policy.

There are also major shortcomings in the terminology. For instance, industrialisation is used indiscriminately to denote the growth of manufacturing activity as part of the secular growth of an economy, but more usually to denote a policy of state subsidisation or state operation of manufacturing. The term investment is also used indiscriminately and at times ambiguously to refer to a transfer of resources from consumption, or to increased resources from improved economic performance, or to resources supplied externally. These are distinctions of analytical and practical significance.

The use of what may be called inappropriate personification is another characteristic of the treatment. For instance, Professor Myrdal writes: . . . south Asia is attempting to close a yawning gap in attitudes and institutions [between it and the west].'[1] But who or what is south Asia?

[1] p. 691.

Here Professor Myrdal implies an identity of interests and uniformity of attitudes throughout south Asia, and he frequently implies that official statements represent and reflect such an identity and uniformity. But as is amply clear from numerous statements throughout the book (including the paragraph immediately preceding the phrase just quoted), there is no such identity or homogeneity. If there were, the drastic measures of standardisation proposed by Professor Myrdal would, of course, be unnecessary. Indeed, differences in outlook, objectives and interests, notably between the intellectuals and the rest of the community, is a major preoccupation of the book.

The practice of personifying large groups leads Professor Myrdal into self-contradiction even within one page. For instance, he writes that all advocates of state economic planning in south Asia agree that it should express the will of the nation as a whole; and he writes in the next paragraph that most people in south Asia are traditionalists in outlook and want to keep things as they are.[1]

Another misleading practice of Professor Myrdal is related to this personification of large groups. This is the habit of referring to a situation as monopolistic when an activity is largely handled by a distinct ethnic group, as for instance the prominence of Chinese in the wholesale and retail trades in certain countries in south-east Asia, or the former prominence of Indian traders in Burma. The indiscriminate use of the term monopoly obscures the essential differences between situations in which decision-making is effectively centralised, which makes possible organised control of supply and restriction on entry, and the wholly different situations when these conditions are absent. There are many other instances in this book where the use of arbitrary and vague terminology obscures or even confuses fundamental differences between situations. And in many places the effects of vague terminology are compounded by the failure to make clear whether a statement refers to actual, probable or possible occurrences, or whether in particular instances Professor Myrdal shares the view he quotes.

Professor Myrdal also frequently implies that his vague and abstract concepts are clear and firm, whereas they are susceptible to widely different, shifting, or even contradictory interpretations. For instance, he explicitly approves of Mr Tarlok Singh's allegedly clearcut support of social justice as a prerequisite of economic progress.

Tarlok Singh, the leading spirit of the Indian Planning Commission since its inception, in a radio discussion with Professor M. N. Srinivas, after some wavering came through with a clearcut statement in the same vein

Professor Srinivas: 'You would then agree with me, Mr Tarlok Singh, that justice is the prerequisite of economic progress?'

[1] p. 710.

Tarlok Singh: 'Yes, economic progress is essential to social justice and ocial justice to economic progress.'[1]

The notion of social justice is completely vague, not to say meaningless, though the context here suggests that social justice is to be interpreted as state-imposed standardisation of material conditions. Such a policy is certainly not a condition of economic development and is indeed, as we have seen, very likely to inhibit it. Some people may, however, still favour such a policy for other reasons. Those who do face a dilemma between two objectives, namely improvement of living standards, and standardisation of conditions, the latter being misleadingly termed social justice. Professor Myrdal ignores this dilemma; yet he freely castigates those who in his view refuse to face up to unpalatable choices.

Professor Myrdal's extensive use of loose and shifting terminology is one of the many examples in this book of the intellectual anarchy and barbarism brought about by neglect or rejection of the distinction between positive and normative economics. The defects of terminology, method, description and analysis are obscured by the unwarranted claim that statement of value premises, even of completely vague and open-ended premises, somehow promotes objectivity. As we have seen this claim is untrue.

We shall have noted in essay 4 certain results and implications of the corruption of language. In this section we instanced Professor Myrdal's use of shifting and arbitrary terminology, which is indeed a characteristic of development literature. The consequences of this practice bear a curious resemblance to the implications of the forcible removal of social and cultural differences. Arbitrary and shifting terminology corrupts the language and undermines that effective discussion and communication on which a moderately free society depends and without which it is likely to be replaced by a command system. The same outcome is also the result of the enforced removal of all differences and distinctions between people except those between rulers and subjects. Effective discussion is impossible between all-powerful rulers and their impotent subjects, and especially so when these subjects are a standardised, undifferentiated mass.

Rejection of economic analysis and empirical evidence. In Professor Myrdal's book, which is addressed both to an academic and a lay readership, there are countless elementary mistakes of analysis and misstatements of fact, which are moverover of a kind often found in widely publicised writings on economic development. Only a few examples can be noted here.

In the treatment of many economic issues and phenomena, relevant and often elementary analysis is disregarded or even dismissed rather

[1] p. 748.

contemptuously. For instance Professor Myrdal writes: 'Higher prices would not call forth greater production as economists reared in western thinking are inclined to suppose.'[1] Why then do governments throughout the region offer higher prices for products whose cultivation they wish to encourage, and why do they protect or otherwise subsidise manufacturing activities they wish to promote? One may readily recognise the importance and relevance of institutional factors as parameters of economic activity. But this recognition does not warrant neglect of simple analysis and obvious empirical evidence.[2]

The discussion of import substitution and industrialisation and the development of heavy industry is almost entirely in physical terms, without any economic analysis and with hardly any references to costs of production and transport or to consumer demand.[3] And, as already noted, there is practically no economic analysis in the discussion of the rural sector, which is by far the largest sector of the economies of south Asia. Prices and incomes, especially in agriculture, are treated as being determined directly by institutions, power structures, custom, convention, bargaining power and the like, without even simple analysis of supply and demand and of their parameters (though these parameters may of course include some of the institutional influences noted by Professor Myrdal). Balance of payments problems and export prospects and earnings are discussed practically throughout without mention of the level of domestic money incomes and prices, monetary or fiscal policies or rates of exchange. Thus, he writes:

Foreign exchange difficulties are not a temporary exigency but a normal and permanent condition in very poor countries, pressing economic development to the limit set by all the attendant circumstances.[4]

The italics are Professor Myrdal's. This passage seems to mean, if anything, that exchange difficulties are unavoidable in the course of the rapid economic development of poor countries. This assertion is untrue, and no amount of italicising will make it true. There are innumerable examples of rapid economic progress of poor countries without exchange difficulties. The frequent balance of payment problems of underdeveloped countries in recent years reflect inflationary monetary and fiscal policies in conditions of fixed rates of exchange.

An alleged lack of suitable economic abilities in the peoples of the region and especially a deficiency of constructive entrepreneurship is one of

[1] p. 1374.
[2] If producers incur costs and personal incomes are limited (both of which follow from the limitation of resources) demand and supply must be functionally related to prices though they may be unresponsive over certain price ranges, especially in the short period.
[3] ch. 24.
[4] p. 2082.

Professor Myrdal's recurrent themes. In his view, these deficiencies necessitate state planning for the development of a variety of activities and enterprises. But he does not ask whether those activities and enterprises developed under state auspices because of alleged lack of private initiative are beneficial or economically efficient; he does not refer either to the costs of these activities and enterprises or to the demand for the output. Nor does he enquire how the state will secure a supply of the necessary abilities, especially a supply of entrepreneurial talent, in the local population.[1]

The frequent references to a supposedly general social and economic rigidity and the effects of this rigidity on progress throughout the region are mostly either ambiguous or simply untrue. Thus:

In south Asia, the inequalities relevant to prospects for economic advance are more deep-seated. They concern not only differences in income, but, more important, differences in status, and in control over productive assets . . . the south Asian case may thus be one in which *the promotion of social and economic equality is a precondition for attaining substantial long-term increases in production.*[2]

The italics are again Professor Myrdal's. This suggestion is in conflict with experience throughout the area, most obviously so for south-east Asia.

Again:

In south Asia, a person's social and economic position tends to be static; the limitations on upward movements are severe.[3]

This statement is certainly not true for south-east Asia, as is obvious from the experience of large numbers of the Chinese and Indian communities there.

The absence of elementary analysis and the disregard of obvious empirical evidence are especially noteworthy in a book which proposes drastic remodelling of man and society. Such a conjunction of neglect of analysis and disregard of empirical evidence, combined with drastic

[1] This point is of general relevance to discussions on development policy. But it is especially pertinent to Professor Myrdal's treatment since he so frequently insists that human beings are equally endowed by nature. Of course they are not. But if they were, how could there be differences in entrepreneurial aptitudes within and between communities?

There are of course many thousands of traders or industrialists in the area. Professor Myrdal quotes Dr T.H. Silcock as saying 'Malaya suffers from an excess rather than a deficiency of enterprise.' Professor Myrdal adds that Dr Silcock 'has to be understood to mean that ideally the overflowing enterprise should be differently directed' (p. 719).

The presence of entrepreneurship in south Asia is indicated also by the imposition of state controls over many activities regarded as undesirable by the political authorities and also by Professor Myrdal. These controls are imposed to prevent rapid expansion of activities which are profitable, but which the authorities wish to discourage, a sequence which implies people's readiness to respond to economic opportunities.

[2] p. 1369.

[3] p. 567.

proposals for revolutionary change, is frequently found in the development literature, but rarely in the extreme form of this book.

External factors and local backwardness. Professor Myrdal discusses international trade and capital flows at some length, especially in chapter 13. The main emphasis is on the allegedly unfavourable external market conditions which the region faces, notably unfavourable and persistently deteriorating terms of trade; low price and income elasticity of export demand, and also competition from substitutes for south Asian exports; and a declining share in world trade. Both in substance and in presentation Professor Myrdal's treatment of these topics is practically identical with the discussion of the same topics by the international organisations, especially by the United Nations Conference on Trade and Development (UNCTAD). The principal ideas of UNCTAD are examined at length in essay 6; thus we shall note them in this appendix only relatively briefly.

Professor Myrdal refers only to the commodity terms of trade, nowhere mentioning the factoral or the income terms of trade, which are in this context the concepts relevant to welfare. The allegations of low price elasticity of export demand are not reconciled with references to the competition from substitutes; nor is it explained why a low price elasticity of demand should be necessarily adverse when the converse is certainly possible and may even be likely. (The bulk of total world capacity and of current production of the major exports from the region is located in a few countries, a situation which facilitates concerted action by governments to curtail exports, a course of action which increases export proceeds if the demand is price inelastic; such concerted action has been undertaken at various times in the region, and is currently being undertaken in the restriction of exports of tin.)

Professor Myrdal does not adduce any evidence in support of his allegations of a low income elasticity of export demand. These allegations are almost certainly invalid for major exports of the region, such as rubber, tin, tea and coconut products. No one knows what is the average income elasticity of demand for the total exports from this huge region. In any case, their diversity makes aggregation largely meaningless, especially since some countries are major net importers of the same commodity (for instance rice) of which others are major net exporters. Speculation about the average income elasticity of demand for the exports from this region is thus of little interest, though it can be said with confidence that with the possible exception of rice the income elasticity of demand for the major exports of the region is not negative (the condition in which the commodity terms of trade would deteriorate for certain when per capita incomes rise in importing countries). And it is also worth noting that for most of the region even the commodity terms of trade have in recent years

more favourable than at almost any time in the past for which
ormation is available. And the factoral terms of trade have been much
ore favourable than the commodity terms.

Nor does Professor Myrdal adduce any evidence for the contention
that the share of the region in world trade has declined, or indicate over
what period the decline is supposed to have occurred. And he does not
note that references to the volume of exports, or to the share of a country
or region in international trade, make little economic sense without
examination of the monetary and fiscal policy and of other factors affecting
the domestic use of commodities previously exported, or of resources
used in the production of these commodities.

These shortcomings are familiar from UNCTAD discussions and from
similar sources. But at times Professor Myrdal presses into service
unusual arguments or forms of presentation to support the contention
that the terms of trade always move against underdeveloped countries
and primary producers, and that somehow the west is responsible for this
unfavourable development, as well as for other damaging influences.
For instance, he writes:

During periods of rising demand in the west, prices of both primary
products and manufactured goods tend to rise; but when aggregate
demand slackens, the former fall while the latter do not, at least not to the
same extent. It is not entirely clear whether the prices of developmental
imports will rise less sharply than the prices of the primary exports of
south Asia during an expansion of economic activity in the west, but it is
apparent that the latter will fall more sharply during a contraction.[1]

If these suggestions were valid the terms of trade of primary producers and
of the underdeveloped world would worsen persistently, and would now
be at their nadir, where as in fact they are unusually favourable.

On the same page Professor Myrdal writes:

The superior adaptability of the more developed countries enables them to
respond more effectively and rapidly to changes in relative prices. Thus
the advanced countries take a larger share of the poorer countries' output
when prices are favourable, but leave them to 'bear the brunt of years of
low prices'.[2]

This passage is so obscure that it defies analysis. One would think that by
taking a larger share of the output of the underdeveloped countries
when prices are favourable, the developed countries confer a special
benefit on them. However, the passage plainly tries to convey the
opposite idea, namely that the activities of the developed countries (that

[1] p. 611.
[2] Ibid.

is of the west) damage the poor countries. Vague though the reason
is, the emotional response this characteristic passage is likely to elici.
clear.

Again, the importance of western Europe and North America a
trading partners of south Asia is said to be a legacy of the colonial perio
and, by implication, to affect the region adversely.[1] In fact, the large and
prosperous economies of North America and western Europe have for
generations been of great material benefit to the region as the principal
markets for its exports and as sources of ideas, skills, capital and imported
commodities. For instance, how could the rubber industry which has
transformed south-east Asia have developed without the motor car
industry of North America and western Europe?

There are indeed countless references to the alleged responsibility
of the west for the material backwardness of south Asia, especially through
colonialism; through the difficulties placed in the way of the progress of
south Asia by the policies or mere presence of the industrialised countries;
and through the alleged adverse developments in the markets for their
exports. In fact, the tenor of most of the long chapter on foreign trade
and capital flows is that these external factors bear a major share of blame
for the poverty of south Asia.

Professor Myrdal also writes that western influences have obstructed
cooperation and integration within south Asia. He does not explain how
closer collaboration among south Asian countries would have occurred
in the absence of western influence, when in fact the transport communication systems of south Asia were established either by colonial
governments (including the government of India) or by companies
financed by the west. Nor does he explain how closer integration would
have promoted material progress. As we have already noted, the material
poverty of south Asia reflects the aptitudes, mores and institutions of its
peoples (and at times also the pursuit of government policies damaging to
economic development). These familiar major determinants of material
progress are not examined by Professor Myrdal in the context of this
argument.[2] The relative backwardness of the areas with few foreign contacts shows how misplaced is Professor Myrdal's emphasis on adverse
external factors.

In fact, the current international economic scene presents exceptional
opportunities for underdeveloped countries. For instance, they can now
benefit from the fruits of technical progress elsewhere, which was not
open to the west at the time of the industrial revolution, for the simple
reason that the western countries were technically far ahead of the rest of
the world at that time. And in spite of various restrictions on international

[1] pp. 594–5.
[2] In other parts of the book Professor Myrdal recognises that the main determinants
of development are domestic.

trade, the advanced countries offer huge markets and represent large and varied sources of supply for the underdeveloped countries, conditions which were not present in the eighteenth and nineteenth centuries.

Allegations that external economic relations damage underdeveloped countries often actually promote policies in these countries, such as restrictions on external economic contacts, which retard their development. They also divert attention from domestic causes for their backwardness, such as objectives, motivations and social institutions, and official policies adverse to material progress. And the suggestion that the more prosperous countries have caused the poverty of the rest tends to translate itself into the idea that at home, too, the more prosperous people are responsible for the poverty of the others, an idea which conduces to political tension and leads to policies damaging to material progress. Finally, such allegations often also obscure the presence of wide discrepancies between the aims of the politicians and planners and the interests and concerns of the people at large: the former often derive political and economic benefits from controls on foreign trade which damage the material interests of the people.

Selection of references and sources. We noted in the introduction to this volume that some of the most influential and widely publicised ideas in the development literature do not represent the unanimous opinion of economists in this field, that indeed there are strong dissenting views, and that the prominence of these ideas in both academic and public discussion has been promoted by the disregard of contrary opinions.

Professor Myrdal's book presents a notable example of this situation. He consistently ignores critical and contrary opinions, even when they are both authoritative and accessible. There are in this book many hundreds and possibly thousands of references to sources, writers and experts on Indian economic policy, especially planning. Many of these references are really dredged up, such as private communications, unpublished theses and popular newspaper articles, always in support of central planning and its components. The critics are ignored, or dismissed in general terms as irrational or obscurantist elements, or as mouthpieces of vested interests. Those so ignored include Professor Shenoy (not mentioned in the book), a systematic and consistent critic of Indian planning policy, who as a member of the Indian government's advisory panel of economists submitted a memorandum of dissent on the Second Five-Year Plan the reasoning of which was subsequently completely vindicated. To its credit, the Indian government officially published this memorandum, thereby showing itself more liberal and objective than Professor Myrdal. Other un-persons include Mr Nirad C. Chaudhuri, that most penetrating observer of the Indian scene, whose opinions on the history and social climate of India and on the activities of visiting western economists bear on this book at many points. Two Indian periodicals, *The Economic Weekly* (moderately left) and *Link* (strongly left) are quoted many times, but the more conservative *Swarajya* and *Commerce* are not mentioned. There are also a number of quotations from the international agencies in support of the argument, some so vague and banal that their reproduction is comic.

5 A Critique of UNCTAD[1]

The ideas canvassed by the United Nations Conference on Trade and Development (UNCTAD) have come to colour much of the discussion on underdeveloped countries and on development policy. These ideas are best studied in the documentation of the first conference in Geneva in 1964.

The most influential document, *Towards a New Trade Policy for Development*, usually known as the Prebisch Report, was published before the proceedings opened. It set the tone for the conference, largely determined its agenda, and substantially influenced its proposals. Dr Rául Prebisch, former executive secretary of the United Nations Economic Commission for Latin America (ECLA), became the first secretary-general of UNCTAD and was head of the permanent secretariat until 1968. The report offers a succinct guide to the ideas of UNCTAD, only some of which can be discussed in this essay. But many other topics raised at UNCTAD are discussed elsewhere in this volume, for example the vicious circle of poverty, in essay 1, and the allegedly ever-widening inequality of incomes, also in essay 1. The papers and proceedings of the conference were published in seven volumes in 1964. The most important were volume 1, *Trade and Development: Final Act and Report*, and volume 2, *Trade and Development: Policy Statements*. These volumes formed the background and starting point for the second UNCTAD in Delhi in 1968.

There is a large measure of unity in the ideas and recommendations of the Prebisch Report, and the subsequent UNCTAD literature. For this reason, and also because so much of this literature is exceedingly vague, I have not quoted specific passages in the text of this essay except

---

[1] The original version of this essay appeared under the title 'UNCTAD and Africa', a study which appeared in *Afrika Spectrum*, 1967/2, published by the Deutsches Institut für Afrikaforschung, Hamburg, at whose invitation it was written. The essay has been greatly enlarged. I am much indebted to Professor Harry G. Johnson for helpful suggestions.

Sections 4 and 5 of this essay are more technical than the general level of discussion in this volume; the nontechnical reader may wish therefore to omit them.

in footnotes; instead I have appended extended passages from t.
Prebisch Report.[1]

1 *Summary of the Main UNCTAD Ideas*

The principal components of the UNCTAD ideas which served as the
basis of the major recommendations of the first conference were as
follows:

The 5 per cent annual growth rate envisaged for the underdeveloped
world in the United Nations Development Decade is a bare minimum
and an inadequate target in view of the extremely low living standards,
near stagnation, rapid population growth, and the ever-widening inequality of incomes between developed and underdeveloped countries.
Its attainment depends critically on an increase in investment expenditure and in the volume of imports, especially of investment goods, in
the underdeveloped world. Even if enough investment could be secured
without external help, which is improbable, the problem would still
not be solved because the export earnings of underdeveloped countries
are not enough for the required imports. The difference between imports
required for minimum acceptable growth on the one hand, and export
proceeds on the other, is termed the trade gap, estimated at about 20
billion dollars for the early 1970s. The chronic payments difficulties of
underdeveloped countries reflect the monetary counterpart of the
problem of securing the imports required for an adequate rate of
development.

The attainment of this modest and indeed inadequate objective
is endangered by external factors outside the control of underdeveloped
countries. External market conditions are held largely responsible for
the inability of these countries to earn sufficient foreign exchange. The
principal adverse factor is the persistent and inherent long-term
deterioration in the terms of trade of underdeveloped countries (a
major theme of the Prebisch Report and of UNCTAD literature as a
whole). This deterioration is in turn due to several factors: the large
increases in the volume of primary production, as a result both of
technical advance and of rapid increases in population in the producing
countries; the relatively stagnant demand for the exports of primary
products, which reflects both low income elasticity of demand for these

---

[1] Even the proposals of UNCTAD are frequently too vague and long-winded to
justify quotation. References to proposals are generally to resolutions passed at the
conference.

orts (a demand which increases less than proportionately to increased ome), and technical progress in developed countries, which has led th to the development of substitutes for many of these exports and to conomies in their use; and the monopolistic nature of the production of the manufactured goods imported by underdeveloped countries, in contrast to the very nearly perfectly competitive nature of the production of primary products which make up the exports from underdeveloped countries. And not only do the terms of trade of underdeveloped countries decline in the long run, but the share of these countries in world trade is also declining.

Both the payments problems and the difficulties of development policy are said to be aggravated by wide fluctuations in export earnings, superimposed on the unfavourable long-term trend. Fluctuations in export proceeds, especially sudden and unpredictable declines, obstruct the process of government development planning, indispensable for economic growth. As these declines are the result of decreases in demand from developed countries, there is here another example of their responsibility for the difficulties of the underdeveloped world.

The problems of underdeveloped countries are further aggravated by the barriers of developed countries against their manufactures. These restrictions not only make it more difficult to earn foreign exchange to pay for imports but also obstruct the growth of their manufacturing industries because the domestic markets of the underdeveloped countries are too small for modern manufacturing techniques.

The importance of current external obstacles to development is the principal explicit theme of the UNCTAD literature. There are also frequent suggestions that the past actions of the developed countries are largely responsible for the present poverty of the underdeveloped world, generally through various types of colonialism, both political and economic.

Domestic factors bearing on economic development are also mentioned, though not discussed systematically. But inequality in the distribution of income and property, especially land, is a subject for frequent adverse comment, both because it is regarded as undesirable in itself and because it is said to retard development in various ways, as for instance by discouraging improvements in agricultural production by poor tenant farmers. Moreover, landlords, and well-to-do people generally, are said to spend their surpluses in luxury consumption instead of investing productively.

The UNCTAD literature takes it for granted that economic deve. ment depends largely on government action, and especially on comp hensive central planning. Even if development were possible witho comprehensive central planning, it would be insufficiently general an deep; material progress other than through central planning is regardec as inadequate if not illusory. There are frequent shifts in this literature in the interpretation of what economic advance is. The many criteria include: income per head, general living standards, the volume of manufacturing industry, the size of the public sector, and political independence. The only form of development which is invariably applauded is the growth of manufacturing industry sponsored or operated by government, usually as part of a programme of comprehensive central planning.

The main policy proposal of the UNCTAD literature is the expansion of intergovernmental foreign aid, which is regarded as a *sine qua non* for an acceptable rate of development of underdeveloped countries. The 1964 UNCTAD formally recommended that official aid should be not less than 1 per cent of the national income of the donors, after deducting certain reverse flows, notably repatriation of foreign capital, and repayment and amortisation of loans.[1] If interest and amortisation payments are unduly burdensome, these payments should be waived, scaled down or postponed.

In addition to this regular and routine flow of aid, other forms of aid, termed compensatory finance, should be provided both to offset any deterioration in the terms of trade and also to compensate for any unforeseeable loss through a decline in export earnings which governments could not reasonably have anticipated when framing their development plans. Payments under all these headings should be made to governments, and not passed on to individual producers, even when the payments are to compensate for a fall in export prices. This stipulation is regarded as important for two reasons. First, if the payments were passed on to individual producers, this would disrupt the development plan; and second, the incentives provided to producers would

---

[1] In most instances, net is interpreted as net of repatriation of capital by residents of developed countries but excluding capital exports by local residents. But certain influential suggestions at the conference envisaged the deduction also of capital exports by residents of the recipient countries.

The 1968 UNCTAD substituted 1 per cent of the gross national product for 1 per cent of the national income as the target for official aid, thereby raising this target by as much as one-quarter. The Pearson Report estimates (p. 144) that depreciation of capital, and indirect taxes (which represent the difference between national product at market prices and the national income), on average inflate the former by one-quarter of the national income.

gravate the deterioration in the terms of trade by encouraging an increase in production.

Developed countries are urged to support commodity agreements designed to raise or maintain prices of primary products so as to improve the terms of trade of underdeveloped countries; and to remove government-imposed obstacles to exports, especially of manufactures, from underdeveloped countries. They should not ask for reciprocity from underdeveloped countries, which should be allowed – indeed encouraged – to protect their manufacturing industries against competition from developed countries and to grant preferences to manufactured exports from other underdeveloped countries.

2 Investment, Import Capacity and Economic Development

The principal proposals of the UNCTAD literature generally assume that economic development is largely limited by the volume of investment expenditure, which in turn depends largely on the capacity to import, especially capital goods, and that this in turn depends largely on external market conditions, especially the terms of trade. Every link in this chain is at best inconclusive or misleading, if not outright erroneous; and the ultimate conclusion, that externally imposed limitations on the capacity to import are the decisive limitations on the rate of development, is wholly invalid.

Economic development is not simply or even largely a function of investment expenditure, least of all of investment expenditure which requires large-scale imports of capital goods. Whilst capital accumulation is a powerful agent of material progress, it is not a necessary condition, still less a sufficient condition. Again, an increase in real capital formation does not depend necessarily on the volume of investment expenditure in the sense of money spent other than on current consumption. More especially, large-scale investment expenditure requiring large-scale imports is neither necessary nor sufficient for economic development. High levels of economic attainment and rates of development have often, indeed generally, been attained without being constrained by the level of imports.

There are countless examples of rapid economic advance without external help and without payments difficulties, both in the early history of now developed countries and recently in many underdeveloped countries. The many obvious examples of the latter include the rapid development of Brazil, Mexico, Peru, Gold Coast–Ghana, Nigeria,

Kenya, Thailand, Malaya and Hong Kong both before and since the second world war.

Nor is it true that adverse external market conditions limit the imports to underdeveloped countries. Most UNCTAD literature (and indeed much development literature generally) discusses foreign trade problems in terms of import requirements on the one hand, and the ability to export or capacity to import on the other. The former is supposed to depend on the level of real income and the rate of development, and the latter on external markets. The unfavourable nature of these conditions is then alleged to cause inherent balance of payments problems.

This line of argument is invalid. It ignores the rates of exchange, the level of prices and costs, and the flow of money incomes, which are the major determinants of the volume of imports and exports. Even elementary discussion of foreign trade and the balance of payments must consider these matters.

In some UNCTAD discussions the stagnant or declining volume of exports from particular countries or groups of countries is instanced as evidence of a sluggish external demand. This all too common reasoning ignores the fact that these exports normally represent only a part and in many instances only a small part of total world exports of these commodities, and an even smaller part of world supplies. Thus the volume of these exports is quite unrelated to the total world demand for the products. Exports of a commodity from a particular country can increase even if total world demand is constant or has declined; and conversely exports from a particular source or sources can decrease even when total world demand has risen. The reasoning quite simply confuses supplies from a particular source with the total demand for the commodity.

The volume of exports from a particular source depends largely on the relative prices at which the commodity is available from alternative sources of supply. These prices depend on the domestic prices of the commodity and the rates of exchange, both of which are commonly ignored in these discussions. So is the level of domestic demand for the commodities in the exporting countries. Altogether this line of reasoning is a characteristic example of economics without prices or costs; it does not recognise that demand and supply are functions of prices, costs and incomes.

Many underdeveloped countries have of course experienced recurrent balance of payments difficulties in recent years. The reason is plain. Balance of payments crises become inevitable if governments pursue

.etary and fiscal policies which inflate their economies faster than
se of their trading partners, while the rate of exchange remains
ed. Such policies account for the balance of payments problems of
any underdeveloped countries since the 1950s. Chronic shortages of
oreign exchange and balance of payment difficulties are not corollaries
of a satisfactory rate of development. Indeed, the policies which result
in these difficulties usually retard rather than promote material progress.

3 Empirical Evidence on the Terms of Trade

The UN–UNCTAD literature[1] (as much of the current literature on this
subject) discusses the terms of trade of underdeveloped countries
largely in terms of global price ratios between primary products and
manufactures; these ratios are put forward as empirical basis for the
suggestion of the unfavourable and declining terms of trade of underdeveloped countries. As the purpose of this essay is an examination of
the UN–UNCTAD conclusions and of the methods by which these have
been reached, we shall mostly follow this literature and refer to the
relative prices and price changes of primary products and manufactures.
However, this is an oversimplification. Countries exporting primary
products are not identical with exporting underdeveloped countries,
because many developed countries are substantial exporters of primary
products, and many underdeveloped countries are substantial exporters
of manufactures. Any systematic discussion ought to take account of the
extreme heterogeneity both of primary producing countries and of the
underdeveloped world. Indeed for most purposes such a discussion
should be confined to the experience of one country or of a very small
group of countries.

Within primary producing countries there are substantial differences
in the movement of the terms of trade between temperate agricultural
foodstuffs, tropical products, agricultural materials, minerals and
petroleum products. Geographically there are substantial differences
between such areas as the middle east, Asia, Africa, Australasia, and
Latin America, which themselves are extremely heterogeneous. One or
two products are predominant in the exports of many underdeveloped
countries. The prices of individual products often move differently
with the result that the terms of trade of individual underdeveloped

---

[1] I shall refer to the literature as UN–UNCTAD literature where there is evident
continuity of ideas in the UN and the UNCTAD literature, and to UNCTAD literature and
discussions when the ideas and proposals are more specific to UNCTAD.

or primary producing countries often show divergent moveme
It is for this reason that for many purposes discussion should
confined to particular countries. For instance, between 1958 and 19
the commodity terms of trade of Chile improved by about one-fifth
while those of Brazil declined by over one-fifth because of widely
different price changes in copper and coffee. But even after allowing for
the required qualifications and reservations it is easy to show that the
UNCTAD allegations about the past course and present position of the
terms of trade of the underdeveloped world are invalid, and are indeed
the opposite of the truth.[1]

The commodity terms of trade of primary producers have in recent
years been more favourable than at almost any time in recorded history.
Sir Arthur Lewis noted recently:

The terms of trade for primary as against manufactured products
averaged higher in the 1950s than at any time in the preceding eighty
years. The first half of the 1950s was especially good because of the
Korean war and heavy stock-piling in the United States and elsewhere.
The terms of trade deteriorated in the second half of the decade and on
till 1962, since when they have moved upwards. However, even in 1962
they were 5 per cent above 1929, which preceded the Great Depression.[2]

After 1962 the terms of trade of primary producers again improved
appreciably. Between that date and the beginning of 1964, the date of the
first UNCTAD, they improved further by about 3 per cent.

The information just presented refers to the terms of trade of primary
producers, as does much of the discussion on this subject in the UN–
UNCTAD literature. However, since 1960 the Statistical Office of the
United Nations has compiled indices of the terms of trade of the underdeveloped world as distinct from the terms of trade of primary producers, outside the communist countries, published in the *Statistical
Year Book*. Although there have been certain changes in coverage and
in the base year, the series is substantially continuous since 1950
(although its compilation began only in 1960, the statistics have been

---

[1] We note at various stages in this essay that the averaging of the trading experience
of countries with widely different patterns of trade produces results which are often of
very limited meaning. But in examining the allegations in UNCTAD discussions about
the position and prospects in international trade of primary producers or of the underdeveloped world we often of necessity have to employ such aggregative concepts.

[2] W. Arthur Lewis, 'A Review of Economic Development' (Richard T. Ely Lecture
at the 75th Annual Meeting of the American Economic Association 1964, published in
the *American Economic Review*, vol. LV, no. 2, May 1965). Sir Arthur Lewis's reference
to the last eighty years looks back to the 1870s when, as will be noted in the next section,
the price ratio was exceptionally favourable to primary producers.

computed for earlier years as well), with the individual years 1938 and 1948 also shown. According to these statistics the commodity terms of trade of the underdeveloped world improved from 80 in 1938 to 95 in 1948 and subsequently to 100 in 1963, the last year before the first UNCTAD.[1] In other words they improved by about one-quarter between 1938 and the last year before the first UNCTAD. From 1963 to 1969 they improved further by 2 per cent.

Thus, there has not been any persistent or long-term decline even in the commodity terms of trade of primary producers or of underdeveloped countries; on the contrary, these terms are now more favourable than at practically any time in history.

The foregoing information refers exclusively to the crude commodity terms of trade. It substantially understates the long-term improvement in the position of underdeveloped countries because it ignores changes in the cost of production of primary products, the emergence of new manufactured products and also improvements in the quality of manufactures. In other words, the factoral terms of trade, the relevant concept here, are ignored. Although the significance of this omission is examined in greater detail in a subsequent section of this essay some observations on it are in order here.

The real cost of production (the volume of resources per unit of output) of many, probably most, primary products exported from underdeveloped countries has been greatly reduced in recent decades. An instructive example is provided by the changes in the conditions of the production of rubber. At the end of the nineteenth century rubber was collected at high cost from naturally growing trees in the jungle; within a few years it came to be produced at a fraction of this cost on estates and smallholdings. Petroleum, cocoa, sugar and vegetable oils are other exports whose costs and methods of production have changed vastly over the last few decades. These influences still operate strongly. For instance, the development of new techniques in the 1950s and their extensive adoption has greatly increased yields on both rubber estates and smallholdings, with a substantial reduction in costs. Thus, in discussions on income and welfare, both absolute and relative, statements about export prices and about the terms of trade of their producers are misleading unless complemented by statements about costs; this point will be further developed in section 4 of this essay.

Substantially similar considerations apply when the volume of

---

[1] This is on the basis of 1963 = 100. According to an earlier series, with 1958 = 100, the improvement from 1938 to 1963 was from 78 to 97.

exports changes greatly. In the early years of the century, a few thousand tons of plantation rubber were exported annually from Malaya and the Netherlands East Indies (the present Indonesia) at very high prices. By the 1920s the price had fallen greatly but annual exports were in hundreds of thousands of tons, with a much greater impact on income and welfare. Much the same applies to the history of the major export crops of both East and West Africa since the early 1900s.

Yet again references to changes in the import prices of manufactures over a long period are of limited meaning even for a single country, because of the heterogeneous and varying nature of manufactured imports and of changes in their quality. Import prices are usually compiled by dividing total value by the weight or numbers of the items imported. This method either ignores altogether changes in quality and in variety or allows for this factor only imperfectly. These limitations apply notably to discussions of the import prices of the underdeveloped world as a whole, that is over one-half of the whole world; indeed, aggregation and averaging at this level are of little meaning.

The significance of the shortcomings of this kind of aggregation is increased by changes in the composition and quality of imports into underdeveloped countries. In recent decades many entirely new products have appeared among the imports of underdeveloped countries, including new technical goods, new consumer durables and a wide range of new chemical products, perhaps the most important of which have been antibiotics. Some of these new products have greatly improved life in many underdeveloped countries. Moreover, the performance and quality of many familiar manufactured imports have changed so greatly over the last fifty years that the products are the same in name only. Locomotives, motor cars, buses and earth-moving equipment are obvious examples of products which have changed out of all recognition since, say, the first world war.

The improvement in quality of imported manufactures is generally not recorded in the import statistics; and the emergence of entirely new products is not reflected in calculations of changes in the terms of trade.[1]

---

[1] For instance, the efficiency of one of the best known makes of earth-moving tractor, widely used in Africa, has increased so greatly in the last few years, as a result of changes in design, that in 1967 it cost appreciably less to move a cubic yard of earth than it had in 1961, although the cost of the tractor was higher. Again, in Nigeria in 1967 the import prices of Italian refrigerators with a capacity of 4·6 cubic feet were 30 per cent lower than the prices of refrigerators with a capacity of 2·8 cubic feet imported from elsewhere a few years earlier. Indices of import prices record the lower price but not the increased capacity.

The emergence of new products provides one illustration of changes in the composition of a country's imports (or exports). All such changes, which occur of course quite apart from the development of new products, greatly complicate the measurement of changes in the terms of trade. They complicate even more the interpretation of changes in the terms of trade as conventionally measured. Thus an apparent deterioration in the terms of trade may reflect no more than a shift in the composition of imports to more expensive varieties or categories of goods, a change which may perhaps have been induced by reductions in their prices relative to those of the displaced varieties or categories. Although the terms of trade as measured may have deteriorated, the purchasing power of a unit of exports may have increased or have remained unchanged.

Changes in the composition of imports can be brought about as a result of government policies introduced for various social, political or ideological reasons. For instance, there has been a widespread development in underdeveloped countries of protectionist policies designed to encourage the establishment or growth of import-substituting manufacturing activities. Such policies tend to change the composition of a country's imports; for example, they tend to increase the share of raw materials, components and equipment in total imports compared to total manufactures. These measures also tend to change the composition of exports, since not all exporting activities will be equally affected by the higher prices of the protected goods or the diversion of resources to their production. Thus such policies may bring about either an improvement or a deterioration in the conventionally measured terms of trade. It is therefore invalid to assume that a deterioration in the conventionally measured terms of trade is a result of adverse changes in external market conditions.

The impact of government policies on the terms of trade usually cannot be determined unambiguously. However, sometimes the direction of the impact is clear, as in certain forms of import control. For instance, early in 1967 transistor radios imported into Nigeria from Japan could be sold at a price about 15 per cent below European sets. However, imports from Japan have come to be restricted by the Nigerian government (as a result of pressure by certain African importers whose business contacts did not extend to Japan). This restriction made the terms of trade of Nigeria worse than they would otherwise have been. And governments of many underdeveloped countries restrict imports from low-cost sources, for a variety of political and ideological reasons.

These considerations illustrate again the limitations of generalised discussions on the terms of trade of underdeveloped countries, and also the lack of homogeneity of interest among the people of any country.

One further point should be noted. In so far as changes in the terms of trade are taken to reflect changes in the income or welfare of a country, one additional relevant type of change is left out of account. In many underdeveloped countries there are taxes on foreign companies and on exports of primary products, including oil royalties. These taxes serve to increase the receipts of these countries from their exports. Increases in the level of such taxes are similar to improvements in the terms of trade in their effect on foreign exchange receipts (although their longer-term effects may be damaging in their discouragement of foreign investment and encouragement of the search for substitutes or alternative sources of supply). However, these improvements are generally not reflected in the conventionally measured terms of trade.

Thus changes in the conventionally measured terms of trade do not serve as a reliable basis for sensible economic argument or policy. This conclusion applies even to arguments based on changes in the factoral terms of trade, and applies with much greater force to arguments based on changes in the commodity terms of trade, to which most current discussion is confined and on which most policy proposals are based.

In discussions on the position of the underdeveloped world, statements about their terms of trade are often coupled with statements about the share of the underdeveloped countries in world trade. As will be explained later, unqualified references to changes in the share of a country or a region or a group of countries in total trade are of limited meaning. However, in view of the UNCTAD allegations on this subject it is noteworthy that the share of the underdeveloped world in total world trade has increased and not diminished over the last half century. According to statistics assembled by P. Lamartine Yates in his large-scale study, *Forty Years of Foreign Trade*,[1] the share of the three poorest continents, Latin America, Africa and Asia (excluding Japan) in total world exports (outside communist countries), increased from about 23 per cent in 1913 to about 28 per cent in 1953. If primary products only are considered (which account for about nine-tenths of the exports of the underdeveloped world), the share of these countries in total exports increased even more over this period, from about 36 per cent to about 49 per cent. Over this long period the under-

[1] London, 1959.

developed world, therefore, gained and did not lose ground in world trade.

The well-known GATT report *Trends in International Trade*[1] found that the share of non-industrial countries in aggregate world exports was practically the same in 1928 and 1957 at about 30 per cent of the world total. This result is especially notable in the face of the inflationary and protectionist policies of many underdeveloped countries. Both 1928 and 1957 were years of generally high economic activity, which adds meaning to the comparison.[2]

4 Terms of Trade: Issues of Concept and Analysis

Allegations of unfavourable and persistently deteriorating terms of trade of underdeveloped countries have for long been a major theme of the publications of the United Nations for about two decades.[3] It was a prominent topic of the literature of the Economic Commission for Latin America; Dr Prebisch, it will be recalled, was executive secretary of ECLA for many years, until he became secretary general of UNCTAD.

The conceptual, analytical and empirical bases of these allegations are invalid; their defects have been exposed repeatedly in the technical literature.[4] Nevertheless they are again prominent in the Prebisch Report and elsewhere in the UNCTAD literature. They are a main basis for the UNCTAD proposals. They also enjoy widespread influence, chiefly as a result of persistent propaganda and sheer repetition. Systematic exposure of these allegations is in order.

[1] Geneva, 1958.

[2] The particular issue of the share of underdeveloped countries in world trade is discussed by Professor Romulo A. Ferrero in an illuminating paper, *Trade Problems of Primary Producing Countries*, International Industrial Conference, San Francisco, 1965 (mimeographed).

[3] The alleged long-term deterioration in the terms of trade of underdeveloped countries and of primary products has been much canvassed by UN economists since the late 1940s. It was widely publicised in a report by the United Nations Department of Economic Affairs entitled *Relative Prices of Exports and Imports of Underdeveloped Countries* (Lake Success, 1949). This report equates underdeveloped countries with primary producers. This in turn drew in part on an earlier League of Nations report entitled *Industrialisation and Foreign Trade* (Geneva, 1945). The Prebisch Report and much of the UNCTAD literature explicitly draw on information provided by the United Nations secretariat for their material in this general area. There is thus a clear continuity of ideas, sources and method.

[4] The numerous criticisms include, among others: P.T. Ellsworth, 'Terms of Trade between Primary Producing and Industrial Countries', *Inter-American Economic Affairs*, Summer 1956; Theodore Morgan, 'The Long-Run Terms of Trade Between Agriculture and Manufacturing', *Economic Development and Cultural Change*, October 1959; Harry G. Johnson, *Economic Policies towards Less Developed Countries*, Washington, 1967.

It is the concept of the factoral terms of trade which is relevant to worthwhile discussion of the effects of changes in the terms of trade on incomes, living standards, welfare and development.[1] This concept, which allows for changes in costs of production, indicates the volume of imports which can be bought with the output of a unit of resources of the exporting country. For instance, a fall in export prices compared to import prices is compatible with an improvement in the factoral terms of trade, if the cost of production of exports has fallen more than the price of imports. The UNCTAD literature refers to commodity terms only. The factoral terms of trade are not discussed, which is a crucial omission.

Except for very short periods the factoral terms of trade normally improve for all or most trading partners. Changes in commodity terms of trade are akin to zero sum games in which gains and losses cancel out. Changes in the factoral terms of trade are more akin to economic activity in general which normally benefits all direct participants.

Changes in the total volume of trade and the causes of such changes are also pertinent to the relation of the terms of trade to economic welfare. Even if factoral terms of trade, corrected for quality changes, have deteriorated, the economic welfare of people in exporting countries can still improve if there is a large increase in total trade. A familiar example is that of the expansion of an industry from small beginnings to large-scale activity under the stimulus of initially high prices.

References to unfavourable terms of trade are, by themselves, meaningless. The terms of trade can be unfavourable only in a comparative sense of being less favourable than at some other time. It is clear from this elementary consideration that a discussion of the terms of trade and of changes in these terms is fundamentally affected by the base period chosen. Different base years yield widely different results (and so do changes in the country or commodity coverage of the discussion).

A large measure of uniformity (or at least substantial similarity in experience) of the components of groups whose position is examined is a condition of the interest and significance of references to changes in the terms of trade of different groups. Aggregation and averaging of widely

---

[1] The concept used here is that of the single factoral terms of trade. In certain specialised contexts some of its variants may be of interest, such as the income terms of trade, or the double factoral terms of trade. In most contexts, notably the discussions of UNCTAD on the position or prospects of underdeveloped countries, the concept here employed is the most relevant, especially since changes in the volume of trade are also noted in the text.

⁣rent experiences produce largely meaningless results. And the more ⁣erogeneous is the composition of the group and the more divergent ⁣ir experience, the less meaningful do the results become. This ⁣nsideration is clearly relevant to the trading experience of the under-developed world, a group which comprises over one-half of the population of the world.[1]

The conceptual ambiguities and problems just noted are enhanced and compounded in discussions about the likely future course of the terms of trade. Such discussions are usually based on extrapolation into the future of changes over certain periods in the past. Practically any result can be obtained by the judicious selection of the period for the basis of extrapolation. And as if this were not enough, changes which contradict a particular forecast can be ruled out as being only temporary, while changes supporting it can be adduced as confirmation.

So far the discussion in this section has borne on the alleged deterioration of the terms of trade of the underdeveloped world. The allegations that the share of the underdeveloped world in world trade shows a long-term decline, which is moreover likely to continue, and that such a decline is damaging, are also subject to radical criticism.

To begin with, as we have noted in the preceding section, there has been no long-term decline in the share of the underdeveloped world in total world trade. But even if there had been such a decline, it could not be discussed sensibly without examining the domestic economic conditions, and especially the domestic economic policies, of the countries under review, since these matters directly and necessarily influence the volume of external trade of these countries and, therefore, their share in world trade.

Further, the share of a region in world trade often changes for extraneous reasons which do not affect its prosperity. Indeed, the share of a region in total world trade can, and often does, decline as a result of developments which affect its prosperity favourably. In recent years the prosperity of western Europe and Japan brought about a decline in the share in world production and trade of many countries and areas

[1] The averaging procedures of the UN–UNCTAD discussions on the terms of trade recall Bohm–Bawerk's comment on some of Marx's averaging methods: 'We might just as well try in this way to prove the proposition that animals of all kinds, elephants and May-flies included, have the same length of life; for while it is true that elephants live on an average one hundred years and May-flies only a single day, yet between these two quantities we can strike an average of fifty years. By as much time as elephants live longer than the flies, the flies live shorter than the elephants. The deviations from this average "mutually cancel each other", and consequently on the whole and on the average the law that all kinds of animals have the same length of life is established!' (quoted by Professor P. P. Streeten, in Gunnar Myrdal, *Asian Drama*, p. 1990).

where the level of incomes benefited from the rapid progress of th. areas.

Thus neither general references to changes in the share of a countr. or a group of countries, in world trade, nor unanalysed statistics on th. subject, can serve as worthwhile basis for discussion or policy.

5 *Alleged Persistent Deterioration of the Terms of Trade of Primary Producers*

The analytical basis for the suggestion of a persistent deterioration in the terms of trade of underdeveloped countries is, as we have noted, derived from the allegedly low income elasticity of demand for primary products;[1] the increase in population in primary producing countries; the technical progress resulting in economies in the use of raw materials in manufacturing processes and in the development of substitutes; and the prevalence of trade unions and business monopolies in the exporting industries of developed countries. These arguments are insubstantial.

(*a*) A low income elasticity of demand (less than one) does not by itself imply a deterioration of the terms of trade, provided that it is not negative (less than zero). The implications of a low income elasticity of demand are frequently confused with those of a negative income elasticity of demand. The income elasticity of world demand for primary products is certainly not negative. It is unlikely even to be low for the major exports of underdeveloped countries. The most important of these exports are raw materials such as oil, rubber and copper, for which the income elasticity of world demand is unlikely to be low. Indeed, it is high (almost certainly significantly more than one) for petroleum products, which are much the most important single export from underdeveloped countries: they are about one-half of total merchandise exports from underdeveloped countries, or one-half of the primary products exported by them, and over four times the value of the next most important export. The income elasticities of world demand are also unlikely to be very low for such high-class foodstuffs as coffee, cocoa and tea, which are again important exports from underdeveloped countries. The suggestion of a generally low income elasticity of demand for exports of underdeveloped countries rests on unwarranted identifica-

[1] That is, the nature of the demand is such that it increases less than proportionately to increases in income.

̇ion of total exports of underdeveloped countries with exports of staple ̇oodstuffs for which the income elasticity of demand is thought to be low at high levels of income.[1]

Whether the income elasticity of world demand for the exports of underdeveloped countries is lower than that for their imports is doubtful, and so far as I know has not been measured. We have already given reasons why the income elasticity of demand for their exports is unlikely to be low; and in comparing this with the income elasticity of their demand for imports it should be remembered that a large proportion of imports of manufactures in underdeveloped countries is strictly controlled and consists of products deemed essential on some criterion or other.

The direction in the movement of the commodity terms of trade of underdeveloped countries as a group depends on the rate of growth of demand for their exports compared to the rate of growth of their demand for imports; and the rates of growth in these demands depend on rates of growth of aggregate incomes multiplied by the income elasticities of the respective demands.[2]

Even if the average income elasticity of demand for exports of underdeveloped countries is lower than the average income elasticity of their demand for imports (which as we have argued is doubtful), their commodity terms of trade will deteriorate for certain only if their incomes grow as fast or nearly as fast as do those of the developed countries.

But the usual complaint is, of course, that in the aggregate their incomes grow less fast. The commodity terms of trade of the underdeveloped world will deteriorate if the ratio of the rate of growth of the aggregate incomes of the developed countries to the rate of growth of the aggregate incomes of underdeveloped countries is less than the ratio of the income elasticity of demand of the underdeveloped countries for the exports of the developed countries, to the income elasticity of the aggregate demand of developed countries for the exports of underdeveloped countries; and they will improve if the relationship

[1] It is doubtful whether the income elasticity of world demand is low for many staple foodstuffs either. The level of incomes and the structure of wants of a large proportion of the world population are such that the income elasticity of demand for internationally traded staple foodstuffs are likely to be comparatively high. Income elasticities of demand for food of near unity have been suggested by some studies of Latin America and India.

[2] Assuming there is no change in the degree of restrictions on trade.

In the formulation in the text there is no reference to changes in costs as an influence on the terms of trade, because the effects of these changes are subsumed in changes in incomes.

between these ratios is the converse.[1] As we have just noted, there is no evidence about the relative average income elasticities of the demand for the aggregate exports and the aggregate imports of underdeveloped countries. Nor is such evidence likely to be available in the near future. But even if it were available it would be largely useless for at least two reasons.

First, it would be useless because what matters for development and welfare purposes are the factoral terms of trade and not the commodity terms of trade.

Second, references to income elasticities of total world demand for imports and exports of all underdeveloped countries imply aggregation and averaging of elements so diverse that any conclusion is meaningless, except of course for the statement which can be made with absolute confidence that the income elasticity of total world demand for the exports of the underdeveloped world is not negative. Yet this condition is the only one that would by itself imply a deterioration of the commodity terms of trade of underdeveloped countries over a period in which average world incomes have risen.

(b) The population of underdeveloped countries is likely to continue to increase rapidly. The real incomes per head in countries with limited supplies of land may be unfavourably affected by a rapid increase in population. But this effect is distinct from unfavourable changes in the terms of trade.[2]

---

[1] The rate of growth of demand by the developed world for the exports of the under-developed world can be written as $R_d E_d$, where R_d is the rate of growth of incomes in the developed world and E_d is the income elasticity of their aggregate demand for the exports of the underdeveloped world. The rate of growth of the aggregate demand of underdeveloped countries for the exports of the developed countries can be written correspondingly as $R_u E_u$. The terms of trade of the underdeveloped world will improve if $R_d E_d > R_u E_u$, that is if $\dfrac{R_d}{R_u} > \dfrac{E_u}{E_d}$; and they will deteriorate in the converse case.

The conditions listed in the text determine the *direction* of changes in the commodity terms of trade. The quantitative extent of the change depends on the elasticities of aggregate domestic supply and demand in the two groups: the higher the numerical value of these elasticities the less will be the change in either direction. For instance, a high elasticity of demand such as is brought about by the possibilities of substitution between different raw materials (much canvassed in UNCTAD discussions) would diminish the extent of changes in the terms of trade by increasing the elasticity of demand for these products.

[2] Rapid rate of increase of population (whether in a particular country or elsewhere) can affect adversely the commodity and factoral terms of trade of exporters of products which are highly labour intensive. Such a result would be analogous to a decline in marginal productivity through the operation of diminishing returns. Such an outcome has nothing to do with reliance on primary products. For instance, production of crude oil, the most important single export of underdeveloped countries, is extremely capital intensive.

Increased total world demand both for primary products and for manufactures brought about by an increased world population and a higher aggregate world income is more likely to favour than to disadvantage those underdeveloped countries which produce and export mineral and agricultural products, because it will tend to increase the comparative scarcity of these commodities.[1] The favourable effects of a larger world population and of higher incomes on both commodity and factoral terms of trade of exports of primary products will be enhanced if the increase in total output of manufactures reduces their cost and improves their quality through the operation of increasing returns.

(c) Technical progress normally affects the terms of trade and living standards of underdeveloped countries in exactly the opposite way to that envisaged in the Prebisch Report and the UNCTAD literature generally. Technical change may well reduce the amount of raw materials required in the productive processes generally. But equally it reduces the real cost of the commodities which the underdeveloped countries import.[2] Technical progress has been a major factor in the material progress of developed countries, in the resulting huge increase in world demand for exports of underdeveloped countries, and in the vast expansion in the range and quality of manufactured exports available to them.

There may be various reasons for the insistence by UNCTAD representatives on the allegedly damaging effects on underdeveloped countries of technical progress in the west, especially the development of synthetic products. These may include the familiar asymmetry of noticing the competitive elements and results of economic phenomena and ignoring their complementary aspects. And it may reflect also the practice of inappropriate aggregation, of treating the underdeveloped world as a broadly homogeneous entity, so that any adverse experience (genuine

---

[1] This last consideration applies only in so far as underdeveloped countries are net exporters of primary products. Exports from the underdeveloped world are not coterminous with primary products. Although about nine-tenths of exports from underdeveloped countries are indeed primary products, there are substantial exports of manufactures from some of these countries and this category may become more important in the future. But this consideration does not affect criticisms of the UNCTAD arguments in the text because these arguments are based largely on the terms of trade of primary producers.

[2] Technical progress in the development of substitutes has often imposed a ceiling on the price of particular exports of underdeveloped countries. But the operation of this fact is again symmetrical and affects the products they import as well as those which they export, though this fact may not be so readily perceived.

or spurious) of any small part can be regarded as typical of the fortunes of underdeveloped countries.

(*d*) It is often argued that the position of the underdeveloped countries is weakened not only by an alleged low income elasticity of demand for their export products but also by a low price elasticity of demand (that is, a comparative unresponsiveness of demand to changes in price). However, it is difficult to reconcile assertions that the price elasticity is low with other assertions that the development of synthetic substitutes in the advanced countries is important: the presence of substitutes makes for relatively high price elasticities. Moreover, a low price elasticity of demand is not necessarily an economic disadvantage. It is true that if the price elasticity is low, an increase in supply such as may result from an unusually large crop will bring about a more than proportionate fall in price and thus reduce total receipts below those obtainable from a smaller supply. But of course the converse also applies, and with a low price elasticity a smaller supply results in higher receipts. And a low price elasticity provides opportunities for increasing total export receipts by the exercise of control over export supplies. Governments acting together can increase export earnings – and simultaneously save domestic resources – by the imposition of export taxes or by restricting supply in other ways, as is done, with varying degrees of success, in the current international commodity control schemes. These opportunities are not present where the demand for a product has a high price elasticity.

(*e*) The suggestion that monopolistic conditions, whether in the labour or product markets, in the developed countries, result in long-term deterioration in the terms of trade of underdeveloped countries is superficial. In the first place it is doubtful whether there now exist effective world monopolies or cartels of exporters of manufactures (to be effective such monopolies would need to be worldwide); there is a great diversity of supplies of practically all manufactured exports. There may have existed isolated instances of effective world monopolies or cartels of particular manufactured exports, but their impact on the terms of trade of the underdeveloped world, even in the past, would have been negligible. But the UNCTAD argument, that monopolies in the export industries of developed countries have served to bring about a persistent deterioration in the terms of trade of the underdeveloped world, is open to a more fundamental objection. The presence of monopolies

1 developed countries would not in itself serve to bring about a long-term *deterioration* in the terms of trade of the underdeveloped world. Such an effect would require an *increase* in the extent or effectiveness of monopoly power through time. No evidence has been adduced of such a trend: in fact there is much *prima facie* evidence to the contrary.

To begin with, while it is true that the governments of developed countries tend to be less hostile to export cartels than to cartels in the home market, the increasing hostility to domestic cartels has further weakened the operations and effectiveness of any export cartels or monopolies (in contrast to the promotion of commodity agreements covering exports of primary products from underdeveloped countries, and of other preferential arrangements for their exports). Again, while there are highly concentrated manufacturing industries in each developed country, there is no evidence that the extent of high concentration has increased over the decades; and in the United States, for which there are reliable estimates for the last half century or longer, concentration in the industrial sector appears to have decreased. And, what is probably the most important influence in this context, the spread of manufacturing industries over the developed world as well as in some underdeveloped countries has meant that importing countries have had progressively wider access to alternative sources of supply, a tendency which has been reinforced by improvements in transport and communications; action by monopolists or near-monopolists in one country has become increasingly ineffective. And the spread of manufacturing activities has also tended to weaken the price effect of national trade unions in international trade.

In short, it may be ruled out that in general there has been any secular increase in the extent or effective exploitation of monopoly power in the supply of goods from developed to underdeveloped countries.

6 *UNCTAD Statistics on the Terms of Trade*

How does the UN–UNCTAD literature substantiate the unfounded allegation that the terms of trade of underdeveloped countries or primary producers have persistently declined?

The easiest way to arrange statistics to show a long-term or systematic deterioration of the terms of trade is simply to omit the years over which they have improved, a device frequently employed in UN–UNCTAD discussions. The alleged secular decline in the terms of trade

of underdeveloped countries was first widely publicised in UN literatur
on the basis of a series beginning with the 1870s and ending in 1938; in
the Prebisch Report and the UNCTAD literature it is derived from a series
beginning with 1950 and terminating with 1961. Between 1938 and
1950 the commodity terms of trade of primary producers improved
by almost two-fifths, even without any correction for the improvement
in the quality of manufactures. It is easy to assert that the terms of
trade of primary producers always decline if the years when they have
risen are omitted.

Quite apart from the disregard of relative price changes between
1938 and 1950, the choice of 1950 as a starting-point of a trend is also
noteworthy. That was the first year of the Korean boom, when the
prices of primary products rose greatly as a result of stockpiling. Thus a
subsequent relative fall was to be expected; the period 1950–61 cannot
be used legitimately as a basis for extrapolation, quite apart from the
fact that it is much too short to serve as a basis for a discussion on long-
term trends.

The unwarranted omission of some products from the list of imports
or exports considered, also helps to promote the desired conclusion;
for instance, petroleum products are omitted from the calculations of
the terms of trade in the Prebisch Report (and from the share of underdeveloped countries in world trade), without any explanation.[1] Yet
petroleum products are by far the most important export from the underdeveloped world, and their volume has increased enormously since the
second world war. This huge increase, together with the much higher
taxation of the foreign-owned oil companies, has greatly benefited these
countries.

In the UNCTAD literature any adverse movement in the terms of
trade of underdeveloped countries is regarded as permanent or likely
to herald a further deterioration, while any improvement is treated as
temporary.[2] By 1964, the date of the first UNCTAD, the prices of primary
products had risen relatively to manufactures since 1961; this movement is either ignored or mentioned as likely to be temporary only.

To provide such a discussion with meaning it would be necessary to
set a time limit for the trend, as it must presumably come to an end

---

[1] Prebisch Report, pp. 18–9.

[2] In a memorandum submitted by FAO to UNCTAD, 'International Commodity Arrangements and Policies' (published in *Trade and Development: Commodity Trade*), there are
estimates of the so-called trade gap in 1970. They are based on various assumptions
about the terms of trade of underdeveloped countries in 1970 which do not even con-
template a possible improvement in the terms of trade.

as the terms of trade approach zero, when trade itself would also come to an end. In fact, such limits are not specified in this literature. Reading the UNCTAD literature (and indeed much of the contemporary literature in this field) one gets the impression that the prices of primary products always fall and never rise, so that it seems surprising that trade in primary products continues, and astonishing that its volume is currently at record levels.

In sum, the allegation of a long-run decline of the terms of trade of primary producers or of underdeveloped countries is untrue. The concepts used in the UNCTAD discussions are practically meaningless and the analysis is invalid. The empirical evidence summarised in the statistical series in the official publications of the United Nations, such as the Statistical Year Book, shows these allegations to be the opposite of the truth.

7 Forerunners of UNCTAD Ideas

Some of these ideas and methods on the subject of the terms of trade of primary producers were advanced in the UN literature before the establishment of UNCTAD, though in a less blatant form.

The alleged secular decline in the terms of trade of underdeveloped countries was widely canvassed in the UN report already mentioned, *Relative Prices of Exports and Imports of Underdeveloped Countries*. The argument was based partly on changes in relative prices of primary products and manufactures in world trade between 1876–80 and 1938, and also on changes in British import and export prices (regarded as typical of primary products and manufactures) over the same period. These changes are taken as evidence of a secular decline in the terms of trade of primary producers, which in turn is regarded as evidence of a decline in the terms of trade of underdeveloped countries. The defects and indeed outright fallacies of this reasoning have often been pointed out in the literature.[1]

These statistics ignore the import and export prices and the large fall in the cost of transport by land and sea, which over several decades appreciably exceeded the fall in British import prices, so that the local prices of primary products rose while their prices overseas fell. Similarly, the cost of imports fell in the primary producing countries. Thus the terms of trade of primary producers improved over this period.

[1] Two of the most thorough and effective criticisms are the studies by Professors Ellsworth and Morgan already mentioned.

British imports over this period were not representative of primary products generally, much less of exports from the present under-developed world. For instance, the bulk of British imports in the 1870s came from North America, Europe, Scandinavia and Australia. Many of today's underdeveloped countries either had no international trade in the 1870s, or only an insignificant amount; at that time there were no exports of plantation rubber or petroleum products at all, nor of cultivated agricultural products or minerals from Africa.

British import and export prices are available from 1801; the price ratio was most favourable to primary products in the 1870s, much more so than in earlier periods, so that a decline from the level of the 1870s does not measure a secular trend. For the nineteenth century as a whole there was a substantial rise in this ratio in favour of the prices of primary products even without allowing for changes in transport costs. If, for instance, 1900 had been chosen as the base, the terms of trade shown in these statistics would have presented a great improvement in the course of the nineteenth century.

It has often been noted in the technical literature, especially by Professor Theodore Morgan, that the primary producing countries are far too heterogeneous a group for sensible aggregation, least of all on the basis of indices of British import prices; that available statistics do not show any general long-term deterioration even in the commodity terms of trade of primary producers, let alone their factoral terms of trade; that over the last hundred years in most countries for which statistics are available the commodity terms of trade between primary products and manufactures moved differently at different times; and that in the few instances of a continuous trend this was in favour of primary products (for instance for New Zealand between 1860 and 1950 and also in certain series relating to American agriculture over most of the last hundred years); that because of the great diversity of underdeveloped countries and the prominence of a relatively small number of products among exports of individual countries, the terms of trade of individual countries often move very differently over the same period; that it is the factoral and not the commodity terms of trade which are relevant to economic development and to economic welfare; and that even this concept has to be supplemented by information on changes in the composition and in the quality of imports and in changes in the total volume of trade.

These fundamental criticisms of the UN allegations of the declining terms of trade of underdeveloped countries were published several years before the Prebisch Report. They are simply ignored in the UNCTAD literature, which repeats and indeed compounds the defects of the earlier publications. Such techniques as the disregard of petroleum products and the outright omission of periods over which the terms of trade of primary producers greatly improved (1938–50) make especially clear the method and purpose of these exercises.

8 Terms of Trade and Material Progress

The assumption that the prospective terms of trade of the under-developed world will show a secular decline is also unfounded.

Even if the evidence were much more carefully and dispassionately collected and assessed, conjectures about the prospective movement of the terms of trade for the underdeveloped world as a whole would be unfruitful. This scepticism derives not only from the inevitable uncertainties but also from the far-reaching diversity in the conditions and the composition of the foreign trade of different underdeveloped countries, and the necessarily widely different movements of their commodity and factoral terms of trade.

However, a limited conjecture is permissible. Because of the certain further increase in world population in coming decades, the virtually certain technical progress in manufacturing industry, and the virtually certain increase in total world income, it is probable that those under-developed countries which produce mineral and especially agricultural products for export will experience an improvement in both commodity and factoral terms of trade. This probability underlines the irony of current discussions which predict a world shortage of food, and simultaneously urge underdeveloped countries to direct their efforts and resources away from agriculture and towards manufacturing.

A more technical point may be noted. The UNCTAD literature emphasises the importance of the trade or foreign exchange gap (said to result largely from the adverse terms of trade) as a key obstacle to development. This obstacle is said to be superimposed on a savings gap, which represents the difference between the investment necessary for an acceptable rate of development and the domestic savings available. Regardless of the validity and meaningfulness of the concept of such a savings gap (that is of the notion that the savings potential is a key bottleneck in development), there is for most purposes no substantial practical significance in the distinction between the two gaps. Certainly, the principal arguments and policy proposals of UNCTAD are not affected by this distinction. The imports obtainable with a country's export proceeds represent the result of the transformation of the country's productive resources into valuable goods and services. The economic position of a group is improved by any favourable change in the terms on which resources can be converted into valuable goods and services, and it is also improved if it receives or discovers additional valuable resources. But this consideration applies equally to the transformation of resources through domestic activity and through foreign trade. The emphasis on a foreign exchange or trade gap is another instance of the emphasis on external responsibility for a country's economic difficulties or for a rate of development deemed inadequate.

This long examination of the alleged secular decline of the terms of trade of underdeveloped countries was necessary because of the prominence of this subject in UNCTAD literature and especially its prominence as basis for the UNCTAD policy proposals. It should not be inferred from the length of the discussion that movements in the terms of trade are likely to be major factors in the development prospects of underdeveloped countries. The terms of trade are, in fact, unrelated to the prime causes of poverty in the underdeveloped world. It would be idle to think that any likely changes in the terms of trade of underdeveloped countries would substantially affect these underlying forces.[1]

9 Shares in World Trade

Many of the criticisms of the UN–UNCTAD allegations about the terms of trade of underdeveloped countries apply also to the arguments of this literature about the alleged decline in the share of the underdeveloped world in world trade.

The share of a country or of a group of countries in total world trade can, and often does, change without affecting substantially its economic position or prospects. For instance, it can and often does decline as a result of an increased volume of trade between other countries which do not compete with its products. What matters in this context are changes in the absolute volume not in relative shares. And even the former are of very limited meaning without examination of the factors behind these changes. The volume of exports from a country can decline for

[1] The significance to a country of changes in the terms of trade depends on the importance of international trade in the national economy and on the costs of import substitution. This point is pertinent to the welfare and development implications of changes in the terms of trade and should therefore be remembered. But it need not be developed further here, as it does not bear directly on the main UNCTAD arguments.

n radically different reasons as an increase in the domestic use of
viously exported products (as a result, for instance, of domestic
flation); or the introduction or intensification of protectionist policies
t home; or a decline in export demand. For instance, the decline in the
exports of Indian groundnuts since the 1940s reflects the increased
domestic use of groundnuts at a time when world demand for oils and
fats increased greatly. The exports of many underdeveloped countries in
Latin America and Asia have been adversely affected by a combination
of domestic inflation and overvalued exchange rates.

The unfounded and meaningless suggestion of the decline in the
share of underdeveloped countries in world trade can, then, be easily
dismissed. The method used in the UNCTAD literature on this subject
is essentially similar to that used in discussions on the terms of trade.
The allegations are based largely on the experience of the years following the Korean boom; at least a short-period decline from this exceptional level was to be expected. As already noted, Dr Lamartine Yates
has shown that the share of underdeveloped countries in world trade has
not decreased but has appreciably increased in recent decades. Again,
in some of the UNCTAD discussions on the share of underdeveloped
countries in world trade petroleum products are excluded and the
exports of these have increased vastly since 1950. Moreover, the 1950s
saw the reconstruction of the economies of western Europe and the
liberalisation of intra-European trade with a consequent large increase
in the external trade of Europe. There was also a very large increase in
the foreign trade of Japan. These developments brought about a
decline in the share of other groups in total world trade. The absolute
volume of the trade of the other groups increased, but proportionately
less than that of western Europe and Japan.[1] Thus, as is indeed obvious
on reflection, a decline in the share of a group of countries in total
world trade has by itself no unfavourable welfare implications whatever.
Without examination of the specific circumstances such a decline
cannot serve as indicator even of historical change in economic welfare,
let alone of development prospects.

10 Major UNCTAD Proposals

The main UNCTAD proposals are designed to increase the foreign
exchange receipts of underdeveloped countries chiefly by expanding

[1] This matter is carefully examined by Professor Ferrero in his paper already mentioned in this essay. Professor Ferrero also shows that since 1957 the share of the United
States in total world trade has declined more than that of underdeveloped countries.

foreign aid; by promoting commodity agreements; and by remov:
the barriers to exports of manufactures of underdeveloped countri¢
as well as by granting preferences to these exports in both develope
and underdeveloped countries. Foreign aid in the sense of intergovern
mental grants or heavily subsidised loans is taken for granted throughout.[1]

I have already argued in essay 2 that foreign aid is clearly neither
necessary nor sufficient for material progress. I have argued further
that this policy, especially as it has operated since the second world war,
is more likely to retard than to promote the material progress of underdeveloped countries, notably when aid is linked either to the adoption
of comprehensive central planning or to balance of payments difficulties
in the recipient countries.

The approach to foreign aid in the UNCTAD literature is much more
likely to retard than promote the economic development of poor
countries. This is so for various reasons: there is the prominence of the
idea that outside forces are responsible for the poverty of the underdeveloped world, and that the rest of the world owes these countries a
living; the neglect of people's abilities, attitudes and values, and also of
external contacts as determinants of development; the neglect of the
difference between resources supplied gratis from abroad and those
generated locally; the encouragement of policies promoting the flight of
capital; the axiomatic acceptance of the necessity for development planning and the linking of aid to it; and the uncritical acceptance of the
investment fetish, the belief that development is largely determined by
monetary investment expenditure, and also that it necessarily entails
payments difficulties.

The implications of most of these defects have been examined in
essay 2. But it seems worthwhile to note certain likely results of the
suggestion that the volume of foreign aid required for development
should be computed after allowing for outflow of capital from the
recipient countries. Acceptance of this suggestion would encourage
the pursuit of policies designed to bring about withdrawal and export
of capital from underdeveloped countries because such capital would be
wholly or partly private while foreign aid accrues to the government. It
is palpable that government action frequently promotes the withdrawal
of capital by actual and threatened expropriation, the imposition of

---

[1] 'While the importance of external private investment in the developing countries is
recognised, the need for the provision of considerable amounts of public resources is
no longer questioned.' Prebisch Report, p. 79. Public resources here refers to foreign
aid, not to funds borrowed by governments on the world's capital markets.

controls or of high taxation, and discrimination against foreign capital. Acceptance of this suggestion would further encourage such policies. It would also induce governments to overstate the outflow of capital, as this would result in increased foreign aid.

In the UNCTAD literature, amortisation, interest and dividend payments are considered as major burdens on underdeveloped countries; these payments are termed drains or even losses. It is repeatedly suggested that these payments should be rescheduled or waived, which is a euphemism for default, and also that foreign aid should compensate both for amortisation and for interest and dividend payments. This approach encourages defaults on contractual obligations and thereby promotes an attitude unfavourable to material advance. The tenor of the discussion also implies that amortisation, dividend and interest payments represent net losses rather than repayment of resources and returns on resources supplied to these countries.

11 *Compensatory Finance*

In addition to routine aid UNCTAD officially proposes 'compensatory finance' to offset losses by underdeveloped countries from deterioration in their terms of trade and to compensate them for a decline in export receipts below the reasonable expectations of governments, especially the reasonable expectations entertained in framing development plans.

The substantive discussions are confined to commodity terms of trade and in practice envisage only their deterioration. There are a few casual remarks to the effect that compensatory payments should not be repayable if by chance the terms of trade were to improve subsequently. There is scope here for unlimited manipulation. By judicious changes in the period reviewed or in the commodities included in the computation of the terms of trade it is always possible to claim a deterioration.

Another form of compensatory finance is designed to offset a reduction in foreign exchange receipts below reasonable expectations. In the context, the idea of reasonable expectation is, of course, inherently ambiguous.[1] A decline in exchange receipts can always be brought about by government policy, as for instance by inflationary monetary and

[1] Both the vagueness of the concept of reasonable expectation and the close link between foreign aid and development planning are apparent in the relevant UNCTAD documents. Here is a typical passage: 'In reply to requests for the clarification of the concept of "reasonable expectations" of export proceeds in their proposal, the sponsors stated that the practical implications of the concept would have to be established empirically, but that it was geared to the desirability of safeguarding the execution of sound development programmes.' *Trade and Development : Final Act and Report*, p. 202.

fiscal policies, which discourage exports and encourage imports besides often also promoting an outflow of capital. The larger and more ambitious is the development plan, the more likely export earnings are to decline below reasonable expectations, particularly in relation to the fulfilment of the plan. The UNCTAD proposals nowhere consider the accumulation of reserves in good times to provide for less favourable conditions, an elementary rule of self-reliance and prudence.

The discussion and advocacy of foreign aid by UNCTAD, especially of compensatory finance, is closely linked to changes in foreign exchange earnings and in the terms of trade. Yet even if foreign aid is thought desirable, there is no reason for adopting as criteria for aid either the level of foreign exchange earnings or the terms of trade or of changes in these. There are other grounds or criteria for the granting of aid which would seem to be less inappropriate, such as general living standards or overall government policy in the recipient countries. As the poorest countries and groups in the underdeveloped world are those with few or no external contacts, allocation of aid on the basis of criteria linked to external trade will ensure that the poorest do not qualify for it. Besides focusing attention on irrelevant criteria, the linking of any substantial part of aid to changes in the terms of trade or to a decline in exchange reserves of the recipients also discourages the accumulation of foreign exchange reserves.

12 *Commodity Agreements*

Another major UNCTAD proposal is the promotion of commodity agreements to stabilise, maintain and raise the export prices of primary products. Although stabilisation is mentioned at times, this rather complex concept is left largely undefined. It is, however, clear that what is envisaged is not a smoothing of fluctuations around a trend but the maintenance or raising of prices above what they would otherwise be in order to improve the terms of trade of underdeveloped countries. This proposal in effect envisages yet another form of foreign aid in the form of income transfers from consumers and consuming countries to the exporting countries. Besides the various objections to foreign aid based on criteria linked to external trade, this proposal is also open to further criticisms.

The governments and producers benefiting from such arrangements are arbitrarily chosen. They are certainly not the poorest countries or groups, nor are the recipient governments and producers most likely to use the funds most productively; and the selection of the consumers who are made to pay the higher prices is also largely arbitrary. Moreover, such agreements usually require organised restriction on production and on the extension of capacity. These measures tend to freeze the pattern of production, protect high-cost producers and restrict the growth of lower-cost suppliers. They also imply barriers to entry into the activities subject to these measures, which often bears harshly on those people who have no suitable alternative source of cash income. These are not minor administrative details but major implications of commodity agreements.

13 *Import Restrictions on Manufactured Exports from Underdeveloped Countries*

UNCTAD urges developed countries to eliminate or at least to reduce their restrictions on imports of manufactures from underdeveloped countries. These restrictions are said substantially to damage the development prospects of poor countries by curtailing their trading opportunities and thus their import capacity, and also by restricting the size of the market for their manufactures and thus obstructing the necessary economies of scale.

Substantial barriers in the form of tariffs and quotas against manufactured exports from poor countries exist in many rich countries. And the height of the barriers is often much greater than appears at first sight. Tariffs are expressed as a percentage of the value of the processed product. If, as is often the case, imports of raw materials enter duty free or at low rates of duty, an apparently moderate rate of duty on the processed product often represents a very high percentage of the value added in processing and thus a correspondingly high degree of protection to these activities.

Although the erection of these barriers does not of course mean that the underdeveloped countries are harmed by the existence of developed countries, the barriers undoubtedly affect adversely the development prospects of several underdeveloped countries, especially in Asia, and their material progress is retarded compared to what it would be without these impediments to trade. The barriers prevent or retard the development of otherwise economically viable activities, and so affect the rate of growth of the national income. What is perhaps more important, they prevent or retard the development of external contacts, which have often helped to promote favourable changes in attitudes, motivations, methods of organisation, and institutions, and which have also served to promote the inflow of foreign enterprise and capital.

The significance of these barriers as obstacles to development should not, however, be overstated, as is done in the UNCTAD literature. Even the complete removal of these barriers would not substantially affect the underlying causes of poverty in underdeveloped countries, as these are largely domestic; indeed, many underdeveloped countries are quite unaffected by the presence of these barriers. Moreover, the barriers are not unsurmountable, as is shown by the success of Hong Kong and Israel which are leading exporters of certain manufactures in spite of the trade barriers facing them. The success of the exporters in these countries is underlined by the fact that neither country has a large domestic market or has important natural resources. Indeed, their success as exporting countries enables them to import raw materials and contributes to the growth of their domestic markets. This sequence confirms that in any causal or functional relationship between the determinants of development and the size of the market, the latter is largely an effect or dependent variable.

The UNCTAD literature enjoins developed countries not to insist on reciprocity from underdeveloped countries when reducing their own barriers against manufactures from these countries. The latter are to be allowed, or indeed encouraged, to protect their own industries. Both developed and underdeveloped countries are advised to grant preferences to imports of manufactures from underdeveloped countries. Underdeveloped countries are advised to try to establish common markets among themselves to secure wider markets for their manufactures.

In enjoining the developed countries to reduce or remove the barriers against manufactured exports from underdeveloped countries, the UNCTAD literature rightly points out that such a policy would benefit the consumers and the economy at large in these countries although it would harm sectional interests. This particular argument is, of course, along familiar free trade lines.

But the argument also applies to the underdeveloped countries. Yet the UNCTAD literature envisages and proposes the maintenance or the increase of similar barriers in underdeveloped countries. Save in unusual circumstances (the presence of which would need to be specified), subsidised manufacturing in underdeveloped countries is unlikely to represent either the most efficient allocation of their resources or the most effective method for promoting their growth. The economic implications of subsidising manufacturing are often obscured by the bit of treating the output as a net addition to the flow of income and ignoring the cost of the resources absorbed by it.[1]

UNCTAD suggests that underdeveloped countries should grant preferences to each other's manufactures and to establishing common markets among themselves. Such policies are likely to lead to the proliferation of high-cost industries at the expense of consumers and of the growth of agricultural production for the market, and thus of the spread of the money economy. The policies are also likely to restrict economic contacts with developed countries, which are the principal channels through which new ideas, methods, wants, resources and attitudes reach the underdeveloped world. Restrictions on these contacts are extremely damaging to material progress.

There is a tendency to exaggerate the benefits to be expected from common markets among underdeveloped countries. In many of these countries there is little point in considering the benefits of international integration when their domestic economies are not integrated because of high, often prohibitive, transport costs, and because of tribal, social and ethnic barriers to occupational or geographical mobility. Many of the larger underdeveloped countries, such as Brazil, the Congo, Nigeria, India, Pakistan, Indonesia, are hardly national markets for most purposes. Further, as already noted, the success of Israel and Hong Kong as manufacturing producers and exporters shows the comparative unimportance of the size of the domestic market as a major factor in economic efficiency. Even when the establishment of common markets among poor countries does not restrict economic contacts with more developed countries, it is still unrealistic to expect it to promote the material progress of underdeveloped countries, since once again we are dealing with a proposal which does not affect the underlying determinants of development. A collection of poor people does not add up to a rich society.

14 UNCTAD Suggestions on Domestic Policy

The UNCTAD literature is inevitably primarily concerned with international issues rather than with domestic policies. There are, however, some remarks on domestic policy, about the axiomatic necessity of

[1] It has been observed by Sir Arthur Lewis (*American Economic Review*, May 1965) that the prospective comparative advantage to poor countries in international trade may shift towards manufacturing. This necessarily speculative possibility does not justify the subsidisation of currently uneconomic activity. It strengthens the case for trying to make the economies of poor countries flexible and adaptable.

development planning, the necessity for institutional change, and th. need to develop manufacturing industry.[1]

The institutional changes envisaged are not changes in basic customs, attitudes and values, such as communal or tribal tenure of land, or the inviolability of animal life, or the restrictions on women working. The changes envisaged refer largely to the expropriation of landowners or of prosperous people in the name of land reform and of the promotion of equality. There are frequent references to the need to eliminate privilege, both on social grounds and also in order to promote development. In fact, however, as we have already noted, the most pronounced instances of material inequality in many underdeveloped countries have nothing to do with privilege in the accepted sense. In many underdeveloped countries and regions the richest people were formerly extremely poor immigrants or descendants of poor immigrants, such as the Chinese, Indians and Levantines, who certainly did not receive official favours and who were usually excluded from major sectors of the economy, notably land-owning and the civil service. The activities of these groups have usually contributed greatly to the material progress of the countries of their adoption and in many cases were even largely responsible for it.

The alleged need for state-sponsored industrialisation derives largely from certain general ideas about manufacturing and about the external economies it is thought to yield, which we have already discussed in the appendix to essay 2. There are, however, certain specific arguments prominent in the UNCTAD advocacy of it.

First, the argument runs, it is necessitated by the secular deterioration of the terms of trade of primary producers. As we have seen, there has been no such secular deterioration. Any uncertainty about the future course of the terms of trade, though it may present a case for increasing the flexibility of the economy, is not a ground for state-sponsored manufacturing.

The second argument for subsidised industrialisation is based on the necessity to relieve population pressure, especially rural unemployment, said to be widespread in underdeveloped countries. Quite apart from

---

[1] It is axiomatic throughout the UNCTAD literature that comprehensive development planning is necessary for economic advance and that foreign aid should be linked to it. For instance: ' . . . as a prerequisite [for foreign aid], developing countries should have properly drawn up development plans with targets and time limits covering all aspects of their economy . . .'. *Trade and Development : Final Act and Report*, p. 45.

'The discussion of problems of development finance focused on the need to increase aid, to link it with development plans and to improve the terms of aid and to ease the existing burden of debt service.' *Ibid.*, p. 170.

e fact that rural unemployment is by no means general in under-
eveloped countries (for instance, it is clearly not a major factor in the
African economies), this argument is inconclusive, because it does not
follow that diversion of resources into manufacturing would provide
more employment than expenditure on the development of agriculture
or on the improvement of communications.[1]

The third argument canvassed by UNCTAD is the usefulness of manufacturing for the spread of technical skills. But for the reasons noted in
the appendix to essay 2, in the conditions of most underdeveloped
countries agricultural production for the market is likely to be more
effective for the development of the changes in attitudes and skills
required for material progress than is subsidised manufacturing.[2]

Manufacturing is simply a type of economic activity, or rather a
miscellaneous bundle of activities. It is not an analytical category; nor
does it offer or represent a clear criterion for activities to be singled out
as particularly promising instruments for material progress.

Most of the UNCTAD discussion on manufacturing is vitiated by
treating its output as a net addition to the flow of income without examining the economic cost or the demand for the output. This familiar
shortcoming of much current discussion on economic issues is
prominent in the UNCTAD literature, especially in its numerous flattering
remarks on the rapid economic progress of Soviet-type economies
without reference to general living standards there.

15 *Conclusion*

Assuming that the criticisms in this essay are substantial, the question
arises whether the UNCTAD meetings or machinery could be reformed
sufficiently to serve the aim of promoting the development of poor
countries. In principle, such a transformation would be possible. The
UNCTAD conference or secretariat could conceivably examine such
matters as the allocation of aid to support those governments whose

---

[1] For most purposes of policy the concept of rural unemployment would need to be
defined carefully, which it is not in the UNCTAD advocacy of sponsored industrialisation.
Further, in the context of policy the question also needs to be asked why such unemployment, where it is present, does not bring about a fall in wages sufficient to encourage
unsubsidised manufacturing.

[2] This last argument noted here often merges into the infant industry argument,
which is also frequent in UNCTAD discussions. This familiar argument is obscure. If the
infants show genuine promise they will be able to be financed by their supporters or by
entrepreneurs without recourse to subsidy by the rest of the community. In fact, the
infants often fail to grow up; and even if they do, they do not usually repay to the
community the subsidies they received.

policies are most likely to promote and raise the general living standard and wellbeing of their populations, rather than promote objectives quite unrelated to these ends. It could also seriously examine such matters as the smoothing of fluctuations in incomes of producers without state control over the economy, or the conditions under which trade barriers are most likely to be reduced or removed. By addressing itself to such matters the UNCTAD machinery could make a minor but perhaps not insignificant contribution to the material progress of poor countries. But the likelihood of such a reconsideration of its outlook and activities is remote.

APPENDIX: EXTRACTS FROM THE PREBISCH REPORT

Apart from minor exceptions, the UNCTAD literature is not quoted in this essay because the vague and devious nature of the principal documents would have made the quotation of representative passages unduly lengthy. This appendix reproduces some typical passages from the Prebisch Report on the related subjects of the declining terms of trade, the role of compensatory finance and the linking of aid to development planning; they are intended to forestall an objection that the opinions or passages discussed in the text are not representative.

In the Prebisch Report the improvement in the commodity terms of trade of primary producers between 1961 and 1964 is briefly noted but dismissed as temporary. The following passages are characteristic:

But can it be argued that the general trend has finally reversed itself and that there is no longer any need to worry about the possibility of further deterioration? Or ought we, on the contrary, to face up to this phenomenon with a great sense of foresight?[1]

However, for the technical discussion to be profitable, it must be preceded by a political decision of the first importance, namely, a decision to transfer, in one way or another, to the countries exporting primary commodities the extra income accruing to the industrial countries as a result of the deterioration in the terms of trade.[2]

From a pragmatic point of view this means recognising that countries experiencing a deterioration in the terms of trade have a *prima facie* claim upon additional international resources – resources over and above those which they would have received in the normal course of events. Some aspects of this matter are rather delicate and might lead the discussion on to barren ground unless we keep these pragmatic considerations uppermost in our minds [*sic*]. Practically speaking, the position is this. The foreign earnings of the developing countries have suffered severely from the deterioration in the terms of trade. Unless these countries succeed in obtaining additional resources, they will be unable to achieve the reasonable rate of growth set as a target in their plans. The situation will be worse still if the terms of trade deteriorate further in the future.[3]

Although the discussion of compensatory finance both in the Prebisch Report and elsewhere in the UNCTAD literature is at times ambiguous, it seems that such finance is envisaged under two headings: compensation for short-period declines in export proceeds leading to balance of pay-

[1] Prebisch Report, p. 16.
[2] *Ibid.*
[3] *Ibid.* The 'normal course of events' here means routine aid, not export earnings.

ments disequilibrium, and compensation for deterioration in the terms of trade. The latter is regarded as the principal category.

The discussion in the Prebisch Report is on pages 80–3. The first type of compensatory finance is envisaged as emerging from certain measures already taken by the International Monetary Fund. Dr Prebisch considers useful those measures designed to tide over short-term declines in export receipts:

... but they do not go to the heart of the longer-term problems associated with a downward trend in the terms of trade ... the international community should recognise that it has a clear responsibility towards developing countries that have suffered a deterioration in their terms of trade.... In relation to what point in time should losses be calculated? Would it suffice to assure the developing countries that they will not be subject to new losses in relation to present prices? Or should losses be calculated in relation to some past year, when the terms of trade were less unfavourable to developing countries than they have recently been? To compensate for new losses is important but it is not enough; something needs to be done to restore the purchasing power of the developing countries, and not simply prevent it from weakening further.[1]

... such an approach would have to be based on a study of the potential investment resources lost by each country as a result of actual past deterioration in the terms of trade, the impact of this deterioration on the balance of payments, the effects of both these phenomena on the rate of growth, and any other factors that it might be advisable to consider in each particular case. This study would be necessary in order to determine what additional international resources would have to be provided in order to compensate developing countries for the adverse effects of the terms of trade.[2]

... all this should be studied by experts.... [However] in order to prevent the experts from proceeding along the wrong track, there must be a prior political decision regarding the transfer of resources....[3]

In other words, the expert study is to be an exercise in public relations in order to make palatable and plausible the political decision to transfer resources from the developed world to the underdeveloped world.

The flow of aid, both of general aid and of compensatory finance, is to be closely geared to development planning:

The pragmatic approach to which reference has just been made would be easier if the countries concerned had a development plan. A development plan is generally based on the assumption that the export and import prices currently prevailing will be maintained during the period of the plan. It is on this assumption that the possibilities of mobilising domestic capital are quantified.[4]

[1] p. 81.
[2] pp. 81–2.
[3] p. 82.
[4] *Ibid.*

The need for compensatory financing to maintain the integrity of development programmes will therefore be apparent.[1]

In the light of this explanation of the close link between compensatory financing and development plans, it will be understood that the resources in question should not normally be allocated directly to individual producers. If that were done, not only would the basic objectives of the development programme be adversely affected, but the problem of deterioration in the terms of trade might be aggravated in the future as a result of the incentive which the higher return would offer to producers.[2]

Compensatory funds should constitute a net addition to that target [the 'accepted target' of 1 per cent of the national income of donors as routine aid], the amount of the addition depending, of course, on the terms of trade.

Moreover, in view of the outright loss that a deterioration in terms of trade represents, the compensatory resources should not take the form of loans subject to amortisation and interest payments.[3]

It is to be hoped that procedures for allocating resources furnished as compensatory financing will help to give developing countries every reasonable assurance that they can rely on the global funds needed for the carrying out of their development plans.[4]

Improvement in the terms of trade of underdeveloped countries or repayment of compensatory financing for declining terms of trade are apparently not envisaged. Moreover, factoral terms of trade are nowhere discussed in the Prebisch Report, nor, as far as I know, in any publication of UNCTAD.

In the face of the actual course of the terms of trade of underdeveloped countries and of their share in world trade over the last few decades, the Prebisch Report must be judged to be mere fiction or political propaganda.

[1] *Ibid.*
[2] p. 83.
[3] *Ibid.*
[4] p. 84.

7 Economics as a Form of Technical Assistance[1]

Has the economist a place in a programme of technical assistance? Is a knowledge of modern economic theory and analysis a useful or necessary input in a programme designed to foster economic growth in a foreign economy? These questions provide the theme for the following observations, which relate to various aspects of this theme, and proceed at different levels of detail and generality.

1 *Some Relevant Theory*

Some years ago Lord Robbins, in an address on 'The Economist in the Twentieth Century',[2] discussed the contribution of economists in government service. He suggested that the command of the somewhat elementary and trite platitudes of economics was particularly useful in this context. More recently, Professor Simon Rottenberg, an economist with extensive experience of development problems, expressed substantially the same view in the field of development economics.[3]

I agree with these assessments. We should note, however, what is meant by these platitudes or simple fundamentals. I take it that they include such matters as the treatment of supply and demand as being functionally related to price, and of cost as opportunity cost; the theory of relative prices; the implications of comparative advantage and costs, and the functional relationships between the flow of money incomes, the volume of employment and the balance of payments.

Such fundamentals are clearly relevant to economic policy-making, notably to the assessment of alternative policies and the efficiency of different specific measures. They apply to public finance, especially to the assessment of the incidence and other effects of different taxes and items of government expenditure. But their scope extends far

---

[1] The original version of this essay appeared in *The Manchester School*, May 1967. That article was in turn a revised version of a talk at the Staff Seminar in the Faculty of Economics and Social Studies of Manchester University, May 1966.

[2] *Economica*, May 1949.

[3] 'Economic Instruction for Economic Growth', *Economic Development and Cultural Change*, October 1964.

beyond these important spheres. For instance, recognition of the effects of prices on supply, or of the presence and relevance of costs, is necessary for assessing the implications of such diverse measures as licensing of transport or processing enterprises; prescription of minimum physical standards for export products; the payment of uniform prices to producers, irrespective of their location; imposition of minimum wages; prescription of rents or leasing of government-owned land at uniform rates, regardless of its fertility and location; and many other measures which affect incomes, opportunities and the efficient use of resources.

The neglect of the importance of cost largely explains the confusion between technical and economic efficiency implicit in such measures as the prescription of minimum physical standards for export products, and other similar measures adopted in many underdeveloped countries, including those whose governments have economic advisers or even lavishly staffed planning units.[1] Yet these are measures which can be assessed largely on the basis of economic reasoning since they do not raise wide political and social issues. They are often costly in the sense that a given volume of output could be produced with an appreciably smaller volume of scarce resources; they serve also to retard the expansion of production for the market and the spread of the exchange economy in many poor countries; and the retardation of the spread of the exchange economy has far-reaching adverse effects on development.

The establishment of minimum wages by statute or by organised labour or by government directive is now almost universal in major activities in the underdeveloped world. Such measures raise wages above the supply price of labour; this supply price indicates its highest contribution to output, which in turn reflects its economic scarcity. Wage regulation affects considerably the rate of development, the prospects of industrialisation, the level of employment, and the pattern of economic activity in many underdeveloped countries. The effects and implications of these measures cannot properly be assessed without reference to elementary economic theory. Even without econometric or statistical investigations it is possible to form some idea of such

[1] An analogous instance of the identification or rather confusion of technical and economic efficiency is the ban on the use or importation of second-hand machinery. For instance, in the 1950s the import of second-hand machinery into Egypt was banned for some years. This type of equipment is often available more cheaply to underdeveloped countries because it has lost its usefulness in advanced countries where wages are higher, while it is still valuable in countries where they are lower. In these circumstances a ban on the import of second-hand machinery deprives the country of a comparatively cheap addition to its productive equipment.

relevant factors as the presence or absence of monopsony, or the factors affecting the elasticity of demand for the product, or the elasticity of supply of complementary resources, or the elasticity of substitution between resources. Without some grasp of elementary economics these factors will be overlooked, as indeed they generally are. This defect in turn makes it impossible to select the industries for the imposition of minimum wages in order to secure the most effective achievement of any specific policy objective.

Elementary economic analysis is also pertinent to many specialised aspects of technical assistance. For instance, prices, costs and returns are clearly relevant when choices are being made between alternative agricultural or industrial techniques. Costs depend on factor prices and resource availabilities, and these often differ for different types of producer even within the same economy or country. Thus, for instance, the most suitable planting density in rubber growing differs between estates operating with large capital and expensive hired labour forces on the one hand, and smallholdings with little capital and without hired labour on the other; and the optimum planting density varies also with differences in expected prices and costs. Thus the optimum planting density can be determined only after taking into account both economic and technical factors.

Restrictionism has become widespread in underdeveloped countries. It is directed primarily against ethnic and tribal minorities distinct from the groups enjoying political power but it operates extensively and is not confined to these categories. These restrictive measures substantially damage the development prospects of these countries; they inflict hardship on many people; and they often exacerbate social and political tensions. A reasonable grasp of the nature and sources of income, of the theory of relative prices, and of the implications of competitive or complementary relationships between resources, helps both to understand the forces behind these tendencies and also to analyse some of their effects and implications.

With few and normally irrelevant exceptions, incomes represent payments to owners of productive resources for services supplied, and not money extracted from others without return. The contrary view that incomes, especially those of certain groups, are somehow extracted from other people, is politically influential, popular and appealing. For familiar reasons, the appeal is particularly pronounced when the income recipients are ethnic minorities, or owners of property, or people engaged in service industries, including trade.

Related to this issue in practical politics, though analytically distinct from it, is that of the complementary or competitive nature of the economic relationship between different groups, in the sense of the effect of a change in the volume of the activities of one group on the real incomes of other groups. People generally are sensitive to the actual or potential competitive element in their economic relationships with other groups; and they are apt to overestimate the competitive and to underestimate the complementary aspect of these relationships. This asymmetry in people's perception of the gains and losses from the activities of others, together with the belief that incomes of certain groups are extracted from others without having any economic rationale, are often major factors behind government support of economic restrictionism and various other measures against particular classes and groups. Other factors behind these measures include a failure to appreciate some of the most important but not immediately obvious effects of restrictionism, such as the incidence of the cost of restrictionism on those excluded from the restricted activity, or the effects of restrictionism on the growth of resources and on development generally.

Another influence behind such measures is the belief that they are required to diminish the poverty or redress the weakness of the bargaining power of the local population against foreigners and minority groups. This belief ignores the incidence of these measures on other poor members of the local population, often poorer than the beneficiaries of these measures. And liability to exploitation depends on absence of alternatives and not, as is often supposed, on differences in wealth or in commercial sophistication. Yet another reason for the ready acceptance of these measures is the oversimplification of the concept of the interest of the local population, as homogeneous and also divergent from or even opposed to the interest of foreigners and minorities. This view ignores many complexities in the concept of group interest; for instance, it ignores the fact that the activities of foreigners or minority groups are usually complementary with those of the majority of the local population, though they may be competitive with those of some groups in it. When restrictionism is directed against ethnic or linguistic groups distinct from the ruling group, tribalism or xenophobia also play a part. These various influences, especially the notion that incomes are extracted rather than earned, have contributed substantially to the policies directed against materially successful but politically powerless groups in many poor countries.

The simple propositions of economics are also necessary for the effective use of its more advanced techniques. Thus the adoption of ostensibly sophisticated planning techniques or techniques of project appraisal is irrelevant if alternative uses of resources are disregarded in the process of applying them to specific projects or sectors. It is not that recent advances in economic analysis may not be relevant for and applicable to the problems of underdeveloped countries. But their use is misconceived or even mischievous when it is accompanied by gross neglect or apparent ignorance of elementary but basic economic considerations and by a disregard of the implications of the institutional background.

As a firm grasp of fundamentals is a hallmark of expert knowledge, so their neglect reflects its absence. It seems paradoxical that in spite of important technical advances in so many branches of economics, and in spite of enormous interest (or at least output) in development economics, there is now a substantial lack of fundamental expertise in this branch of the subject. The eagerness with which the latest refinements in economic theory and analysis are – or appear to be – embraced by the practitioners of development economics is misplaced if at the same time they disregard elementary economic and institutional considerations.

2 *Some Ambiguities*

As do many other scientific disciplines, the social sciences rely extensively on general abstract concepts. But while in some other disciplines, notably in mathematics and the natural sciences, the abstract concepts are generally used consistently and precisely, the same is not true in economics. For instance, terms such as capital, investment, stabilisation or planning are widely used in a number of different senses. Planning and stabilisation in particular are often given widely different or even diametrically opposed interpretations. To borrow from Sir Isaiah Berlin, these concepts are so porous that there is practically no interpretation which they are capable of resisting. The porosity of these concepts implies that without closer definition they are useless to serve as guides to policy or detailed decision-making; quite different courses of action can be justified by reference to one or other of these conflicting interpretations. These inconsistencies bring about confusion of different objectives of policy and this in turn leads to ineffective policies, that is to say policies not designed to promote their specified objectives. Consistency in the use of terms and concepts may help to avoid pitfalls such as the familiar juxtaposition of the suggestion that producers in poor countries do not respond to incentives with the insistence that certain activities should be subsidised to encourage their expansion.

Examples abound in contemporary economic discussion of inconsistencies in interpretation and resulting confusion of objectives. For instance, a confusion of objectives has been manifest in both national and international discussions of price and income stabilisation: on a national level between the smoothing of price and income fluctuations on the one hand and compulsory saving or disinflation on the other; on the international level between the relief of poverty, the smoothing of fluctuations and the monopolistic raising of prices.

3 The Value of Economic History

The historical experience of some economies cannot necessarily serve as a basis for policy elsewhere, at other times. Yet for many purposes knowledge of history in some depth is required. In the widest sense, some knowledge of history, whether of the particular economy or of other economies, is required to get the record straight on aspects and phases of development; on the origins and operation of institutions; on the background, operation and results of policies; and on the conduct and responses of individuals and groups. Generally, a correct record of empirical evidence is necessary for the formulation of fruitful hypotheses, including hypotheses about the likely results of different policies.

A knowledge of economic history is also helpful in its own right for the illumination of development problems. Some knowledge of a country's history is usually required for an understanding of the strength and operation of many of its institutions which affect its material advance. The origins, development and significance of caste and of the sanctity of cattle in Hindu India are examples. Again, a reasonable working knowledge of European and Mediterranean economic history since the Middle Ages is helpful to the understanding of social and economic transformation in many parts of the contemporary world. Examples include, among others, the role of minorities (including minorities without political rights) in economic development; the social and political arrangements most likely to promote material advance; the effects of international economic contacts on the development of technically more backward societies; the interrelationships between social, political and legal institutions; the influences most likely to modify traditional attitudes and values; the role of different types of external capital in economic development; and so on.

Recognition of the many centuries of material advance in western Europe before the dates conventionally assigned to the industrial revolution, and of the advanced state of social, economic and technical development in Europe by the seventeenth and eighteenth centuries, or in Japan in the nineteenth century, bear on many problems of the present-day underdeveloped world. Again, in assessing the applicability and relevance to underdeveloped countries of the experience of other countries, whether western Europe, North America, the Soviet Union, China or Japan, reasonable knowledge of the history of these economies is necessary. These matters cannot be appraised on the basis of formal analysis, *a priori* reasoning, or observation confined to the contemporary scene.

Quite generally, a knowledge of economic history is helpful or even necessary for an understanding both of the requirements of material progress and its time perspective. This consideration covers such diverse but relevant matters as the human qualities required for the transformation of North America from an empty continent into the most advanced economy in the world; the long period of development in Europe and the Mediterranean area before the industrial revolution; and the numerous instances of the decline of advanced economies in the course of history. This latter is a phenomenon almost wholly ignored in contemporary development literature. Incidentally, this phenomenon is incompatible with the much canvassed notion of generally operative cumulative causation.

There are many further specific matters within the field of economic technical assistance which need the perspectives of economic history if they are to be appreciated. Acquaintance with the history of many underdeveloped areas over the last century, for instance West and East Africa and Burma since the 1880s, helps the observer to recognise the problems posed by the impact of rapid and uneven change. Again, an appreciation of economic history will also help to put into focus such notions as the widely canvassed suggestion that economic contacts between developed and poor countries damage the prospects of the latter (the alleged adverse operation of the international demonstration effect), or that poverty itself sets up insurmountable obstacles to its own conquest (the vicious circle of poverty).

At times it may also be possible to apply successfully relatively sophisticated techniques of economic and econometric analysis to a situation illuminated first by careful historical study, that is, after the ground has been prepared by historical study, including work with primary sources. When successful, this procedure can shed light on the process of development at crucial stages in the economic advance of a country, including an analysis of the provenance of some of the resources which have promoted or accompanied these changes.[1]

Altogether, a reasonable command of economic history is an important element in the equipment of an economist acting as an adviser on general development matters (though not for those economists acting in a restricted capacity, for instance as advisers on specific technical projects).

4 *The Problem of* Ceteris Paribus

The relevance of historical experience is germane to an important and wide issue which straddles the methodology of economics on the one hand and major matters of development policy on the other. This issue is the appropriate use of the device of *cet. par.,* 'other things being equal': what are the variables appropriately selected for discussion, and conversely what influences and factors can be disregarded legitimately, either in the sense of being noted explicitly as parameters or ignored altogether?

The device of *cet. par.* in economic analysis is required to reduce to manageable proportions the complex reality of economic life, that is to make possible the analysis of the relation between a limited number of specified variables selected from among the numerous factors which may affect the situation. The acceptance of this device has often been accompanied by some uneasiness based on the recognition that all elements of an economy are interrelated, so that every change affects everything else, that is other things cannot remain equal, together with the recognition that conditions constantly change, notably so in the process of development. There have also been recurrent doubts whether, granted the necessity for the adoption of *cet. par.,* the variables ignored may not be of greater operational significance than those selected for study. These considerations may limit substantially the explanatory power of a method which relies heavily on *cet. par.* This limitation applies both to partial equilibrium analysis (which ignores both the repercussions of the variables studied on the rest of the system and also the changes in the basic conditions of the system), as well as

---

[1] A notable example of such a successful attempt is a recently published book by Dr R.Szereszewski, *Structural Changes in the Economy of Ghana, 1891–1911*, London, 1967.

to macroeconomic models (which ignore relationships between the variables aggregated for the purpose of macroeconomic analysis and also the changes in the basic conditions of the system). These problems and doubts about the appropriateness and limitations of the choice of variables selected for analysis against those treated parametrically are particularly significant in development economics, which deals with whole systems in which the elements are interrelated and which examines these systems in conditions of change.

Wants, resources (especially human resources) and technology are often treated parametrically in economic discussion. In many contexts this practice is legitimate, though even in the partial equilibrium analysis of comparative statics it is not always helpful. For instance, the well recognised phenomenon of irreversible demand and supply curves suggests the limitations of parametric treatment of wants or technology in some applications of partial equilibrium analysis. And when we consider problems of economic development, especially those of development policy, we must note that the usual variables of modern micro- and macroeconomic analysis, and policy measures designed to operate on these variables, very often, and perhaps generally, affect the factors treated parametrically in economic theory. Manipulations of the variables also affects the parameters.

In the choice of variables for examination, convenience of analysis and exposition, the nature of the system to be investigated, and the relative operational significance of its elements in the problem examined, all play a part. In much of contemporary literature on development planning and technical assistance, notably in contemporary growth models, which have greatly influenced the literature, the principal variables examined are usually total output, capital stock, investment expenditure, consumption and population. Wants, resources and technology are often (though not invariably) treated parametrically.[1] Human abilities and behaviour, social institutions, customs and attitudes, and external contacts, which are patently important and often decisive factors in material progress, are either consciously impounded within cet. par. or are more usually ignored altogether.

---

[1] When wants are admitted as variables the treatment is usually misleading, as in the well known suggestion that the emergence of new wants through external contacts retards development by raising the propensity to consume. Apart from the question of the meaning of development if divorced from consumer wants, this suggestion, which is influential in planning literature, ignores the obvious effects of new wants in inducing a higher economic performance. Technological change is sometimes introduced formally into the discussion, usually however without examining how it comes about, a procedure which is not illuminating.

Such a treatment may perhaps be appropriate (though even this is doubtful) in the analysis of highly developed industrialised societies pervaded by the money economy. It is certainly insufficient for explaining the rate of development of underdeveloped countries, or for the design of policies for its promotion.

These parameters and their interaction with the conventional variables change through time in ways which it is generally difficult and often impossible to predict. A reasonable command of economic history and extensive direct observation of particular societies are often indispensable for worthwhile discernment and prediction of the interaction of variables and parameters, of changes in these parameters, and also of changes in their interaction with the variables.

5 Variables and Parameters

The operation of conventional variables, and of the policies designed to influence these variables, usually affect, often substantially, determinants of development. These repercussions are apt to be ignored in conventional discussion. Again, the emphasis on aggregates in macroeconomic models has obscured the interaction of the components of these aggregates which, at times, is highly significant for the promotion of development. The emphasis on growth models and on aggregates has also promoted the spread of an economics in which absolute or relative prices and costs find no place, and are simply ignored.

Let me elaborate on some of these matters which are relevant to the value of economics as a form of technical assistance. When assessing the principal results of changes in the level and direction of taxation, or of government expenditure, or of the imposition or removal of specific controls, on development, it is insufficient to examine the direct effects on conventional variables, such as the volume of investible funds, or the level of consumption, or the supply of effort. As we have already emphasised in various contexts, such measures affect occupational and geographical mobility (including the incentive and ability of people to set up new enterprises), as well as the direction and volume of interregional and international contacts, and also the movement of people, goods and ideas. These contacts and flows in turn affect the spread of new wants, methods and crops, and they also influence established attitudes, customs and values. The repercussions on these determinants of material progress are often much more far-reaching and pervasive than the direct effects operating through the conventional variables.

Again, when examining the likely effects (favourable or adverse) on economic development of a substantial extension of government control over economic life, one should take into account such factors as the repercussions on the position and prospects of ethnic minorities; the diversion of the energies of enterprising men from economic to political life; the effects on social cohesion; the strengthening or disintegration of traditional attitudes; and the likely effects on different social institutions.

There are familiar difficulties in the way of systematic or formal treatment of some of these major determinants of economic development, notably human capacities, social institutions and attitudes, and the role of ethnic minorities and immigrants. The difficulties include the problem presented by the time span over which these effects operate or become manifest. However, it may eventually prove possible to incorporate at least some of these factors into systematic development economics, even if quantification should prove impracticable. For instance, empirical work on the type of commodity or service likely to serve as an incentive good in various societies might yield interesting results.

The dangers of oversimplification in aggregative analysis must also be remembered. The important role of a higher and more varied level of consumption in inducing a higher economic performance in saving, investment, innovation and enterprise is particularly apt to be forgotten when consumption is treated as a homogeneous aggregate without examining its composition or the interrelation of its components, or the question whether consumption and investment are competitive or complementary in total economic activity (in the sense that an increase in one is likely to bring about an increase or decrease in the other).

6 Selection of Variables

Economics as a form of technical assistance faces a number of limitations. The first limitation, or set of limitations, is inherent in any technical subject, namely the impossibility of conclusive assessment of the merits of any policy solely on the basis of technical reasoning. The merits of any policy compared to other policies depend on their probable result on the total social situation. These likely results cannot normally be assessed with certainty on the basis of technical reasoning only, notably on the basis of expertise in any particular field. Technical reasoning can help to assess the operation of specific variables and influences which the policy is designed to affect. But these variables usually interact with other factors, some of which are outside the purview or special competence of the expert, who cannot therefore assess correctly the likely effects of the policy on the total social situation. Moreover, the evaluation of the merits of different courses of action depends on value judgments, notably on preferences between different types of societies. And these value judgments often influence not only opinions about the relative merits of different results; they can also influence covertly or subconsciously the assessment of the likely costs, results and repercussions of different policies.

This limitation does not bear equally upon all policy measures, proposals or discussions. For instance, such measures as the prescription of minimum physical standards for exportable produce can be assessed much more effectively from economic reasoning than can such far-reaching and pervasive policies as special taxation to increase government investment expenditure (compulsory saving). But even when technical reasoning alone is insufficient for assessing the merits of a policy, it is often legitimate to use technical reasoning to point out that arguments in support of particular policies ignore costs, or are inconsistent with arguments invoked in support of other policies, or are susceptible to widely different or even inconsistent interpretations. More generally, when policies are supported by arguments based on technical reasoning it is legitimate to examine the arguments on the same level.

There is an analytical framework behind economics which confers on it at least a potential firmness, which used to justify its claim to be the queen of the social sciences. But it also engenders certain characteristic habits and attitudes of mind in economists, especially theoretical economists, which affect their judgment on social and political issues, somewhat similar to the outlook and attitudes of physicists when they examine such issues. For reasons which are the staple of the textbooks, economists often have to work with highly simplified models of the real world in which a few assumptions are put forward to provide a predictive framework by isolating factors implicitly or explicitly regarded as crucial or critical. In fact, however, the variables selected are often chosen for their logical convenience and their susceptibility to treatment by modern economic analysis, rather than for their relevance or significance as determinants. The latter characteristics are often difficult to establish conclusively or convincingly in the absence of contrived experiments. This difficulty adds to the attractions of simplicity. In particular, the choice of variables is apt to be biased in favour of those which both permit and promote simplicity in analysis. The predilection for simplicity and for tractability by formal analysis has also induced a disregard of direct observation of the complexity of situations, and also of the importance and relevance of historical antecedents, and of the operation of chance factors. While the choice of variables on the basis of logical convenience, simplicity, or elegance of analysis, is often fruitful in the natural sciences, this is not usually so in social studies, where recognition of the complexity of a problem is indispensable for valid results, especially results with predictive value.

These considerations are particularly pertinent when the analysis is to serve as basis for action and, more especially, when it is applied to an unfamiliar institutional situation. In practice, the whole process of model-building, especially the inferences drawn from the models, often goes far beyond useful and necessary simplification and issues in conclusions so unrelated to reality that they are a travesty and not an elucidation of the matters at issue. In much of the development literature these conclusions, designed to serve as a basis of action, are often unrelated to reality, first because the assumptions abstract from the most important determinants, but also because a solution, in the sense of a resolution or development of social and political situations, cannot be derived from technical reasoning alone. These problems are complex: they are affected by innumerable variables of differing significance which operate with different time lags; they are subject to shifting parameters; the parameters are often affected by the variables and by policies designed to modify them; and they involve conflicts of interest which cannot be resolved on the basis of logic.

The major determinants of material progress are at present outside the concern of formal economic analysis: human capacities and attitudes; social institutions and customs; political systems and arrangements; access to external contacts; and possession of natural resources or access to them. As I have already suggested, it is difficult to say whether these significant determinants can be made amenable to the prevailing techniques and approach of economic analysis, but they are certainly not so at present. Abstraction of these factors is appropriate in most modern micro- and macroeconomic theory, the validity of the conclusions of which are not affected thereby. But this does not warrant their neglect in development economics. There is here a significant limit to the potentialities of economics, especially of contemporary economics, as an instrument of technical assistance. Its application can even be harmful when it ignores the repercussions on the major determinants of development of policies designed to influence the conventional but less critical variables.

The purport and implications of the preceding passages do not constitute criticism of theory, abstraction and simplification, nor of the inclusion of unrealistic or the exclusion of realistic assumptions in economic analysis. Simplification and abstraction are what we strive after in scientific work and their fruitfulness is beyond dispute. The criticism is directed at the construction and elaboration of models which ignore demonstrably pertinent factors and forces. Moreover, these models have not yielded testable predictions which can be falsified by the facts. Nor have they served to produce hitherto unsuspected explanations of historical developments and contemporary situations, or even provoke interesting insights. And these models or their derivatives have come to be used operationally: major policies and plans are based on the models before their relevance has in any way been established, and despite the fact that in many respects the relationships implied by the models either ignore or do violence to readily ascertainable facts.

Several of the most prominent contributors to the development of growth models appreciate the limitations of their models, especially those limitations deriving from their highly aggregative and abstract character. My criticism is largely that many other (and often influential) writers have ignored these limitations and have tried to apply such models in practice to situations in which the abstraction and aggregation involved render them irrelevant: instead of being useful simplifications which expose the essentials of problems and phenomena, they become travesties which divert attention from the essentials and obscure the issues. Moreover, these models are sometimes used to provide a spurious intellectual basis for policies likely to defeat their own ostensible purposes. Examples include the use of models which emphasise increased capital formation as a condition for higher incomes and improved living standards, an emphasis which is used to justify conscription of labour, special taxation, or restriction of external contacts or of emigration, on the argument that the increased investment expenditure made possible by these policies will, at some future date, improve the living standards of the people who are being subjected to these policies.

7 *Importance of Fundamentals*

I noted earlier the importance of a grasp of simple but basic propositions of economics. I shall suggest two reasons for my insistence on this point. But I should like first to emphasise a characteristic of economics which may forestall certain objections to what follows.

This characteristic is that in economics progress is often followed by serious relapse, by renewed acceptance of demonstrated errors. This phenomenon has been noted by economists as different in outlook and interests as D. H. Robertson, Professor Milton Friedman and Mr G. D. N. Worswick. This characteristic reveals a difficulty in the use of economics as a form of technical assistance. In technology or in a technical subject the practitioners rely on agreed and established ideas and methods, and advance from these established bases. This condition is much less true of economics, even on an elementary level.

The first reason for insisting on the simple elements of economics is the frequent failure of economists to appreciate the difficulties of laymen (even intelligent, educated and experienced laymen) in handling economic ideas and concepts. Non-economists generally, and politicians and administrators in particular, often find it difficult to envisage supply, demand and price as functional relationships; or to recognise or acknowledge the concept of foregone alternatives; or to remember the related consideration that because the economic problem is one of allocation and not one of priorities, the economic significance of a unit of a commodity depends on number rather than on class. They also often overlook the relevance of distinctions such as that between scarcity rents on the one hand and monopoly profits on the other.

These difficulties partly explain the elusive character of elementary economics which, though it does not present severe intellectual challenges, often eludes laymen who try to tackle it, somewhat as a piece of soap which has fallen into the bath tub slips through the fingers of the person trying to grasp it.

The second and much more disturbing reason for the necessity of emphasising the importance of apparently trite elementary propositions is that in the last twenty years or so economists themselves have often ignored them. This neglect is particularly notable in development literature, especially so in the literature on technical assistance, which abounds in examples of the neglect of the simple relationships of elementary economics.[1]

The practice of treating an activity or an output as a net addition to total output, income or welfare, without considering the alternative uses of resources, that is cost, is also widespread. This treatment is almost universal in contemporary literature on government sponsored industrialisation and on the establishment of government operated or supported national trade corporations, where alternative sources or uses of the required capital are seldom brought into the discussion. Another notable example of the practice of disregarding costs is presented by the terminology or nomenclature of the numerous official organisations and institutions termed development banks or development boards in underdeveloped countries. Their funds are usually derived largely from the taxation (at times by the raising of officially guaranteed loans) of productive activities, chiefly the production and marketing of cash crops, a prime instrument of material progress in underdeveloped countries. These institutions often finance politically popular but uneconomic activities or political parties, or the expenditures of influential people. To term them development organisations prejudges the results of their operations. Neglect of the cost of the resources at the disposal of these organisations (in the sense of the alternative uses of these resources) precludes worthwhile assessment of their activities.[2]

Yet firm recognition that resources are limited and that their uses have to be assessed in terms of foregone alternatives is perhaps the most fundamental single idea in economics. Its oversight strikes at the root of the subject as a systematic discipline. Quite generally one reads about needs, requirements and supplies (almost in military language, and out-of-date military language at that), rather than about supply and demand as function of costs, prices and incomes.

The neglect of elementary economic propositions has now spread to macroeconomics. An example, or series of examples, is provided by the frequent – almost habitual – practice of discussing the balance of

[1] To mention but one of many examples: in a well-known World Bank Report on Nigeria there is a prolonged discussion of factors influencing agricultural output in that country. The factors listed include climatic conditions, water supply, plant disease, cultivation methods, and agricultural research. The price received by the producer is not mentioned. This report is discussed at length in essay 11.

[2] Another example of costless economics, analogous to those instanced in the text, is the much publicised suggestion that the infant industry argument for protection applies to them generally because they are infant economies. The infant industry argument, whatever its merits, envisages assistance to an infant sector of the economy at the expense of the rest of the economy. If the entire economy is regarded as an infant, there can be no fully grown sector to be taxed for the benefit of the infants.

payments position and prospects of underdeveloped countries without reference to monetary policies, or to the effects of domestic prices, incomes or exchange rates on the volume of imports or exports. Again, a reduction in the volume of exports of a commodity from one country is often instanced as evidence of a decline in the demand for it, which confuses the supply from one source with total demand. These transgressions often occur in ostensibly sophisticated and technical writings. These defects and others noted in this essay are, of course, not universal in the development literature, but they are widespread, especially in the most publicised and influential academic and official literature.

There are two points related to this disregard of elementary methods and propositions of economics on which I should like to touch lightly. The first is perhaps one of clarification. The burden of my criticism is that these relevant considerations are simply ignored, and not that they are re-examined and rejected in the light of subsequent information, or that they are deemed inapplicable in a particular situation. Second, this disregard of elementary economics is often accompanied by an equally pronounced disregard of simple empirical evidence. For instance, a frequent theme of the most influential literature on development is the alleged presence of a generally operative vicious circle of poverty, the suggestion that poverty itself sets up insurmountable obstacles to its own conquest which can be remedied only by the inflow of free or subsidised external resources. This thesis is inconsistent with the most obvious empirical evidence, including the phenomenon of development as such. Such oversights prevent the establishment of a reasonable empirical basis for development economics. They also have various important implications for policy. For instance, during the last half century acute problems calling for government action in many poor countries have arisen from the impact of rapid and uneven change. They would clearly not arise in a stagnant society caught in a vicious circle of poverty.

Disregard of accepted propositions of elementary economics and of obvious empirical evidence has brought it about that many of the major publications in the development literature are irrelevant or confusing travesties of reality: instead of illuminating the scene they confuse the issues. They also divert attention from the relevance of economics and from the possibilities of strengthening the sources of material progress. In this manner, much of the literature of development economics has not promoted but has retarded the progress of a field of study of much potential intellectual interest and practical relevance.

8 *Disregard of Standards*

There are serious difficulties in the introduction and perhaps even more in the maintenance of firm and agreed standards in economics, in the use of concepts, procedures and acceptance of conclusions. The difficulties stem largely from the absence of contrived experiments, the shifting of parameters, the problems of selecting the appropriate variables, the uses and limitations of direct observation, and the intrusion of political influences into ostensibly technical discussion. In development economics the operation of these factors is reinforced by the obvious importance of determinants not readily susceptible to economic analysis; by the interaction of variables and parameters; by the unfamiliarity of the institutional setting; and by the special costs and difficulties of direct observation, and also the inadequacies of relying from afar on statistics collected by others, often in unpropitious circumstances. Direct observation and primary sources have come to be neglected in much of the development literature. As a result of this neglect, development economists often analyse societies, systems and situations which they do not know: they literally do not know what they are talking about.

The obstacles to the adoption of technical reasoning and the attitudes appropriate to it are accentuated in this sphere by an overwhelming concern with policy, even more intense and pervasive than in other branches of economics. The concern is so intense that it has often lent a missionary and almost messianic tenor to much of the discussion, which is inappropriate to a technical subject.[1]

Economics owes much, including its birth and much of its present

---

[1] Two examples from the ostensibly technical or at any rate academic literature will illustrate this point. Professor Myrdal writes (in *An International Economy*, p. 322): 'Not merely to save the world, but primarily to save our own souls, there should again be dreamers, planners and fighters . . . to avoid the unbearable discomfort for reformers of a climate of substantial agreement.' As substantial agreement is a condition for the effective application of techniques, this approach, widely shared in contemporary discussion, is almost by definition incompatible with economics as a form of technical assistance.

Our second example is from *A Proposal*, by Professors Max F. Millikan and W. W. Rostow (p. 151), to which we have already referred. The authors write: ' . . . the execution of the proposals presented in this book requires an active rededication to the fundamental principles which have given American life its distinction, its transcendent quality. . . . All this is to the good, for America at its best has never wholly lost a sense of the community of human destiny:

One thought ever at the fore –
That in the Divine Ship, the World, breasting Time and Space,
All peoples of the globe together sail, sail the same voyage,
Are bound to the same destination.'

financial support, to preoccupations with problems of policy, both by its practitioners and by the public at large. The connection between public interest and resources available for study and research is obvious in development economics. This interest has also served at times to focus attention on the examination of substantive issues and away from trivia. But this concern with policy has contributed to the confusion between the promotion of policy and the advancement of knowledge (or, more nearly, the confused identification of these two distinct pursuits), and has done much damage in economics, conspicuously so in the economics of development. While these shortcomings and problems are present in other branches of economics also, they are particularly evident in the economics of underdeveloped countries, which at times threatens to become intellectually impoverished and squalid. This impoverishment is often concealed behind a façade of quasi-mathematical language, in much the same way as the slums of the cities of poor countries are sometimes concealed behind a line of modern buildings, or specially erected hoardings along the main streets or on the roads from the airports.

An unwarranted belief in the centrality of economics for the analysis and promotion of the forces of material advance, and even more in its immediate usefulness for these purposes, has thwarted the realisation even of its limited but considerable potentialities. There are, however, certain encouraging signs. Some of the recent work by young scholars has proved illuminating and rewarding: it reflects the recognition of the prerequisites of scholarly study and also of the limitations and potentialities of the subject.

8 The Study of Underdeveloped Economies[1]

1 *The Relevance of Economics*

Economic analysis is widely relevant to the explanation of many phenomena in the underdeveloped world and to the assessment of many measures of policy. On the other hand, it cannot explain so readily the various factors behind economic progress, let alone forecast the likelihood of their occurrence, though it may eventually succeed better in the former task, especially if it were to work with other disciplines. In discussing these matters I shall touch on several topics lightly, rather than try to discuss one subject more thoroughly. This may help to convey some feeling of the vastness and diversity of the underdeveloped world, of the range and variety of the intellectual and practical problems it presents, and perhaps also of the amorphous nature of this branch of economics.

Although dissentient voices are still heard, the relevance of economic analysis to poor countries is now more readily accepted than a decade or two ago. Over a wide range of issues this relevance is not in question, since some of the propositions of economics derive directly from the universal limitation of resources. Their relevance is recognised in the practice of governments in underdeveloped countries of taxing commodities and activities to be discouraged and subsidising those to be encouraged. This practice makes sense only if the demand for particular commodities is a positive and their supply a negative function of price and reward (that is, if people wish to attain their objectives, whatever these may be, at least cost in terms of scarce resources), which accords with the postulates of elementary economic theory. Indeed, the applicability of economic analysis emerges in unexpected contexts. In the 1940s bride prices in Nigeria rose greatly with the general rise in the prices of assets. Government control over bride prices was widely

[1] The original version of this essay, now revised and somewhat expanded, appeared in *Economica*, November 1963. This article was in turn the published version of an inaugural lecture given at the London School of Economics and Political Science in May 1963.

canvassed and officially considered but was rejected when the difficulties of allocation were perceived.

Simple macroeconomics has also been successfully applied in under-developed countries. In the Gold Coast in 1947 the late H. S. Booker in an unpublished paper predicted that unless taxation were raised or import controls relaxed, an acute shortage of consumer goods would develop in the forthcoming cocoa season, so severe that it might lead to civil disturbances. The prediction, based largely on the technique of national income and expenditure analysis, was ignored but was completely fulfilled.

2 *Difficulties and Opportunities*

The study of underdeveloped economies encounters certain special but familiar difficulties, yet at the same time may offer rather unsuspected opportunities.

An obvious difficulty is the inadequacy or absence of certain types of statistics, especially demographic, national income and occupational statistics. Even when available, these are often subject to conceptual and practical limitations, notably statistics of national income where subsistence output is important, and occupational statistics where specialisation is incomplete. On the other hand, as I shall suggest shortly, there are often excellent and illuminating statistics for certain sectors of these economies.

Another difficulty is to find one's way and to observe uniformities in the often unfamiliar social landscape, unfamiliar because the institutions, and especially the values and mores, often differ from our own, which requires an adjustment of our sights. In East Africa cattle are often kept for aesthetic reasons or for prestige. But in the west also substantial resources are absorbed in the maintenance of animals not designed for work or food. Differences in values and institutions may affect the comparative importance of different economic variables, making it more difficult to discern their operation, without affecting the relevance and validity of economic analysis. Thus, for example, within the opportunities open to them, the responses of people to changes in the relevant variables, for instance prices and wages, are over a wide range of countries and activities much the same as in the west, and, as I have just suggested, this is recognised in government policy throughout the underdeveloped world. And when new profitable opportunities arise the responses are often massive and rapid, as in the spread of the cultivation of profitable cash crops by Asian and African smallholders, or in the large-scale migration of south Indian labourers to Malaya and Ceylon, which, when it was permitted, responded very closely to the changes in relative economic conditions. These major changes occurred in communities supposedly rigorously subject to the sway of custom and tradition.

Nevertheless, the conditions of underdeveloped countries offer some useful and possibly unexpected opportunities for the economist.

Much of the information in underdeveloped economies, or about them, is suitable for the examination of economic hypotheses and for the establishment and even measurement of the relationships between economic variables. This is so for at least two reasons. First, a large part of output in these countries is in unprocessed primary products, which avoids some of the difficult or intractable problems presented by differences and variations in the quality of commodities and in the composition of output. Second, costs of transport are often heavy and communication between local markets difficult. This results in situations identical in all, or most, relevant aspects, except one or two variables whose operations and relationship can be investigated.

A single illustration suffices here. In the purchase of Nigerian groundnuts, the combination of a standardised commodity with clearly separate submarkets, and differences in the number of buyers, has made possible investigations into the effects of the number of buyers on the prices received by the producers. In Nigeria groundnuts for sale are produced in two widely separated regions. In 1949–50, when the enquiry was conducted, in one region there were only two merchants buying groundnuts; in the other region there were about twenty merchants buying (although the numbers in each town or village were appreciably fewer). In both regions minimum prices payable by merchants were officially prescribed. In the first region the actual market prices nowhere exceeded the official minima, while in the other region they much exceeded them in many markets. There was a very high positive correlation in the individal markets between the number of merchants and the excess of actual over prescribed prices. This example at any rate bears on the often heard suggestion that an increase in the number of merchants tends only to inflate costs, without improving the terms of trade of their customers.

The interaction of economic variables and the general environment, a notable aspect of development, can also be well observed in underdeveloped countries, that is to say the interaction of incomes, prices, quantities and other familiar economic variables, with other factors or influences, such as attitudes, wants and institutions, variations in which are deliberately ignored for most purposes of economic analysis. For example, in many underdeveloped countries the cultivation of profitable cash crops has provoked the emergence of individual tenure of land. In Malaya and Ghana rubber or cocoa trees are already individually owned, while much of the adjoining land under subsistence crops is still under some sort of communal tenure, though this can be seen to be losing ground. Thus one can observe, and at times vividly, processes on the contemporary scene similar to those which happened centuries ago in the now developed countries.

Altogether, economics explains satisfactorily much of what goes on in underdeveloped countries. It readily explains the very wide seasonal and year-to-year price fluctuations in local agricultural produce, a general phenomenon in the underdeveloped world which reflects the marked degree of inelasticity of short-period supply and demand. This in turn reflects the narrowness of markets in space and time, due largely to the low level of transport and storage facilities. Moreover, economic analysis helps to assess the effects of certain specific measures of policy, often encountered in underdeveloped countries, such as charging rents on officially alienated land which vary only with the crop cultivated and not with location or fertility, or the prohibition of exports falling below certain standards, and many others. It is also obviously relevant to an assessment of the simpler effects of tax changes and, indeed, of some of the major implications of more far-reaching policies, such as taxation for development by way of compulsory saving.

3 Two Unsuccessful Approaches

These matters are often of considerable interest. But they are not the main reason for the interest of economists and others in poor countries. Since the eighteenth century at least, the primary interest in this sphere has been and still is in the determinants of economic progress, in fact in the causes of the wealth of nations.

Two widely canvassed approaches to this range of problems have, I think, been unsuccessful.

The first approach regards development as largely or wholly determined by capital accumulation, an approach often expressed in formal growth models. (Such models usually derive from the growth models of Harrod and Domar. But these pioneers and their immediate followers were not primarily concerned with the long-term historical development of societies. Their main concern was with the conditions of steady growth in advanced industrial societies.)[1] In their emphasis on capital these models bear some family resemblance to discussions in classical economics. But this similarity is rather superficial. The classical writers, including Adam Smith and Marx, closely related capital accumulation as an engine of development to the activities and conduct of particular groups, organisations and classes, such as traders, governments and the bourgeoisie, and to social attitudes, relationships and institutions, and to changes in these. Some of the most influential growth models abstract these forces, and apparently treat long-term progress as dependent on capital expenditure alone; and this abstraction differentiates this modern approach from that of the classical writers.

More recently this emphasis on capital has increasingly come to be regarded as inadequate, for various reasons, including the obvious failure of many large-scale investment programmes, especially in under-developed countries; recognition of the very limited explanatory power of the capital-output ratio; renewed emphasis on the dependence of the productivity of physical assets on the market for their output, and on the presence of complementary factors, notably skills and appropriate attitudes; and, more generally, recognition that expenditure does not become productive simply because it is termed investment.

These and other grounds for scepticism have been confirmed by statistical studies showing that neither in Britain nor America can the growth of physical capital possibly account for all or even most of the secular growth of income. And it is not obvious how the special but not unusual case of economic decline can fit into a theory of development based largely or wholly on the growth of capital.

The recognition of the inadequacy of physical capital, and *a fortiori* of investment expenditure, as an instrument of development has come to influence policy; for instance, foreign aid proposals and programmes increasingly acknowledge that money expenditure by itself will not achieve much without changes in institutions and attitudes.

---

[1] These models are largely Keynesian in their main aims and assumptions. They are chiefly concerned with the conditions of long-run full employment, notably the rate of growth of income necessary for this; and they disregard changes (and the effects of different kinds of change) in tastes, knowledge and other resources, attitudes and customs, the degree of monetisation of the economy, political systems, and often also in population and techniques. These limitations greatly reduce their relevance to the study of economic development since the models treat as given its primary determinants. Keynes's own formulation of his assumptions, which we quoted in essay 2, shows this clearly.

Thus while the accumulation of physical capital can contribute substantially to economic progress, it is certainly not a sufficient and often not a major factor. The opening of new markets, the establishment of external contacts, changes in attitudes, conduct, customs and wants, the spread of knowledge and of skills, generally play at least as great a part in development as does the growth of physical capital, particularly in pre-industrial societies, and especially before the society has been pervaded by the money economy.

The other widely canvassed but I think unfruitful approach to a general theory of development is the stages-of-growth approach, which seeks to express history as a predictable sequence of necessarily successive stages. The approach is not new. But economic historians generally have not found it illuminating in explaining the progress (or decline) of societies. In some of the most widely canvassed recent formulations it is not clear what the theory has to say about the causes of development, since at times it emphasises certain key variables, while at others it suggests that development depends on an indefinite number of often unspecified factors, saying in effect that growth depends on the presence of factors making for growth. It is precisely because the long-term movement of any society depends in large part on unpredictable forces and events that the stages-of-growth approach may necessarily involve formulations so vague and open-ended as to be unserviceable. This consideration points to important limitations in the applicability of techniques and methods of thought, including economic analysis, which are appropriate to the study of phenomena which in practice or in principle are repeated or repeatable, as are most phenomena studied by the natural sciences and many which are studied by the social sciences. The historical process of entire societies is, however, unique in its major elements. This problem is an aspect of the radical difference between the assessment of a situation or the prediction of the probable result of a change in specified variables on the one hand, and the forecasting of the unknown future on the other. I need not labour this point, since it would be only an inadequate reflection of Professor Popper's classic treatment of this problem.[1]

4 *Some Instances of Progress*

Neither formal growth models nor stages-of-growth theories help to

[1] Especially *The Poverty of Historicism*, London, 1957. This issue is examined at greater length in essay 9.

explain or predict the long-term development of entire societies. But this does not preclude the possibility of specific generalisations about some of the major aspects or determinants of material progress. Indeed, such specific generalisations about these matters, rather than the framing of complete systems, are in the tradition of the literature, even though they may not be expressed in terms of conventional or formal analysis. Examples include the relationship between the extent of the market, specialisation and productivity, and the importance for development of the habits of 'order, economy, and attention, to which mercantile business naturally forms a merchant'.[1] Generalisations of this type are not so narrow as growth models preoccupied with capital expenditure, nor so ambitious as the well-nigh universal theory of history reflected, for example, in the stages-of-growth approach. But such generalisations, even apparently simple ones, may reveal some factors in the process of development.

To begin with a straightforward though negative suggestion. Physical natural resources, notably fertile soil or rich minerals, are not the only or even major determinants of material progress, though differences in the bounty of nature may well account for differences in levels and ease of living in different parts of the underdeveloped world. It has always been known that physical resources are useless without capital and skills to develop them, or without access to markets. And the diminishing importance of land and other natural resources in production is also familiar. But the recent rapid development of some underdeveloped countries poorly endowed with natural resources has come as a surprise, though perhaps it should not have done so, in view of the Japanese experience. A recent but already classic case is that of Hong Kong, which has practically no raw materials, very little fertile soil, no fuel, no hydroelectric power, and only a very restricted domestic market, but which in spite of these limitations has progressed phenomally.

The natural rubber industry, which has been the mainspring of the rapid development of Malaya and indeed of the economic transformation of that country and of much of south-east Asia, owes little to scarce natural resources, or to any *local* resources. The rubber tree, which is indigenous in South America, does not require particularly fertile soil and thrives practically anywhere in the tropical rain forest. The soil of Malaya and Sumatra, the two principal producing countries, is generally poor, nor had their territories appreciable labour forces or

[1] Adam Smith, *Wealth of Nations*, Book III, ch. 4.

supplies of capital when the rubber industry began there only about sixty years ago. The main reasons for its development there were the presence of European merchants and of a stable administration, and access to large reservoirs of labour in southern India, China and Java, and to the capital markets of western Europe.

5 *Differences in Economic Aptitudes*

Another range of issues concerns the conspicuous differences between individuals and groups in economic aptitudes, such as industry, enterprise, curiosity and ability to perceive and exploit economic opportunity. In a subsistence economy they are largely irrelevant and unobtrusive. But they come into play quite soon in emerging economies, especially with the advance of the money economy. There are obvious examples in the progress of certain distinct ethnic groups, especially, but not only, immigrants, in a number of underdeveloped countries. Throughout the underdeveloped world, originally penniless and often quite uneducated immigrants have within a few years completely outdistanced the local population.

Two examples will suggest that the special circumstances of migration alone do not explain this. In Malaya there is a large Indian as well as a large Chinese population. The great bulk of both communities came within recent decades as very poor, illiterate coolies. Within a few years the Chinese drew far ahead of the Indians. The other example is from Israel. The authorities there established a number of separate villages in the same region for recent immigrants from different countries, whom they provided as nearly as possible with the same amount of capital and identical facilities per family. Within a year or two substantial differences in prosperity emerged, in the same region, between villages inhabited by European and by Indian Jews.

Differences in economic abilities bear on many aspects and problems of economic development, including, for instance those of overpopulation. The Chinese can make a living in areas often regarded as hopelessly overcrowded, as for instance Hong Kong and the West Indies. In the latter, which are generally considered as severely overpopulated, prospective Chinese and Lebanese migrants have to be statutorily excluded.

Very little is known about the climatic, biological, cultural and social factors which may lie behind these differences in economic qualities and performance, and their emergence, persistence or disappearance.

It is probable that climatic and other geographical factors play an important part. It is noteworthy that with the exception of a few small areas with which the developed world has established direct and intimate contacts all tropical countries are underdeveloped. Conversely, almost all countries in the temperate zone are comparatively highly developed. Even allowing for the much lower requirements for shelter and clothing, the concentration of poverty within the tropics is notable. Differences in general material achievement, as distinct from the construction of outstanding monuments, between the tropical world and the temperate zones go back for many centuries.[1]

Again, much of the now widely canvassed difference in prosperity between north and south Italy goes back at least to the Middle Ages. Since then the north has been well ahead of the south in scientific, intellectual, artistic, commercial and industrial achievement, and it was also the source of the Italian voyages of discovery. It seems to be unknown how much of the northern advantage reflects ethnic or climatic factors, or how much was contributed by migrants from the south or from other countries.

Although some of these differences in economic qualities are long-standing, some others, especially the capacity to handle technical objects and processes, can change comparatively quickly. The rapid emergence of Japan as an industrial nation in the nineteenth century is well known.[2] Less familiar and in some ways even more striking was the economic transformation of Sweden in the latter part of the nineteenth century. And again, the peoples of sub-Saharan Africa had neither invented the wheel nor, until very recently, taken to it even when it was brought to their notice. By now they are readily accepting modern equipment and modern technology. Some attitudes and customs which much affect economic development seem very tenacious at home, while they are largely absent abroad. The south Indian communities in Malaya come from parts of rural Madras where caste is strictly observed,

---

[1] There is a curious contrast which is perhaps worthy of note in this context, as well as in others. There has been much travel and exploration from the west (including at times the Levant) to Asia and Africa since at least the time of Herodotus, and on a large scale since the fourteenth century. There was little reverse movement, even though throughout the ages there have been rich and powerful individuals and groups in many areas of Asia and Africa.

[2] The material progress of Japan over the last hundred years has indeed been phenomenal. But there is a major consideration to be taken into account before assessing its relevance to the contemporary underdeveloped world. The economic and social prerequisites of material progress were present to a far greater extent than in the present underdeveloped world. For instance, very sophisticated financial institutions had developed in Japan by the seventeenth century.

as it has been for many centuries; yet they largely abandon it when they leave India.

The study of the often pronounced ethnic differences in economic performance, and of the geographica, climatic, genetic and other factors that may underlie them, might now be more illuminating and rewarding than in the past because of advances in biology, biometrics, genetics and climatology. These should enable us to observe, assess and perhaps even control some of the effects of climate on economic performance, even long-term performance.

There is no cause for surprise, much less for indignation, at this explicit recognition of the pronounced and often sustained differences in economic faculties between persons and groups, any more than at noting differences in physical or intellectual attributes and qualities between persons and groups. Moreover, even if it is found that such differences are deep-seated and persistent, this would not point to any specific prescriptions for policy.

6 *External Contacts and Economic Progress*

Over most of the underdeveloped world, in the tropics and elsewhere, the most prosperous regions and sectors at present are those with which the developed world has established contacts: the cities and ports of India and their vicinity; the cash crop-producing areas and the entrepôt ports of south-east Asia, West Africa and Latin America; and the mineral-producing areas of Africa, the middle east and the Caribbean. Conversely, in Africa, Asia and Latin America the poorest and most backward are usually populations with few or no external contacts, the aborigines being the extreme case. Although there may be odd exceptions, in the nature of curiosa perhaps, the general connection between external contacts, at any rate peaceful contacts, and economic advance is familiar from economic and social history. In the Middle Ages the more advanced regions of backward eastern and central Europe and Scandinavia were those in touch with France, the Low Countries and Italy. And the difference in the material prosperity of the coastal regions and the centre of Spain has been a notable feature of Spanish history and one of the determinants of its course.

The connection in underdeveloped countries between comparative material prosperity and external contacts is not surprising. These are the channels through which human and material resources, skills and capital from developed countries reach the underdeveloped world. These contacts open up new markets and sources of supply and bring new commodities, wants, crops and methods of cultivation to the notice of the local population. They also engender a new outlook towards material possessions and the means of obtaining them. And perhaps most important, they undermine customs, attitudes and values which obstruct material advance. Again, in poor countries the sectors in contact with richer communities also attract groups and individuals from the local population most responsive to economic opportunities. Such matters obviously greatly affect economic performance in underdeveloped countries, especially in the early stages of development. In the widest sense such contacts promote that dissatisfaction with the existing situation which has been termed the first condition of progress. Their importance can hardly be exaggerated.

Some of the pervasive changes engendered by external contacts in the contemporary underdeveloped world, notably in south-east Asia and West Africa, are familiar. External contacts have largely transformed these areas. I might perhaps mention a much less familiar instance of change brought about by external contacts, which is nevertheless noteworthy and substantial, to which Professor H. M. Robertson of the University of Cape Town has drawn attention.[1] He has repeatedly stressed the revolutionary effects of the activities of European traders on the life of the Bantu of South Africa. The use of the blanket as a garment is often thought of as typical of the tribal Bantu. In fact, until the late nineteenth century they were unknown to these people, who used a skin covering known as the *kaross*. Enterprising traders brought blankets to the notice of the tribal Africans and had blankets specially made for them in Yorkshire. What are regarded as traditional tribal patterns were in fact designed in England at the instigation of merchants wishing to differentiate their products.

Altogether, these contacts draw parts of the underdeveloped world into a wider system of international economic life; and, by enabling their peoples to draw on the resources of the outside world, they help to raise and maintain the economy above subsistence production.

These simple considerations reflect on the curious and influential argument that the presence of developed countries and contacts with them somehow prejudice the advance of poorer countries, a suggestion which is contrary to massive empirical evidence, including the clear connection between economic prosperity and progress in the underdeveloped world and contact with richer countries, which I have

[1] In *South Africa: Economic and Political Aspects*, London, 1957, pp. 19–20.

already mentioned. They also show up certain implications of the severance of contact between the underdeveloped countries and the developed countries through restrictions on migration, trade and capital movements, whether from pressure of sectional interests or wider political motives.

Indeed, at present these contacts offer exceptional opportunities. Because of the presence of advanced countries and highly developed communications, the underdeveloped world has readier access to the fruits of scientific and technical progress elsewhere than the now developed countries had in the past. Access to this accumulated knowledge could be as helpful as access to unused land was to other countries in times past. The ability of underdeveloped countries to take advantage of this depends greatly on the attitudes and skills of their own peoples, as well as on government policies promoting or restricting international contacts.

External contacts by themselves are of course not sufficient to ensure progress if other factors are missing. The spread of material progress from advanced sectors to others depends on human, institutional, cultural and political factors, besides physical and occupational obstacles to mobility. In Latin America the Peruvian Indians have remained very poor in spite of external contacts, while in Mexico Indians are often prominent and prosperous. Again, in the Middle Ages North Africa had extensive contacts with the prosperous regions of Europe, but these contacts did not prevent its decline. Ibn Khaldun, the Arab philosopher-historian of the fourteenth century, attributed the decay of North Africa, and the failure of the advanced city civilisations to pervade the Arab world, to a feckless and careless attitude of the rural population reflected in a nomadic life and reinforced by it.

Societies, groups and persons differ in their inclination and ability to take advantage of economic opportunities presented by contacts with more advanced economies, through new ideas, methods, groups, commodities and sources of supply or markets. These differences in extent or speed of response to externally presented opportunities (which are examples of differences in the ability and willingness to perceive and exploit economic opportunity generally) may reflect such influences as differences in interest in material progress or in attachment to various customs and institutions adverse to it.

7 *The Limitations of Formal Theory*

Some of these observations have taken the reader far from the usual preoccupations of contemporary economics. The economist may well ask whether they can help him in his academic or professional pursuits. I think they are relevant both to the explanation of much of the scene, and to the assessment of policies for the promotion of economic development of poor countries generally, or of particular areas. But of course they are no more than tentative generalisations and they share this tentative quality with most other generalisations on the process of economic development. Whatever their validity, consideration of these topics seems necessary for any worthwhile study of development.

Many of these observations and generalisations are largely unrelated to conventional formal economic reasoning (at least to the formal economic analysis of recent decades). Insistence on the wide relevance of economic reasoning in explaining phenomena in underdeveloped countries, and in illuminating situations or explaining some aspects and conditions of development, is quite consistent with recognition of its limitations in predicting the course of development. This is because long-term development depends so largely on general conditions not susceptible to economic analysis, and, what is equally important, on unpredictable changes in these conditions. It would, therefore, be preferable to speak of material progress or advance, rather than of economic development. And further, the economist is not particularly qualified to assess the wider implications of economic development or of the different methods of attempting to promote it, either in terms of personal happiness or in terms of social and political results.

The late von Karman, a distinguished physicist, used to say that prophecy was not a scientific activity and therefore not the task of science. This observation certainly applies to the social sciences. Our task is in some ways similar to that assigned by Collingwood to historians, that is 'to reveal the less obvious features hidden from a careless eye in the present situation'. This is very different from speculation about the remote unknown future of a society. The claims of chemistry have always been more modest than those of alchemy. I believe that in economics, especially in the economics of underdeveloped countries, as in other disciplines, it is a sign of maturity and not of obscurantism when the practitioners recognise the limitations of their subject.

8 *Cooperation between Disciplines*

In the study of underdeveloped economies there may be scope for interdisciplinary cooperation, especially between anthropologists, economists and historians. Various situations and phases of development, as yet imperfectly understood, might be fruitfully studied through such cooperation. They might include parts of the vast field of the responses of different groups to changes in economic conditions and opportunities. Again, within the extremely important and interesting range of issues in the transmission of knowledge, skills, attitudes and inducements between countries and groups, there are many examples which might perhaps be usefully investigated jointly by anthropologists, economists and historians.

There are more specific episodes or phenomena the interdisciplinary study of which might prove illuminating. Instances would include the rapid spread of cash crops produced by the local population, or the present organisation of some of these industries, such as smallholders' rubber in the present Indonesia (where millions of acres were put under rubber by smallholders in a few years in the 1920s and 1930s) or kola nuts in Nigeria. These are among the examples of massive development of cash crop production which passed unnoticed for many years, and which in kola nuts at any rate has involved a high degree of organisation of production, transport and trade, entirely by the local population. Another possible example of such worthwhile study would have been the Gold Coast cocoa hold-up of 1937–8, which was a remarkable farmers' strike by well over 100,000 producers, who for seven months sold practically no cocoa to the merchants. Close interdisciplinary enquiry into this episode might well have yielded interesting results on the transmission of information, the organisation by a few people of large numbers of producers, and on the ability of farmers and labourers to obtain food and other necessities. Again, the frequently reported wide differences in prices of local foodstuffs in near-by areas could also be examined on an interdisciplinary basis, to ascertain how far they are illusory or real, and if they are real how far they are explained in different instances by transport costs, inertia, ignorance, custom, lack of response or quasi-monopoly, which have widely different implications. In suggesting these topics, I may add that serious discussion of underdeveloped countries and their problems is much affected by an acute dearth of scholarly monographs and essays on particular countries or subjects. The investigation of these subjects or similar matters might produce illuminating results; and the process of enquiry is likely to yield worthwhile insights into the economy.

In the study of these other aspects of underdeveloped economies and of economic development, interdisciplinary cooperation may perhaps yield another incidental but possibly important benefit. It may help to convey the value of direct observation and of unprocessed material, and conversely, the pitfalls of reliance on second-hand or third-hand material, including reliance on statistics without examination of their sources or background. Statistics are necessarily a form of abstraction and they are most effectively used if other aspects of the situation are also known, that is other than those quantified in the statistics.

Some may fear that this approach or method of study will tempt us into excessive detail. However, concern with detail, whether in inter-disciplinary studies or otherwise, can be very fruitful in our particular field of study. I think the emphasis in recent years has been too far in the opposite direction. Perhaps we would do well to remind ourselves of the Baconian maxim (recently quoted by Professor C. H. Philips) that it 'cometh often to pass that mean and small things discover great better than great can discover small'.

List of Works Cited

P. A. Baran, *The Political Economy of Growth* (New York 1957).

P. K. Bardhan and T. N. Srinivasan, 'Cropsharing Tenancy in Agriculture: A Theoretical and Empirical Analysis', *American Economic Review* (March 1971).

A. K. Cairncross, *Factors in Economic Development* (London 1962).

A. K. Cairncross, 'The Place of Capital in Economic Progress', in L. H. Dupriez (ed.), *Economic Progress* (Louvain 1955).

Steven N. S. Cheung, *The Theory of Share Tenancy* (Chicago 1969).

Nirad C. Chaudhuri, *The Autobiography of an Unknown Indian* (London 1951).

Nirad C. Chaudhuri, *The Continent of Circe* (London 1965).

Kenneth Clark, *Civilization* (London 1970).

Commission on International Development, *Partners in Development* (Pearson Report) (New York 1969).

L. H. Dupriez (ed.), *Economic Progress* (Louvain 1955).

P. T. Ellsworth, 'Terms of Trade between Primary Producing and Industrial Countries', *Inter-American Economic Affairs* (Summer 1956).

G. R. Elton, *The Practice of History* (Sydney 1967).

Stephen Enke, *Economics for Development* (Englewood Cliffs, N.J. 1963).

Alexander Erlich and Christian R. Sonne, 'The Soviet Union: Economic Activity', in Z. Brzezinski (ed.), *Africa and the Communist World* (Stanford 1963).

Leonard B. Eron, *The Classification of Behavior Disorders* (Chicago 1966).

Romulo A. Ferrero, *Trade Problems of Primary Producing Countries* (San Francisco 1965).

S. Herbert Frankel, *The Economic Impact on Underdeveloped Societies* (Oxford 1953).

J. S. Furnivall, *Colonial Policy and Practice, A Comparative Study of Burma and Netherlands India* (New York 1956).

GATT, *Trends in International Trade* (Geneva 1958).

D. V. Glass and D. E. C. Eversley (eds), *Population in History* (London 1965).

E. H. Gombrich, *The Tradition of General Knowledge* (London 1962).

John Hajnal, 'European Marriage Patterns in Perspective: The Uniqueness of the European Pattern', in D. V. Glass and D. E. C. Eversley (eds), *Population in History* (London 1965).

R. J. Hammond, 'Economic Imperialism, Sidelights on a Stereotype', *Journal of Economic History* (December 1961).

W. K. Hancock, *Survey of British Commonwealth Affairs*, vol. II: *Problems of Economic Policy 1918–1939* (part 2) (London 1942).

F. A. Hayek, 'The Intellectuals and Socialism', in George B. de Huszar (ed.), *The Intellectuals* (Glencoe 1960).

George B. de Huszar (ed.), *The Intellectuals* (Glencoe 1960).

Nona Jabavu, *Drawn in Colour* (London 1960).

Harry G. Johnson, *Economic Policies Towards Less Developed Countries* (Washington 1967).

N. Kaldor, 'The Role of Taxation in Economic Development', in E. A. G. Robinson (ed.), *Problems in Economic Development* (London 1965).

J. M. Keynes, *General Theory of Employment, Interest and Money* (London 1936).

H. Kitamura, 'Foreign Trade Problems in Planned Economic Development', in Kenneth Berrill (ed.), *Economic Development with Special Reference to East Asia* (London 1964).

Anne O. Kreuger, 'Factor Endowments and Per Capita Income Differences among Countries', *Economic Journal* (September 1968).

League of Nations, *Industrialisation and Foreign Trade* (Geneva 1945).

V. I. Lenin, *Imperialism, the Highest Stage of Capitalism* (Moscow 1934).

W. Arthur Lewis, 'A Review of Economic Development', *American Economic Review* (May 1965).

S. B. Linder, *The Harried Leisure Class* (New York 1970).

Herbert Luthy, 'Fragmente zu einem Instrumentarium des geistigen Terors', in *Nach dem Untergang des Abendlandes* (Cologne 1964).

Karl Marx, *Address to the Communist League of Germany* (1850).

A. McPhee, *The Economic Revolution in British West Africa* (London 1926).

Max F. Millikan and Walt W. Rostow, *A Proposal: Key to an Effective Foreign Policy* (New York 1957).

Czeslaw Milosz, *The Captive Mind* (London 1953).

Kenneth Minogue, *The Liberal Mind* (London 1963).

E. J. Mishan, *The Costs of Economic Growth* (London 1967).

Theodore Morgan, 'The Long-Run Terms of Trade between Agriculture and Manufacturing', *Economic Development and Cultural Change* (October 1959).

Gunnar Myrdal, *An International Economy: Problems and Prospects* (London 1956).

Gunnar Myrdal, *Asian Drama: An Inquiry into the Poverty of Nations* (London 1968).

Gunnar Myrdal, *Development and Underdevelopment: a Note on the Mechanism of National and International Inequality* (Cairo 1956).

Gunnar Myrdal, *Economic Theory and Underdeveloped Regions* (London 1957).

H. Myint, 'The "Classical Theory" of International Trade and the Underdeveloped Countries', *Economic Journal* (June 1958).

H. Myint, *The Economics of the Developing Countries* (London 1964).

Kwame Nkrumah, *Africa Must Unite* (London 1963).

Kwame Nkrumah, *Neo-Colonialism* (London 1965).

Kwame Nkrumah, *Towards Colonial Freedom* (London 1962).

Ragnar Nurkse, *Problems of Capital Formation in Underdeveloped Countries* (Oxford 1953).

Prabhakar Padhye, 'The Intellectual in Modern Asia', in George B. de Huszar (ed.), *The Intellectuals* (Glencoe 1960).

Karl Popper, *The Poverty of Historicism* (London 1957).

I. Potekhin, *Problems of Economic Independence of African Countries* (Moscow 1962).

A. R. Prest, *Public Finance in Underdeveloped Countries* (London 1962).

A. R. Prest, *The Investigation of National Income in British Tropical Dependencies* (London 1957).

A. R. Prest and I. G. Stewart, *The National Income of Nigeria 1950–1951* (London 1953).

H. M. Robertson, *South Africa: Economic and Political Aspects* (London 1957).

Simon Rottenberg, 'Economic Instruction for Economic Growth', *Economic Development and Cultural Change* (October 1964).

Paul A. Samuelson, *Economics: An Introductory Analysis* (2nd ed.) (New York 1951).

Helmut Schoeck, *Envy* (London 1969).

B. R. Shenoy, *Indian Economic Policy* (Bombay 1968).

Adam Smith, *The Wealth of Nations* (1776).

Study submitted by the Center for International Studies of the Massachusetts Institute of Technology to the State Committee investigating the operation of Foreign Aid (Washington 1957).

T. Szamuely, 'Russia Fifty Years After', *The Spectator* (20 October 1967).

Thomas S. Szasz, 'The Psychiatric Classification of Behavior: A Strategy of Personal Constraint', in Leonard D. Eron (ed.), *The Classification of Behavior Disorders* (Chicago 1966).

R. E. Szereszewski, *Structural Changes in the Economy of Ghana 1891–1911* (London 1966).

Prakash Tandon, *Punjabi Century 1857–1947* (London 1961).

Alexis de Tocqueville, *On the State of Society in France* (London 1873).

Peter Townsend (ed.), *The Concept of Poverty* (London 1971).

United Nations, Department of Economic and Social Affairs, *Analysis and Projections of Economic Development. 1: An Introduction to the Technique of Programming* (New York 1955).

United Nations, Department of Economic and Social Affairs, *Economic Survey of Latin America 1955* (New York 1956).

United Nations, Department of Economic and Social Affairs, *Relative Prices of Exports and Imports of Underdeveloped Countries* (Lake Success 1949).

United Nations, *Monthly Bulletin of Statistics*, vol. xviii (New York, December 1964).

United Nations, *Year Book of National Accounts Statistics 1963* (New York 1964).

Dan Usher, *The Price Mechanism and the Meaning of National Income Statistics* (Oxford 1968).

Dan Usher, 'The Transport Bias in National Income Comparisons', *Economica* (May 1963).

P. Lamartine Yates, *Forty Years of Foreign Trade* (London 1959).

A. J. Youngson, *Overhead Capital: A Study in Development Economics* (Edinburgh 1967).

Index